AT HOME
with the WORD
2 0 0 8

Sunday Scriptures and
Scripture Insights

Margaret Nutting Ralph
Anne Elizabeth Sweet, OCSO
Mary Ellen Hynes
Jennifer Willems

ALSO AVAILABLE IN A LARGE PRINT EDITION

LITURGY
TRAINING
PUBLICATIONS

Acknowledgments

Nihil Obstat
Reverend Brian J. Fischer
Censor Deputatus
April 20, 2007

Imprimatur
Reverend John F. Canary, STL, DMIN
Vicar General
Archdiocese of Chicago
April 23, 2007

The *Nihil Obstat* and *Imprimatur* are official declarations that a book is free of doctrinal and moral error. No implication is contained therein that those who have granted the *Nihil Obstat* and *Imprimatur* agree with the content, opinions, or statements expressed. Nor do they assume any legal responsibility associated with publication.

Prayers in the seasonal introductions are from *Prayers for Sundays and Seasons, Year A* by Peter Scagnelli, Chicago: Liturgy Training Publications, 1998.

The paper used to print this year's *At Home with the Word* was carefully chosen with our customers in mind and with a commitment to the environment. After extensive searching, we found a highly opaque paper that fits both of those needs. The 40# Remarque Offset paper that this book is printed on is 100% recycled and contains a minimum of 40% postconsumer waste. The non-postconsumer portion consists of pre-consumer recycled fiber. Although many de-inking processes use highly toxic bleach, this paper was processed using PCF (Processed Chlorine Free) technologies. This paper is also acid-free to reduce yellowing as it ages. ✿

Printed in the United States of America.

ISBN 978-1-56854-613-1
AHW08

The cover art for this year's *At Home with the Word* is by Jeanne Troxel. The interior art is by Kathy Sullivan. The book was edited by Lorie Simmons with assistance from Mary Fox. Carol Mycio was the production editor. The design is by Anne Fritzinger and M. Urgo. Mark Hollopeter typeset the book in Matrix and Minion.

Welcome to At Home with the Word 2008

The Authors of the Introductions

Martin F. Connell teaches liturgical theology at St. John's University in Collegeville, Minnesota. Michael Cameron teaches scripture and theology at the University of Portland in Oregon.

Scripture Readings

For each Sunday you will find full texts of the three readings, as well as (on most Sundays) the psalm from the Lectionary for Mass proclaimed in Roman Catholic churches in the United States.

Scripture Insights

Two scripture scholars share the fruits of their studies and reflection on scripture. Margaret Nutting Ralph, PHD, is a teacher, having taught grade school, high school, college, graduate school, and adult education groups throughout the country. Presently she directs the Master of Arts in Pastoral Studies program for Catholics at Lexington Theological Seminary. Margaret is the author of ten books on scripture, including Paulist Press's bestseller, *And God Said What?* She has written Scripture Insights for the seasons of Advent, Christmas, Lent, and Easter, and for the solemnities of the Most Holy Trinity and Body and Blood of Christ.

Sister Anne Elizabeth Sweet has an MA in theology from the Catholic Theological Union and a PHD in New Testament from the University of Notre Dame. She has lived the monastic life for 38 years, 25 as a Benedictine sister, working as a religious educator and college teacher, then as a Trappistine nun of Our Lady of the Mississippi Abbey, most recently at the abbey's foundation in Norway, Tautra Mariakloster. Sister Anne Elizabeth has contributed articles to *Homily Service, Celebration, The Bible Today, Cistercian Studies Quarterly,* and the *Seasons of Faith* religious education series. She has written Scripture Insights for Ordinary Time.

Practice of Prayer

Here, on most Sundays, you will find at least a part of the responsorial psalm. Seasonal prayers for beginning and ending your scripture study are provided at the opening of each season of the year.

Practice of Virtue (Faith, Hope, and Charity)

Two writers focus on practicing virtue. Mary Ellen Hynes holds master's degrees in pastoral studies and religious education from Loyola University Chicago. She is a theology teacher and freelance writer. Her work appears in the seasons of Advent and Christmas, and the Second through the Fourth and the Twentieth through the Thirty-fourth Sundays in Ordinary Time. Jennifer Willems is the assistant editor of the *Catholic Post,* Peoria, Illinois. She has been a freelance writer, pastoral associate, and director of the Rite of Christian Initiation of Adults. Find her practices in the seasons of Lent and Easter, the solemnities of Most Holy Trinity and Body and Blood of Christ, and the Ninth through Nineteenth Sundays of Ordinary Time.

Weekday Readings

The opening of each season provides a list of scripture texts read at Mass on weekdays and on feasts falling on weekdays.

Art for *At Home with the Word 2008*

On the cover, Jeanne Troxel depicts a family kitchen, suddenly quiet after a lively meal. Christ on the cross overlooks the scene and *At Home with the Word* waits for its readers to return. Jeanne, a Chicago resident, works in oils and pastels. She earned a bachelor of arts degree in visual communications at Indiana University, Bloomington, and studied painting and drawing at the Art Institute of Chicago.

Kathy Ann Sullivan uses a scratch board technique in the interior designs to evoke the liturgical seasons—from our ancestors in faith on the Jesse tree to the oil lamps for Ordinary Time in the fall. Kathy Ann designed the scenes in the baptismal font at St. Mary's Cathedral, Colorado Springs.

Table of Contents

The Lectionary

by Martin F. Connell

WHAT IS A LECTIONARY?

A Lectionary is an ordered selection of readings, chosen from both testaments of the Bible, for proclamation in the assembly gathered for worship. Lectionaries have been used for Christian worship since the fourth century. Before the invention of the printing press in the fifteenth century, the selection and order of the readings differed somewhat from church to church, often reflecting the issues that were important to the local communities of the time.

For the four centuries between the Council of Trent (1545–1563) and the Second Vatican Council (1963–1965), the readings in most Catholic churches varied little from year to year and were proclaimed in Latin, a language that many no longer understood. Vatican II brought dramatic changes. It allowed the language of the people to be used in the liturgy and initiated a revision of the Lectionary. The Bible became far more accessible to Catholics and once again a vibrant source of our faith and tradition.

THE THREE-YEAR LECTIONARY CYCLE

The new Lectionary that appeared in 1970 introduced a three-year plan that allowed a fuller selection of readings from the Bible. During Year A, the Gospel readings for Ordinary Time are taken from Matthew, for Year B from Mark, and for Year C from Luke. This liturgical year, 2008, begins on the First Sunday of Advent, December 2, 2007, and ends with the celebration of Christ the King, November 23, 2008. It is Year A, the year of Matthew.

YEAR A: THE GOSPEL ACCORDING TO MATTHEW

Most of the Gospel readings proclaimed in your Sunday assembly this year and printed in *At Home with the Word 2008* are from the Gospel according to Matthew. The introduction to this Gospel on pages 14–17 and the Scripture Insights for each week will help you recognize and appreciate the contribution this Gospel makes to our faith.

THE GOSPEL ACCORDING TO JOHN

You might ask, What about the Fourth Gospel? The Gospel according to John is not assigned a year of its own because it constitutes so much of our reading during certain seasons and times of the year.

The readings for Year A on the Third, Fourth, and Fifth Sundays of Lent are from the Gospel according to John, and they are proclaimed every year in parishes celebrating the Rite of Christian Initiation of Adults (RCIA) when the elect are present. These three wonderful stories from this Gospel—the woman at the well (on the Third Sunday), the man born blind (on the Fourth Sunday), and the raising of Lazarus (on the Fifth Sunday)—accompany the celebration of the Scrutinies in the process of Christian initiation. During Years B and C, you will find two sets of readings on these Sundays in *At Home with the Word:* one set for Sunday Masses at which the Scrutinies of the RCIA are celebrated and another set for Masses at which they are not celebrated.

The Gospel according to John also appears for the Mass of the Lord's Supper on Holy Thursday and for the long Passion reading on Good Friday. And on most of the Sundays of Easter—during the Fifty Days from Easter Sunday until Pentecost—this Gospel is proclaimed at the liturgy.

THE DIFFERENCE BETWEEN THE BIBLE AND THE LECTIONARY

Because the Lectionary uses selections from the Bible, arranged according to the seasons and feasts of the liturgical year, the assembly often hears a selection of texts "out of order" from their position in the Bible. However, the overall shape of the Lectionary comes from the ancient Church practice of *lectio continua,* a Latin term that describes the successive reading through books of the Bible from Sunday to Sunday.

You can see *lectio continua* in practice if you consider the Gospel texts for the Twelfth Sunday in Ordinary Time, June 22, through the Feast of Christ the King, November 23. Though not every verse is included (and excepting Sundays when feasts interrupt the flow of the Gospel according to Matthew with other Gospel texts), the Lectionary moves from chapter 9 in Matthew through chapter 23.

Although Christians hold the Gospels in particular reverence, the first two readings provide strong teaching as well and comprise nearly two-thirds of the material in the Lectionary. The first reading often echoes some image or idea in the Gospel, as is the Church's intention. The second reading often stands on its own and comes from a letter of Paul or another letter from the New Testament. Notice, for example, that the second readings from mid-June through November take us through Romans, Philippians, and 1 Thessalonians. The stretch of Ordinary Time in summer and autumn provides a perfect opportunity for sustained attention to one or a few sections of the Bible.

UNITY WITH OTHER CHRISTIAN CHURCHES IN THE WORD OF GOD

The basic plan of the Lectionary for Catholics is universal. The readings proclaimed in your parish on a particular Sunday are the same as those proclaimed in Catholic churches all over the globe. The Lectionary is one of the main things that makes our liturgy so "catholic," or universal.

The revision of the Roman Catholic Lectionary has been so well received that other Christian churches have begun to follow its three-year cycle. Catholics and their neighbors who attend other Christian churches often hear the same word of God proclaimed and preached in the Sunday gathering. We may not talk about the Sunday readings with our neighbors and therefore don't realize that their readers read the same scripture passages and their preachers preach on the same scriptural texts. This is really a remarkable change when you consider how very far apart from one another Catholic and Protestant churches were before the Second Vatican Council.

Although Roman Catholics in the United States always hear the New American Bible translation in their liturgy, and that is what you will find in this book, the Church has approved other translations for study, such as the New Revised Standard Version (NRSV) and the New Jerusalem Bible. When preparing to hear the readings on Sunday, it is helpful to read more than one translation, and also to read more than the Lectionary passage so that you understand the context in which it occurs in the Bible. Consulting various Bibles, and perhaps a few Bible study tools, will enrich your preparation. (See Studying and Praying Scripture on page 22.)

May your experience of the liturgy in your parish be deepened by the preparations you make with this book. And may the time you spend with scripture during the liturgical year help you feel ever more "at home with the word" of God.

YOUR RESPONSES INVITED

The LTP staff appreciates your feedback. E-mail: ahw@ltp.org.

An Introduction to the Gospel According to Matthew

by Michael Cameron

The first Gospel is anonymous, but early tradition ascribed it to Matthew, the tax collector who became an apostle (Matthew 9:9). Most scholars today read it as an expanded "second edition" of the Gospel according to Mark. Readers quickly notice great blocks of Jesus' spoken teaching. It might be that this Gospel was placed first in the New Testament because it stood out as the "teaching Gospel."

Scholars' best estimates date Matthew's composition to the 80s of the first century and place it possibly at Antioch in Syria (Acts 11:26). That multicultural city would have nurtured this Gospel's passionate devotion to Jesus as well as its profound knowledge of ancient Jewish traditions, ethical concerns, and cultural coloring.

The Gospel according to Matthew came out of a circle of converted scribes (teachers of Jewish tradition) who had been "instructed in the kingdom of heaven" (13:52). This Gospel shows a teacher's touch. Between the stories of the Messiah's birth (chapters 1–2) and death (chapters 26–28), this Gospel is organized into "five books" (perhaps imitating the five books of Moses). Each features a narrative section leading into one of Jesus' five great teaching discourses (chapters 5–7, including the Sermon on the Mount, and 10, 13, 18, 24–25). Most outstanding are the Sermon's Beatitudes (5:3–10), the Lord's Prayer (6:9–13), and the Golden Rule (7:12).

Matthew's view of Jesus is exalted. Genealogically descended from Abraham and David (1:1–17), Jesus carries a prophetic name, *Emmanuel*, "God with us" (1:23; Isaiah 7:14). He is a king from birth (2:2), who effortlessly conquers disease and evil "by a word" (8:16). That word rings with majestic authority ("You have heard it said . . . but I say to you . . ." six times in 5:21–48), and will never pass away (24:35). Because Jesus has received "all power in heaven and on earth" (28:18), he decides to whom he will reveal the Father (11:27), who will ". . . inherit the kingdom" (25:34), or who will hear "I never knew you" (7:23). Yet he is "humble of heart" (11:29), saying "I am with you always, until the end of the age" (28:20).

Jesus' first concern to restore "the lost sheep of the house of Israel" (10:6; 15:24) widens into this Gospel's universal outlook that embraces "all nations" (24:14; 28:19). Matthew links Jewish and Christian perspectives by the theme of "fulfillment," wherein Old Testament events, characters, laws, and prophetic visions are renewed in Jesus. Fulfillment of the prophets is a constant refrain in the stories of Jesus' birth (1:23; 2:6, 15, 18, 23), ministry (4:14–16; 8:17; 12:16–21; 13:35; 21:4–5), and Passion (27:9–10). His Sermon on the Mount presumes a new law written on the heart (Jeremiah 31:31–34), but it neither destroys nor weakens the old: "I have come not to abolish but to fulfill," he says (5:17). Far from repealing the law, Jesus' Gospel intensifies its demands to include inner motivations and attitudes (5:20–48). His disciples are to reflect in kind, if not in degree, God's own indiscriminate love for others (5:43–48). This love and its corresponding just relationships epitomize the law and prophets (7:12; 22:36–40). The first covenant thus remains the deep root from which the new covenant continually flowers.

At first Matthew's strong Jewishness seems at odds with its vehemence against Jewish leaders and their practices (15:1–14; 23:1–36), but Matthew expresses the characteristic Jewish concern for final accountability before God, who renders rewards according to one's works. The prophets similarly denounced those who fail to practice God's commands (Isaiah 29:14).

Jesus' demands on his community are just as exacting. Half-hearted Christians are sternly warned: Those who do good only for show will be excluded from the kingdom (6:1–18; 7:21). Only serious disciples can expect to enter 22:1–14; 25:1–31).

Yet Matthew mixes severity and sweetness. A childlike attitude is extolled (18:3–4). Latecomers to the kingdom are welcomed if they are earnest (20:1–16; 21:28–32). Sinners can be forgiven if they forgive others (6:14–15; 18:21–35). Despite its rigors, Jesus' way is so appealing that disciples find his yoke "easy," and his burden "light" (11:28–29).

Unique among the Gospels, Matthew pays attention to the community of Jesus' followers; this Gospel alone uses the word *church* (*ekklesia*; 16:18; 18:17). The apostles and especially Peter serve as models, yet often they seem to slouch toward glory. Several times Jesus chides them for their lack of faith. "O you of little faith" (6:30; 8:26; 14:31; 16:8) sounds solemn in English, but actually translates Jesus' needling one-word nickname for the disciples, *oligopistoi* ("little-faiths"). Peter embodies the paradox of the beloved stumbling disciple (perfectly captured in Matthew's unique story about Peter walking on water only to sink and be rescued; 14:28–31). Peter spoke before he thought, slept at his post, and denied the Lord. But because he was the first to confess Jesus' true identity as Son of God, Jesus poetically renamed him (Peter means "rock") when he spoke of building his Church (16:18). Warts and all, the Twelve are foundation stones of the kingdom community (19:28). Faltering yet faithful, they were appropriate first hearers of the Savior-King's call, "Come to me, all you who labor and are burdened, and I will give you rest" (11:28).

Finally, Matthew contains many treasures found nowhere else. His Christmas stories uniquely tell of Joseph's dreams, the adoring Magi, the star, Herod's murderous fury, and the holy family's flight into Egypt (chapters 1–2). Matthew's pithy phrases, "salt of the earth" (5:13), "pearls before swine" (7:6), "wolves in sheep's clothing" (7:15), "wise as serpents" (10:16), "strain at a gnat and swallow a camel" (23:24), are part of our language. Certain parables are found only in Matthew: the Wheat and the Weeds (13:24–30), the Good and Bad Fish (13:47–48), the Unforgiving Servant (18:21–35), the Workers in the Vineyard (20:1–16), the Two Sons (21:28–32), and the Ten Virgins (25:1–13). Matthew alone tells of Peter finding the coin to pay his temple tax in a fish's mouth (17:24–27), and recounts Judas's final remorse (27:3–10), the dream of Pilate's wife (27:19), and the earthquakes (27:51; 28:2). All of these make Matthew's account of the Gospel a powerful teaching resource.

An Introduction to the Gospel According to John

by Michael Cameron

This Gospel has no year of its own in the Lectionary's three-year cycle, but it is strongly represented *every* year during seasons of Christmas, Lent, and Easter; it also appears in Ordinary Time in Mark for Year B, Sundays 17–21. John shares some features of the first three Gospels (called "synoptic" for "seeing together"). Some stories overlap, characters seen in the synoptics reappear, and John clearly voices the evangelistic, instructional purpose of all the Gospels: that you may believe and receive life in Jesus' name (20:31).

But its vision stands majestically apart, like the eagle that became this Gospel's symbol. It is rooted in the teaching of a mysterious unnamed figure, the "disciple whom Jesus loved" (13:23; 19:26; 20:2; 21:7, 20), who authenticates this Gospel's "testimony" (19:35; 21:24). It uniquely portrays the divine Word acting with God and as God to create all things (1:1–5,), taking human flesh to reveal the Father's glory (1:1, 14–18). It is an oversimplification to say that while the synoptics portray an extraordinary *human* with God-like powers, John pictures *God* wearing human flesh, but it carries an instructive grain of truth.

John communicates in distinctive ways. The synoptics tell Jesus' story in compact vignettes; John constructs chapter-long dramas (see especially chapters 4, 9, and 11). The first three Gospels contain pithy, memorable sayings about God's kingdom; John's Jesus speaks hypnotically repetitive discourses focused on eternal life (for example, 6:22–59; 10:1–18; chapters 14–17). The synoptics' homespun parables pique curiosity about Jesus' message; the Johannine Jesus poetically develops elements like water (4:7–15), bread (6:25–35), and light (3:19–21; 9:4–5; 12:35–36) into metaphors for contemplating divine truth.

John tells unique stories about Jesus: He changes water to wine (2:1–11), disputes with Nicodemus (3:1–21), engages the Samaritan woman at the well (4:4–26), heals a man born blind (9:1–41), raises dead Lazarus (11:1–45), chides the doubting Thomas (20:24–29), and cooks post-Easter breakfast for the disciples (21:1–14). John also varies details from some familiar synoptic stories, among which: Jesus "cleanses the Temple" early in his ministry rather than late (2:13–22); the synoptics' Passover meal ("the Last Supper") is a meal *before* Passover where Jesus washes the disciples' feet (13:4–15); the synoptic Jesus anguishes before death, but in John goes to the cross with serenity (12:27; 18:11); and unlike the synoptics, John has Jesus die on the day of preparation for Passover when the Passover lambs are sacrificed. These repeated references to Passover heighten the sacrificial symbolism of Jesus' death. Likewise, a strong liturgical symbolism makes Jesus' death the true Passover lamb sacrifice (1:29), his risen body the true temple (2:21), and his sacramental body and blood the true food and drink of Israel's wilderness journey (6:53–58).

John's hallmark strategies of indirectness and double meanings entice characters to move from surface earthly meanings to encoded heavenly meanings. Some catch on, like the woman at the well (4:4–26), but others miss the point, like Nicodemus, (3:3–10), the crowds (7:32–36), and Pilate (18:33–38). This indirectness separates truly committed disciples from the half-hearted window shoppers (2:23–25). Jesus performs "signs" (not "miracles") that lure people up the new ladder of Jacob arching from earth's pictures to heaven's glory (1:51; Genesis 28:12). This imagery of signs ends in a plain revelation about Jesus' divinity not found in the synoptic Gospels. His seven solemn "I AM" statements (6:35; 8:12; 10:7; 10:11; 11:25; 14:6; 15:1) recall God's revelation to Moses as "I AM" (Exodus 3:14) and testify to Jesus as the only source of life. So the inner truth of the blind man seeing is, "I am the light of the world" (9:5), and of the dead man rising, "I am the resurrection and the life" (11:25).

Jesus' signs hint at his divine glory (2:11) to be fully revealed at his "hour" (2:4; 7:30; 8:20; 13:1). Like the disciples, readers put things together only after the Resurrection (2:22); then we realize that as Jesus was "lifted up" for crucifixion by the Romans he was lifted up to glory by his Father (3:14; 8:28; 12:32). He mounted his cross like a King ascending his throne, as Pilate's placard unwittingly proclaimed (19:19–22). The Son's mission was to re-unite the world to its source of eternal life in God (3:16; 4:34; 17:4). He died with satisfaction that this work was accomplished, and announced, "It is finished!" (19:30).

In the Gospel according to John, God the Father is unseen and mostly silent, but pervasively present. The Father sent the Son, loves him (5:20; 15:9), bears him witness (5:37; 8:18), glorifies him (8:54), and dwells with him (14:11). The Father grants the Son to have life in himself, to judge the world, and to raise the dead (5:19–30). Father and Son together gave life to the world at creation (1:1–2), and continue to do so (5:17). God the Son in human flesh has "explained" the Father, literally "brought God into the open" (1:18). The Son does this so completely that Jesus says, "Whoever has seen me has seen the Father" (14:9; 12:45).

But divine life emanates from a third mysterious presence, "the Spirit of truth" (14:17). The Father and the Son together send the Spirit (15:26), who teaches the disciples about what Jesus said and who he was (14:26; 16:13). By the Spirit's indwelling, divine life flows through them like a river (7:38–39; 14:17).

John depicts the disciples as fruitful vine branches that the Father lovingly tends (15:1–5). Omitting all other ethical instruction, this Gospel says that the only measure of the disciples' fruitfulness is their love for one another. (13:34–35; 15:12–17).

True to character, this Gospel is sometimes one-sided. John's sense of Jesus' real humanity is relatively weak; and though teaching that "salvation is from the Jews" (4:22), it can be hostile toward Judaism, (8:21–26, 37–59). John must be balanced by the rest of the New Testament and the Church's later teaching. But its profound spiritual theology of the Word made flesh (1:14) has decisively shaped Christian theology, spirituality, and art, ever since it was written in the late first century.

Studying and Praying Scripture

by Michael Cameron

A recent study claimed that only 22 percent of American Catholics read the Bible regularly, and just 8 percent are involved in scripture groups. Not many know how profoundly biblical the Roman Catholic Church has been from its very roots, steeped in the words and spirit of the Old and New Testaments, "always venerating the divine scriptures as she venerates the Body of the Lord" (Vatican II). How may Catholics learn to read scripture? What follows briefly sketches a path for seekers.

PREPARING TO READ

Become an apprentice to the Bible. Ordinary people can reach a good level of understanding, but at a cost: the Bible yields its riches to those who give themselves to the search for understanding. Start by reading daily, even if only for a few minutes. Join a group that reads and discusses scripture together.

You will need tools. Think of yourself as a prospector for the Bible's gold. Nuggets on the ground are easily picked up, but the really rich veins lie beneath the surface. Digging requires study, commitment, and skills.

Invest in tools that reap the harvest of others' labors. Buy a study Bible with introductions, explanatory notes, and maps. Use another translation for devotional reading and comparison. Get access to a Bible dictionary with detailed information on biblical books, concepts, geography, outlines, customs, and other topics. Bible concordances will help you find all occurrences of particular words. A dictionary of biblical theology will give guidance on major theological ideas. A Bible atlas will give a sense of the locations and movements in the biblical stories. Recent Church documents on the Bible offer rich instruction to seekers.

READING FOR KNOWLEDGE

Get to know historical contexts suggested by a passage. Learn all you can about the Bible's basic story line, its "salvation history," beginning with Israel and continuing in the Church. Salvation by God's grace, obedience to God's will, and judgment on sin are basic to both Old and New Testaments. Learn particularly about the covenants with Abraham and David that emphasize God's grace. The covenant with Moses presumes God's grace and emphasizes obedience. Both covenant traditions re-emerge and are fulfilled in the new covenant in Jesus, who pours out his life to save all people (grace) but is extremely demanding of his disciples (obedience).

Read entire books of the Bible in order to gain a sense of the "whole cloth" from which the snippets of the Sunday Lectionary are cut. Try to imagine what the books meant for their original authors and audiences. Ask how and why a book was put together: What is its structure, outline, main themes, literary forms, overall purpose?

Get to know the Old Testament narratives and the psalms, but learn the Gospels especially. The Lectionary's yearly focus on Matthew, Mark, or Luke offers an opportunity to learn each one. John is the focus during the Church's special seasons.

READING FOR WISDOM

Read as one who seeks God, like the writer of Psalm 119. Ask what the text is asking you to believe, do, or hope for. Jesus' powerful proclamation in Mark 1:15 gives a strong framework: "This is the time of fulfillment" (now is the time to be attentive and ready to act); "the kingdom of God is at hand" (God is about to speak and act); "repent" (be willing to change your mind and move with fresh direction); "believe in the gospel" (embrace the grace that has already embraced you).

Read books straight through, a self-contained section at a time, carefully, slowly, and meditatively. Stop where natural breaks occur at the end of stories or sequences of thought.

Beware the sense that you already know what a text is going to say. Read attentively, asking what God is teaching you through this text at this minute about your life or about your communities— family, church, work, neighborhood, nation. Trust the Holy Spirit to guide you to what you need.

READING FOR WORSHIP

The goal of reading the Bible is not learning new facts or getting merely private inspiration for living, but entering into deeper communion with God. Allow the Bible to teach you to pray by giving you the words to use in prayer. The psalms are especially apt for this, but any part of the Bible may be prayed. This practice dating back more than fifteen hundred years is called *lectio divina*, Latin for "sacred reading."

Read scripture in relation to the Eucharist. The Bible both prepares for Jesus' real presence and helps us understand it. The same Jesus who healed the lepers, stilled the storm, and embraced the children is present to us in the word and in the sacrament.

The Bible is a library of spiritual treasures waiting to be discovered. The Church intends that this treasury be "wide open to the Christian faithful" (Vatican II).

RESOURCES

Brown, Raymond E., ss. *Responses to 101 Questions on the Bible*. Paulist Press, 1990.

Casey, Michael. *Sacred Reading: The Ancient Art of Lectio Divina*. Triumph, 1996.

Magrassi, Mariano. *Praying the Bible*. Liturgical Press, 1998.

Martin, George. *Reading Scripture as the Word of God*. 4th ed. Servant, 1998.

McKenzie, John L., sj. *Dictionary of the Bible*. MacMillan, 1965.

Paprocki, Joe. *God's Library: Introducing Catholics to the Bible*. Twenty-Third, 1999.

The Bible Documents: A Parish Resource. Liturgy Training Publications, 2001.

The Bible Today. (periodical for general readers) Liturgical Press.

The Catholic Study Bible. General editor, Donald Senior, cp. New York: Oxford, 1990.

The Collegeville Bible Commentary. Ed. Dianne Bergant and Robert J. Karris. Liturgical Press, 1990.

The Collegeville Pastoral Dictionary of Biblical Theology. Ed. Carroll Stuhlmueller, cp. Liturgical Press, 1996.

Advent

Prayer before Reading the Word

Sustain us, O God,
on our Advent journey
as we go forth to welcome
the One who is to come.

Plant within our hearts
your living Word of promise,
and make haste to help us
as we seek to understand
what we went out to see in the Advent wilderness:
your patience nurturing your saving purpose
　　　to fulfillment,
your power in Jesus making all things new.

We ask this through our Lord Jesus Christ, your Son,
who lives and reigns with you
in the unity of the Holy Spirit,
one God for ever and ever. Amen.

Prayer after Reading the Word

Joy and gladness, O God,
attend the advent of your reign in Jesus,
for whenever the Good News is proclaimed
　　　to the poor,
feeble limbs are made steady,
and fearful hearts grow strong.

Give us strength for witnessing,
that we may go and tell others what we see and hear.
Give us patience for waiting,
until the precious harvest of your kingdom,
when the return of your Son
will make your saving work complete.

Grant this through our
　　　Lord Jesus Christ,
who was, who is, and who is to come,
your Son, who lives and reigns with you
in the unity of the Holy Spirit,
one God for ever and ever. Amen.

Weekday Readings

December 3: *Isaiah 4:2–6; Matthew 8:5–11*
December 4: *Isaiah 11:1–10; Luke 10:21–24*
December 5: *Isaiah 25:6–10a; Matthew 15:29–37*
December 6: *Isaiah 26:1–6; Matthew 7:21, 24–27*
December 7: *Isaiah 29:17–24; Matthew 9:27–31*
December 8: Solemnity of the Immaculate Conception of
the Blessed Virgin Mary
Genesis 3:9–15, 20; Ephesians 1:3–6, 11–12;
Luke 1:26–38

December 10: *Isaiah 35:1–10; Luke 5:17–26*
December 11: *Isaiah 40:1–11; Matthew 18:12–14*
December 12: Feast of Our Lady of Guadalupe
Zechariah 2:14–17; Luke 1:26–38
December 13: *Isaiah 41:13–20; Matthew 11:11–15*
December 14: *Isaiah 48:17–19; Matthew 11:16–19*
December 15: *Sirach 48:1–4, 9–11; Matthew 17:9a, 10–13*

December 17: *Genesis 49:2, 8–10; Matthew 1:1–17*
December 18: *Jeremiah 23:5–8; Matthew 1:18–25*
December 19: *Judges 13:2–7, 24–25a; Luke 1:5–25*
December 20: *Isaiah 7:10–14; Luke 1:26–38*
December 21: *Song of Songs 2:8–14; Luke 1:39–45*
December 22: *1 Samuel 1:24–28; Luke 1:46–56*

December 24: *2 Samuel 7:1–5,*
8b–12, 14a, 16; Luke 1:67–79

December 2, 2007

READING I   *Isaiah 2:1—5*

This is what Isaiah, son of Amoz, saw concerning Judah and Jerusalem.

> In days to come,
> the mountain of the LORD's house
>   shall be established as
>   the highest mountain
>   and raised above the hills.
> All nations shall stream toward it;
>   many peoples shall come and say:
> "Come, let us climb the LORD's mountain,
>   to the house of the God of Jacob,
> that he may instruct us in his ways,
>   and we may walk in his paths."
> For from Zion shall go forth instruction,
>   and the word of the LORD from Jerusalem.
> He shall judge between the nations,
>   and impose terms on many peoples.
> They shall beat their swords into plowshares
>   and their spears into pruning hooks;
> one nation shall not raise
>   the sword against another,
>   nor shall they train for war again.
> O house of Jacob, come,
>   let us walk in the light of the Lord!

READING II   *Romans 13:11—14*

Brothers and sisters: You know the time; it is the hour now for you to awake from sleep. For our salvation is nearer now than when we first believed; the night is advanced, the day is at hand. Let us then throw off the works of darkness and put on the armor of light; let us conduct ourselves properly as in the day, not in orgies and drunkenness, not in promiscuity and lust, not in rivalry and jealousy. But put on the Lord Jesus Christ, and make no provision for the desires of the flesh.

GOSPEL   *Matthew 24:37—44*

Jesus said to his disciples: "As it was in the days of Noah, so it will be at the coming of the Son of Man. In those days before the flood, they were eating and drinking, marrying and giving in marriage, up to the day that Noah entered the ark. They did not know until the flood came and carried them all away. So will it be also at the coming of the Son of Man. Two men will be out in the field; one will be taken, and one will be left. Two women will be grinding at the mill; one will be taken, and one will be left. Therefore, stay awake! For you do not know on which day your Lord will come. Be sure of this: if the master of the house had known the hour of night when the thief was coming, he would have stayed awake and not let his house be broken into. So too, you also must be prepared, for at an hour you do not expect, the Son of Man will come."

Practice of Prayer

Psalm 122:1–2, 3–4, 4–5, 6–7, 8–9

R. Let us go rejoicing to
    the house of the Lord.

I rejoiced because they said to me,
    "We will go up to the house of the LORD."
And now we have set foot
    within your gates, O Jerusalem. R.

Jerusalem, built as a city
    with compact unity.
To it the tribes go up,
    the tribes of the LORD. R.

According to the decree for Israel,
    to give thanks to the name of the LORD.
In it are set up judgment seats,
    seats for the house of David. R.

Pray for the peace of Jerusalem!
    May those who love you prosper!
May peace be within your walls,
    prosperity in your buildings. R.

Because of my brothers and friends
    I will say, "Peace be within you!"
Because of the house of the LORD, our God,
    I will pray for your good. R.

Practice of Hope

Beating swords into plowshares is the mission of Pax Christi International. In 1945, a small group of people in France, troubled by the fact that French Catholics and German Catholics had fought each other in two disastrous world wars, met regularly to pray. Their spiritual advisor, Bishop Pierre Marie Theas, had begun working for reconciliation while imprisoned by the Germans. Soon after the war, Pax Christi centers were established in France and Germany, then in many countries. Now Pax Christi International maintains a presence at the United Nations as a recognized non-governmental organization (NGO).

The Pax Christi USA Web site, www.paxchristiusa.org, offers fine resources for Advent.

Scripture Insights

During Advent we prepare once more for the coming of our Lord, Jesus Christ. In today's Gospel reading Jesus is telling his disciples that since they do not know when the Son of Man will come they must be ready always. The phrase *Son of Man*, of course, refers to Jesus himself. So, at the same time that Jesus is instructing his disciples to prepare for his future coming, he is already with them. The same is true for us. During Advent we prepare not only for a future coming of the Son of Man when God's purposes in human history will be fulfilled, but for a present coming into our lives right now. Now is the time to prepare for the risen Christ to dwell with us more fully.

Paul, in his letter to the Romans, tells us how to prepare. We examine our lives to make sure that the everyday choices we make are helping us grow in discipleship, helping us "put on the armor of light . . . put on the Lord Jesus Christ." We avoid behaviors such as drunkenness and any action motivated by lust, rivalry, or jealousy. We treat ourselves and others with the dignity due to a beloved child of God.

Isaiah's great prophecy of hope and peace describes the fruit of living as children of the light. When we are instructed in God's ways and choose, with God's grace, to walk in God's path, we will experience joy and peace. Not just individuals, but nations, will find peace when we learn to walk in the light of the Lord.

Today's readings remind us that we must be ready for the coming of the Lord always, because the Lord is always coming. Are we ready?

◆ What words in today's Gospel communicate the urgency of Jesus' teaching to his disciples?

◆ At this moment in your life, in what ways do you experience Christ as already present? How do you envision his Second Coming and how are you preparing for it?

◆ What specific actions can you take this Advent to invite Christ more fully into your life?

READING I   *Isaiah 11:1—10*

On that day, a shoot shall sprout
     from the stump of Jesse,
   and from his roots a bud shall blossom.
The spirit of the LORD shall rest upon him:
     a spirit of wisdom and of understanding,
a spirit of counsel and of strength,
     a spirit of knowledge and
       of fear of the LORD,
   and his delight shall be the fear
       of the LORD.
Not by appearance shall he judge,
     nor by hearsay shall he decide,
but he shall judge the poor with justice,
     and decide aright for the land's afflicted.
He shall strike the ruthless
     with the rod of his mouth,
   and with the breath of his lips
       he shall slay the wicked.
Justice shall be the band around his waist,
     and faithfulness a belt upon his hips.
Then the wolf shall be a guest of the lamb,
     and the leopard shall lie down
       with the kid;
the calf and the young lion shall
       browse together,
     with a little child to guide them.
The cow and the bear shall be neighbors,
     together their young shall rest;
     the lion shall eat hay like the ox.
The baby shall play by the cobra's den,
     and the child lay his hand on
       the adder's lair.
There shall be no harm or ruin
     on all my holy mountain;
     for the earth shall be filled
       with knowledge of the LORD,
     as water covers the sea.
On that day, the root of Jesse,
     set up as a signal for the nations,
the Gentiles shall seek out,
     for his dwelling shall be glorious.

READING II   *Romans 15:4—9*

Brothers and sisters: Whatever was written previously was written for our instruction, that by endurance and by the encouragement of the Scriptures we might have hope. May the God of endurance and encouragement grant you to think in harmony with one another, in keeping with Christ Jesus, that with one accord you may with one voice glorify the God and Father of our Lord Jesus Christ.

Welcome one another, then, as Christ welcomed you, for the glory of God. For I say that Christ became a minister of the circumcised to show God's truthfulness, to confirm the promises to the patriarchs, but so that the Gentiles might glorify God for his mercy. As it is written:

> *Therefore, I will praise you among the Gentiles*
> *and sing praises to your name.*

GOSPEL   *Matthew 3:1—12*

John the Baptist appeared, preaching in the desert of Judea and saying, "Repent, for the kingdom of heaven is at hand!" It was of him that the prophet Isaiah had spoken when he said:

> *A voice of one crying out in the desert,*
> *Prepare the way of the Lord,*
> *   make straight his paths.*

John wore clothing made of camel's hair and had a leather belt around his waist. His food was locusts and wild honey. At that time Jerusalem, all Judea, and the whole region around the Jordan were going out to him and were being baptized by him in the Jordan River as they acknowledged their sins.

When he saw many of the Pharisees and Sadducees coming to his baptism, he said to them, "You brood of vipers! Who warned you to flee from the coming wrath? Produce good fruit as evidence of your repentance. And do not presume to say to yourselves, 'We have Abraham as our father.' For I tell you, God can raise up children to Abraham from these stones. Even now the ax lies at the root of the trees. Therefore every tree that does not bear good fruit will be cut down and thrown into the fire. I am baptizing you with water, for repentance, but the one who is coming after me is mightier than I. I am not worthy to carry his sandals. He will baptize you with the Holy Spirit and fire. His winnowing fan is in his hand. He will clear his threshing floor and gather his wheat into his barn, but the chaff he will burn with unquenchable fire."

Practice of Prayer

Psalm 72:1—2, 7—8, 12—13, 17 (see 7)
R. Justice shall flourish in his time,
and fullness of peace for ever.

O God, with your judgment endow the king,
and with your justice, the king's son;
he shall govern your people with justice
and your afflicted ones with judgment. R.

Justice shall flower in his days,
and profound peace, till the moon be no more.
May he rule from sea to sea,
and from the River to
the ends of the earth. R.

For he shall rescue the poor when he cries out,
and the afflicted when
he has no one to help him.
He shall have pity for the lowly and the poor;
the lives of the poor he shall save. R.

May his name be blessed forever;
as long as the sun his name shall remain.
In him shall all the tribes of the earth be blessed;
all the nations shall proclaim
his happiness. R.

Practice of Charity

In war-ravaged Paris, Armand Marquiset devoted his life to neglected elderly people. In 1946 he founded Little Brothers of the Poor, who provided many services for the elderly, including holiday dinners made memorable by candles and flowers.

Now the Little Brothers serve the elderly in 11 countries, including the United States. Learn how to help: www.littlebrothers.org.

Scripture Insights

In today's Gospel, repentance is an essential preparation for the Lord's coming. John the Baptist calls out, "Repent, for the kingdom of heaven is at hand!" But when some Pharisees and Sadducees present themselves for baptism, John calls them a "brood of vipers" and says, "Produce good fruit as evidence of your repentance."

Pharisees and Sadducees, two Jewish sects, would later be adversaries of Jesus. Pharisees interpreted the law rigidly; Sadducees rejected the idea of resurrection. John is warning them that their status as "children of Abraham" is not enough. They must be open to the Spirit, to the fulfillment of God's promises to the children of Abraham. The one who is to come will baptize them "with the Holy Spirit and fire."

In Isaiah's prophesy, we hear the kind of promises that God made the children of Abraham. God would send the people a future leader who would be open to new understandings of God's power. This future king would be so full of the spirit of the Lord, "a spirit of wisdom and of understanding," that even non-Jews would seek him out. Jesus was the fulfillment of God's promises to the patriarchs. Through Jesus, the Gentiles too came to know and glorify God.

To bear good fruit we must do more than call ourselves Christian and present ourselves for worship. We must truly repent and open our hearts to the Spirit in order to fully welcome Christ into our lives.

◆ In the Isaiah passage, what words and images speak to you most vividly about the Lord who will come?

◆ Paul speaks of the scriptures giving us encouragement and hope. Which ones have especially helped you?

◆ In your experience, how does repentance prepare us and open us to the Spirit?

December 16, 2007

READING I   *Isaiah 35:1—6a, 10*

The desert and the parched land will exult;
    the steppe will rejoice and bloom.
They will bloom with abundant flowers,
    and rejoice with joyful song.
The glory of Lebanon will be given to them,
    the splendor of Carmel and Sharon;
they will see the glory of the LORD,
    the splendor of our God.
Strengthen the hands that are feeble,
    make firm the knees that are weak,
say to those whose hearts are frightened:
    Be strong, fear not!
Here is your God,
    he comes with vindication;
with divine recompense
    he comes to save you.
Then will the eyes of the blind be opened,
    the ears of the deaf be cleared;
then will the lame leap like a stag,
    then the tongue of the mute will sing.

Those whom the LORD has ransomed
      will return
    and enter Zion singing,
    crowned with everlasting joy;
they will meet with joy and gladness,
    sorrow and mourning will flee.

READING II   *James 5:7—10*

Be patient, brothers and sisters, until the coming of the Lord. See how the farmer waits for the precious fruit of the earth, being patient with it until it receives the early and the late rains. You too must be patient. Make your hearts firm, because the coming of the Lord is at hand. Do not complain, brothers and sisters, about one another, that you may not be judged. Behold, the Judge is standing before the gates. Take as an example of hardship and patience, brothers and sisters, the prophets who spoke in the name of the Lord.

GOSPEL   *Matthew 11:2—11*

When John the Baptist heard in prison of the works of the Christ, he sent his disciples to Jesus with this question, "Are you the one who is to come, or should we look for another?" Jesus said to them in reply, "Go and tell John what you hear and see: the blind regain their sight, the lame walk, lepers are cleansed, the deaf hear, the dead are raised, and the poor have the good news proclaimed to them. And blessed is the one who takes no offense at me."

As they were going off, Jesus began to speak to the crowds about John, "What did you go out to the desert to see? A reed swayed by the wind? Then what did you go out to see? Someone dressed in fine clothing? Those who wear fine clothing are in royal palaces. Then why did you go out? To see a prophet? Yes, I tell you, and more than a prophet. This is the one about whom it is written:

> *Behold, I am sending my messenger*
>   *ahead of you;*
>   *he will prepare your way before you.*

Amen, I say to you, among those born of women there has been none greater than John the Baptist; yet the least in the kingdom of heaven is greater than he."

Practice of Prayer

Psalm 146:6—7, 8—9, 9—10 (See Isaiah 35:4)

R. LORD, come and save us.
or: Alleluia.

The LORD God keeps faith forever,
    secures justice for the oppressed,
    gives food to the hungry.
The LORD sets captives free. R.

The LORD gives sight to the blind;
    the LORD raises up
        those who were bowed down.
The LORD loves the just;
    the LORD protects strangers. R.

The fatherless and the widow
    he sustains,
    but the way of the wicked
    he thwarts.
The LORD shall reign forever;
    your God, O Zion,
        through all generations. R.

Practice of Faith

Like many Hispanic neighborhoods, and like towns all over Mexico, Olvera Street in Los Angeles will be vibrant with activity tonight. Every night between now and Christmas, it will host the colorful candlelight procession called *Las Posadas*. In this beloved tradition, "shepherds" and "angels" of all ages accompany Mary and Joseph as they seek shelter. They are turned away from every place where they request lodging—until Joseph bursts out with the news that his wife, the Queen of Heaven, is about to give birth. Then a door is flung open and joyous carols in Spanish and English are sung. Spicy hot chocolate and sweet breads are served. Children break open a piñata, perhaps shaped like a Christmas star, and dive for the candy, toys, and sugar cane that spill out. On Christmas Eve, *Noche Buena*, everyone will proceed to a late-night *Misa de Gallo*—Mass of the Rooster.

Scripture Insights

All three of our readings—from Isaiah, James, and the Gospel according to Matthew—are about people anxiously awaiting the coming of the Lord. However, as the Gospel makes clear, it is not always easy to recognize the Lord when he comes. John the Baptist, who prepared the way for Jesus, had to send his disciples to ask Jesus, "Are you the one who is to come, or should we look for another?"

As we read last Sunday, John was expecting a messiah who would judge the human race, who would "gather his wheat into his barn, but the chaff he will burn with unquenchable fire" (Matthew 3:12). Instead of judging and condemning people, Jesus was reaching out in love and power to heal the blind, the lame, and the deaf, and to preach the good news to the poor. Could Jesus be the messiah?

By pointing to his mighty signs of healing as an answer to the question, Are you the messiah? Jesus is reminding John of the words of the prophet Isaiah that we read today. Isaiah was offering hope to those who felt separated from their God because they had been separated from the holy land, from Zion. Isaiah is assuring the Israelites that God will come in power to save them. The signs of God's coming will be that the blind will see, the deaf will hear, the lame will walk, and the mute will speak. Jesus, who is performing these signs, is the Messiah.

Like John, we too bring false presumptions with us as we prepare the way of the Lord. Our false presumptions hinder our ability to see. In Advent we remember that Jesus can heal the blind, and we ask that our eyes be opened to the many ways in which Jesus is present in our lives.

◆ According to the Isaiah passage, what are all the signs and events people will experience when their God comes to them?

◆ What can the readings from Paul and Isaiah teach us about waiting?

◆ How has your concept of God changed over the years?

READING I   *Isaiah 7:10—14*

The LORD spoke to Ahaz, saying: Ask for a sign from the LORD, your God; let it be deep as the netherworld, or high as the sky! But Ahaz answered, "I will not ask! I will not tempt the LORD!" Then Isaiah said: Listen, O house of David! Is it not enough for you to weary people, must you also weary my God? Therefore the Lord himself will give you this sign: the virgin shall conceive, and bear a son, and shall name him Emmanuel.

READING II   *Romans 1:1—7*

Paul, a slave of Christ Jesus, called to be an apostle and set apart for the gospel of God, which he promised previously through his prophets in the holy Scriptures, the gospel about his Son, descended from David according to the flesh, but established as Son of God in power according to the Spirit of holiness through resurrection from the dead, Jesus Christ our Lord. Through him we have received the grace of apostleship, to bring about the obedience of faith, for the sake of his name, among all the Gentiles, among whom are you also, who are called to belong to Jesus Christ; to all the beloved of God in Rome, called to be holy. Grace to you and peace from God our Father and the Lord Jesus Christ.

GOSPEL   *Matthew 1:18—24*

This is how the birth of Jesus Christ came about. When his mother Mary was betrothed to Joseph, but before they lived together, she was found with child through the Holy Spirit. Joseph her husband, since he was a righteous man, yet unwilling to expose her to shame, decided to divorce her quietly. Such was his intention when, behold, the angel of the Lord appeared to him in a dream and said, "Joseph, son of David, do not be afraid to take Mary your wife into your home. For it is through the Holy Spirit that this child has been conceived in her. She will bear a son and you are to name him Jesus, because he will save his people from their sins." All this took place to fulfill what the Lord had said through the prophet:

> *Behold, the virgin shall conceive and bear a son,*
> *and they shall name him Emmanuel,*

which means "God is with us." When Joseph awoke, he did as the angel of the Lord had commanded him and took his wife into his home.

Practice of Prayer

R. Let the LORD enter; he is king of glory.

The LORD's are the earth and its fullness;
    the world and those who dwell in it.
For he founded it upon the seas
    and established it upon the rivers.   R.

Who can ascend the mountain of the LORD?
    or who may stand in his holy place?
One whose hands are sinless,
        whose heart is clean,
    who desires not what is vain.   R.

He shall receive a blessing from the LORD,
    a reward from God his savior.
Such is the race that seeks for him,
    that seeks the face of the God of Jacob.   R.

Practice of Faith

In Jesus's time, shepherds usually were people who didn't fit well into village life. Nor did they have much in the way of earthly goods. These facts make all the more poignant the hospitality extended to them by Mary and Joseph. However, as Archbishop Oscar Romero observed in a Christmas Eve homily, "No one can celebrate a genuine Christmas without being truly poor. The self-sufficient, the proud, those who, because they have everything, look down on others, those who have no need even of God—for them there will be no Christmas. Only the poor, the hungry, those who need someone to come on their behalf, will have that someone. That someone is God, Emmanuel, God-with-us. Without poverty of spirit there can be no abundance of God." How will you share your Christmas hospitality with those who need it most this year?

Scripture Insights

Today we read the annunciation of Jesus' birth as it appears in the Gospel according to Matthew. Here the annunciation is not to Mary, but to Joseph. Stories surrounding Jesus' birth are Christological; they teach the identity of Jesus Christ as that identity was understood after the Resurrection.

In today's story we learn that Jesus is divine; that is, he was conceived through the Holy Spirit: "For it is through the Holy Spirit that this child has been conceived in her." We also learn Jesus' role in salvation history: ". . . he will save his people from their sins."

Since Matthew is writing primarily to fellow Jews, he constantly emphasizes that Jesus is the fulfillment of God's covenant promises to the Israelites. Here he quotes the passage from Isaiah that we read in today's first reading. When Isaiah told King Ahaz that "the virgin shall conceive, and bear a son, and shall name him Emmanuel," he was assuring King Ahaz that God would be faithful to his promise to the house of David. A young woman would bear Ahaz a son, and that son would be a faithful king. God would be with that son as he had promised to be with David's descendents.

In the light of later events (Mary's virginal conception of Jesus; Jesus' Resurrection from the dead) the early Church saw more meaning in Isaiah's words. God's purposes in history were now understood more fully; the words of the prophet were fulfilled.

Paul, in meditating on these truths and on his own call, reminds us that we are the great beneficiaries of Jesus' saving acts. We are called to belong to Jesus Christ. We are called to be holy.

◆ In the story of the annunciation to Joseph, what persuaded Joseph to change his plan? What things in the story help you to understand Jesus' identity?

◆ In what ways do you belong to Jesus Christ?

◆ How have you responded to your call to be holy this Advent? How would you do so in the future?

Christmas

Prayer before Reading the Word

Almighty God, Creator of all,
whose Word was present with you
      in the beginning
and whose wisdom was placed
at the service of your plan:
Enlighten us to know the glorious hope
to which you have called us;
fill us with faith in Jesus and
with love toward all your people,
that we who have seen in Christ
the glory of your Word made flesh
may bear into the world you so love,
the Light no darkness can extinguish:
your Son, our Lord Jesus Christ,
who lives and reigns with you
in the unity of the Holy Spirit,
one God for ever and ever. Amen.

Prayer after Reading the Word

Your Word, O God of ageless glory,
dwelling with you from before time,
has become flesh and lived among us,
and we have seen the glory of your Christ.

Place on our lips the word of salvation,
in our hearts a love that welcomes all,
and, in the depths of our being,
the light of faith and hope,
which the darkness can never overcome.

We ask this through our Lord
      Jesus Christ, your Son,
who lives and reigns with you
in the unity of the Holy Spirit,
one God for ever and ever. Amen.

Weekday Readings

December 25: Solemnity of the Nativity of the Lord
    Day: *Isaiah 52:7–10; Hebrews 1:1–6; John 1:1–18*
December 26: Feast of Saint Stephen
    Acts 6:8–10; 7:54–59; Matthew 10:17–22
December 27: Feast of Saint John
    1 John 1:1–4; John 20:1a, 2–8
December 28: Feast of the Holy Innocents
    1 John 1:5—2:2; Matthew 2:13–18
December 29: Fifth Day in the Octave of Christmas
    1 John 2:3–11; Luke 2:22–35

December 31: Seventh Day in the Octave of Christmas
    1 John 2:18–21; John 1:1–18
January 1: Solemnity of the Blessed Virgin Mary,
    the Mother of God
    Numbers 6:22–27; Galatians 4:4–7; Luke 2:16–21
January 2: *1 John 2:22–28; John 1:19–28*
January 3: *1 John 2:29—3:6; John 1:29–34*
January 4: *1 John 3:7–10; John 1:35–42*
January 5: *1 John 3:11–21; John 1:43–51*

January 7: *1 John 3:22—4:6; Matthew 4:12–17, 23–25*
January 8: *1 John 4:7–10; Mark 6:34–44*
January 9: *1 John 4:11–18; Mark 6:45–52*
January 10: *1 John 4:19—5:4; Luke 4:14–22a*
January 11: *1 John 5:5–13; Luke 5:12–16*
January 12: *John 5:14–21; 1 John 3:22–30*

READING I   Isaiah 9:1—6

The people who walked in darkness
    have seen a great light;
upon those who dwelt in the land of gloom
    a light has shone.
You have brought them abundant joy
    and great rejoicing,
as they rejoice before you as at the harvest,
    as people make merry when
        dividing spoils.
For the yoke that burdened them,
    the pole on their shoulder,
and the rod of their taskmaster
    you have smashed, as on the day
        of Midian.
For every boot that tramped in battle,
    every cloak rolled in blood,
    will be burned as fuel for flames.
For a child is born to us, a son is given us;
    upon his shoulder dominion rests.
They name him Wonder-Counselor,
    God-Hero,
    Father-Forever, Prince of Peace.
His dominion is vast
    and forever peaceful,
from David's throne, and over his kingdom,
    which he confirms and sustains
by judgment and justice,
    both now and forever.
The zeal of the LORD of hosts will do this!

READING II   Titus 2:11—14

Beloved:

The grace of God has appeared, saving all and training us to reject godless ways and worldly desires and to live temperately, justly, and devoutly in this age, as we await the blessed hope, the appearance of the glory of our great God and savior Jesus Christ, who gave himself for us to deliver us from all lawlessness and to cleanse for himself a people as his own, eager to do what is good.

GOSPEL   Luke 2:1—14

In those days a decree went out from Caesar Augustus that the whole world should be enrolled. This was the first enrollment, when Quirinius was governor of Syria. So all went to be enrolled, each to his own town. And Joseph too went up from Galilee from the town of Nazareth to Judea, to the city of David that is called Bethlehem, because he was of the house and family of David, to be enrolled with Mary, his betrothed, who was with child. While they were there, the time came for her to have her child, and she gave birth to her firstborn son. She wrapped him in swaddling clothes and laid him in a manger, because there was no room for them in the inn.

Now there were shepherds in that region living in the fields and keeping the night watch over their flock. The angel of the Lord appeared to them and the glory of the Lord shone around them, and they were struck with great fear. The angel said to them, "Do not be afraid; for behold, I proclaim to you good news of great joy that will be for all the people. For today in the city of David a savior has been born for you who is Christ and Lord. And this will be a sign for you: you will find an infant wrapped in swaddling clothes and lying in a manger." And suddenly there was a multitude of the heavenly host with the angel, praising God and saying:

"Glory to God in the highest
    and on earth peace to those
        on whom his favor rests."

Practice of Prayer

Psalm 96:1—2, 2—3 11—12, 13 (Luke 2:11)

R. Today is born our Savior, Christ the Lord.

Sing to the LORD a new song;
  sing to the LORD, all you lands.
Sing to the LORD; bless his name. R.

Announce his salvation, day after day.
  Tell his glory among the nations;
  among all peoples, his wondrous deeds. R.

Let the heavens be glad and the earth rejoice;
  let the sea and what fills it resound;
  let the plains be joyful and all that is in them!
Then shall all the trees of the forest exult. R.

They shall exult before the LORD, for he comes;
  for he comes to rule the earth.
He shall rule the world with justice
  and the peoples with his constancy. R.

Practice of Faith

In the words of the late Peter Mazar, "No sooner does the winter sun turn in its course back toward the summertime than we Christians latch on to this tiny sign of hope and make midwinter our second spring. Birth is, after all, a springtime event. How harsh a paradox to celebrate birth when winter is just beginning! Yet 'new birth' is our cry: *Noel!* So we banish the long nights with firelight and candles. We defy the winter by festooning summer's green from our rafters. We spread our tables with the abundance of the harvest, all signs of God's graciousness, signs of the bounty of heaven itself. We gather around the sparkling tree of life and declare this place, no matter how humble, to be paradise." Tonight, as we trek to Midnight Mass, then home for a joyous feast, celebrate God's graciousness in your life. *Noel!*

Scripture Insights

Mary "gave birth to her firstborn son. She wrapped him in swaddling clothes and laid him in a manger, because there was no room for them in the inn." In this simple statement Luke is teaching his Gentile audience the identity of Jesus Christ, an identity that was understood only after the Resurrection.

To call Jesus Mary's "firstborn" is not to suggest that Mary had other children. Rather it gives Jesus a title that emphasizes his divinity. We see this title used in several other New Testament books, including the letter to the Colossians: "He [Jesus] is the image of the invisible God, the / firstborn of all creation. / For in him were created all things in heaven and on earth. . ." (Colossians 1:15—16a).

To say that Mary laid Jesus in a manger, a feeding trough for the flock, reminds us that Jesus is still food for the flock. The Gospel according to John teaches this same mystery when Jesus says, "I am the bread of life" (John 6:35). We experience Jesus as food for us, Jesus' flock, every time we receive Jesus in Eucharist.

To say that there was no room for Jesus in the inn says that Jesus has come to dwell with us. An inn shelters a traveler, not one who has come to dwell with the people.

What is the good news of great joy that we celebrate on Christmas? Paul sums it up in today's letter to Titus: "The grace of God [Jesus] has appeared, saving all and training us to reject godless ways and worldly desires and to live temperately, justly, and devoutly . . . ." The child given to us this day has redeemed all humans from sin and has given us the knowledge and the power to live in right relationship with God and each other.

◆ In today's Gospel, which words or phrases point you to Christ's divinity? Which ones point you to his humanity?

◆ How do Paul's words relate to your celebration of Christmas this year?

◆ In your experience, how has Jesus been food for the flock?

READING I   Sirach 3:2—6, 12—14

God sets a father in honor over his children;
 a mother's authority he
  confirms over her sons.
Whoever honors his father atones for sins,
 and preserves himself from them.
When he prays, he is heard;
 he stores up riches who reveres his mother.
Whoever honors his father
 is gladdened by children,
 and, when he prays, is heard.
Whoever reveres his father will live a long life;
 he who obeys his father brings
  comfort to his mother.

My son, take care of your father when
 he is old;
 grieve him not as long as he lives.
Even if his mind fail, be considerate of him;
 revile him not all the days of his life;
kindness to a father will not be forgotten,
 firmly planted against the debt of
  your sins
 —a house raised in justice to you.

READING II   Colossians 3:12—21

Shorter: Colossians 3:12–17

Brothers and sisters:

Put on, as God's chosen ones, holy and beloved, heartfelt compassion, kindness, humility, gentleness, and patience, bearing with one another and forgiving one another, if one has a grievance against another; as the Lord has forgiven you, so must you also do. And over all these put on love, that is, the bond of perfection. And let the peace of Christ control your hearts, the peace into which you were also called in one body. And be thankful. Let the word of Christ dwell in you richly, as in all wisdom you teach and admonish one another, singing psalms, hymns, and spiritual songs with gratitude in your hearts to God. And whatever you do, in word or in deed, do everything in the name of the Lord Jesus, giving thanks to God the Father through him.

Wives, be subordinate to your husbands, as is proper in the Lord. Husbands, love your wives, and avoid any bitterness toward them. Children, obey your parents in everything, for this is pleasing to the Lord. Fathers, do not provoke your children, so they may not become discouraged.

GOSPEL   Matthew 2:13—15, 19—23

When the magi had departed, behold, the angel of the Lord appeared to Joseph in a dream and said, "Rise, take the child and his mother; flee to Egypt, and stay there until I tell you. Herod is going to search for the child to destroy him." Joseph rose and took the child and his mother by night and departed for Egypt. He stayed there until the death of Herod, that what the Lord had said through the prophet might be fulfilled,

Out of Egypt I called my son.

When Herod had died, behold, the angel of the Lord appeared in a dream to Joseph in Egypt and said, "Rise, take the child and his mother and go to the land of Israel, for those who sought the child's life are dead." He rose, took the child and his mother, and went to the land of Israel. But when he heard that Archelaus was ruling over Judea in place of his father Herod, he was afraid to go back there. And because he had been warned in a dream, he departed for the region of Galilee. He went and dwelt in a town called Nazareth, so that what had been spoken through the prophets might be fulfilled,

He shall be called a Nazorean.

Practice of Prayer

Psalm 128:1—2, 3, 4—5 (see 1)

R. Blessed are those who fear the Lord and walk
    in his ways.

Blessed is everyone who fears the LORD,
    who walks in his ways!
For you shall eat the fruit of your handiwork;
    blessed shall you be, and favored. R.

Your wife shall be like a fruitful vine
    in the recesses of your home;
your children like olive plants
    around your table. R.

Behold, thus is the man blessed
    who fears the LORD.
The LORD bless you from Zion:
    may you see the prosperity of Jerusalem
    all the days of your life. R.

Practice of Charity

Two thousand years of progress have not eradicate the plight of refugees. Millions today are enduring the same fate suffered by the Holy Family as they fled the wrath of Herod. Today's refugees around the world are usually escaping from political oppression or destructive forces of nature, just as in ancient times. In the past few years, many people have been made refugees by weather-related events within our own nation, such as Hurricane Katrina. Families in these situations face grave stresses. In responding to Katrina, Habitat for Humanity (HFH) has made a difference. Each family assisted by the organization invested 350 hours of labor to help build their own new home—an exercise in empowerment and hope. The HFH program Gifts from the Heart offers the opportunity to make a donation in honor of a friend or loved one. Learn more at www.habitat.org.

Scripture Insights

The readings for the feast of the Holy Family teach us, as God's chosen and redeemed ones, how to treat the members of our own family *and* the whole human family.

The Gospel shows us Joseph and Mary fleeing to Egypt to protect their child. While the Lectionary presents this as an example of family life, the Gospel writer's purposes were theological. He was teaching his primarily Jewish audience that Jesus is not only the fulfillment of the words of the prophets, but the fulfillment of the history of his people. Using a teaching device of the time called *midrash*, the author weaves Old Testament allusions around his account of New Testament events. He reminds us of Moses when he describes a slaughter of children at Jesus' birth, and of the nation, Israel, as he describes Jesus being called out of Egypt.

The author of Sirach the urges children of all ages to treat their parents with deep respect. Those who treat their parents with love and respect all their lives will reap benefits in both their relationship with God and their bond with their own children.

When Paul addresses the Colossians as "God's chosen ones, holy and beloved," and tells them how to act toward one another, he is speaking in the context of the whole Christian community. However, what he says is just as applicable to families. Paul emphasizes that forgiveness is absolutely necessary. Since we have been forgiven, we must forgive.

Protection, respect, and forgiveness are all necessary components of our family lives, but most important is love: "And over all these put on love, that is, the bond of perfection."

• How does Paul advise Christians to cultivate forgiving hearts?

◆ From your experience, why is forgiveness essential to family life?

◆ Why do you think Paul calls love "the bond of perfection"?

January 6, 2008

READING I   *Isaiah 60:1—6*

Rise up in splendor, Jerusalem!
     Your light has come,
     the glory of the LORD shines upon you.
See, darkness covers the earth,
     and thick clouds cover the peoples;
but upon you the LORD shines,
     and over you appears his glory.
Nations shall walk by your light,
     and kings by your shining radiance.
Raise your eyes and look about;
     they all gather and come to you:
your sons come from afar,
     and your daughters in the arms
          of their nurses.

Then you shall be radiant at what you see,
     your heart shall throb and overflow,
for the riches of the sea shall be
          emptied out before you,
     the wealth of nations shall be brought
          to you.
Caravans of camels shall fill you,
     dromedaries from Midian and Ephah;
all from Sheba shall come
     bearing gold and frankincense,
     and proclaiming the praises of the LORD.

READING II   *Ephesians 3:2—3a, 5—6*

Brothers and sisters:

You have heard of the stewardship of God's grace that was given to me for your benefit, namely, that the mystery was made known to me by revelation. It was not made known to people in other generations as it has now been revealed to his holy apostles and prophets by the Spirit: that the Gentiles are coheirs, members of the same body, and copartners in the promise in Christ Jesus through the gospel.

GOSPEL   *Matthew 2:1—12*

When Jesus was born in Bethlehem of Judea, in the days of King Herod, behold, magi from the east arrived in Jerusalem, saying, "Where is the newborn king of the Jews? We saw his star at its rising and have come to do him homage." When King Herod heard this, he was greatly troubled, and all Jerusalem with him. Assembling all the chief priests and the scribes of the people, he inquired of them where the Christ was to be born. They said to him, "In Bethlehem of Judea, for thus it has been written through the prophet:

And you, Bethlehem, land of Judah,
     are by no means least among
          the rulers of Judah;
since from you shall come a ruler,
     who is to shepherd my people Israel."

Then Herod called the magi secretly and ascertained from them the time of the star's appearance. He sent them to Bethlehem and said, "Go and search diligently for the child. When you have found him, bring me word, that I too may go and do him homage." After their audience with the king they set out. And behold, the star that they had seen at its rising preceded them, until it came and stopped over the place where the child was. They were overjoyed at seeing the star, and on entering the house they saw the child with Mary his mother. They prostrated themselves and did him homage. Then they opened their treasures and offered him gifts of gold, frankincense, and myrrh. And having been warned in a dream not to return to Herod, they departed for their country by another way.

Practice of Prayer

Psalm 72:1—2, 7—8, 10—11, 12—13 (see 11)

R. Lord, every nation on earth will adore you.

O God, with your judgment endow the king,
　　and with your justice, the king's son;
he shall govern your people with justice
　　and your afflicted ones with judgment.　R.

Justice shall flower in his days,
　　and profound peace, till the moon be no more.
May he rule from sea to sea,
　　and from the River to the ends of the earth.　R.

The kings of Tarshish and the Isles shall offer gifts;
　　the kings of Arabia and Seba
　　　　shall bring tribute.
All kings shall pay him homage,
　　all nations shall serve him.　R.

For he shall rescue the poor when he cries out,
　　and the afflicted when
　　　　he has no one to help him.
He shall have pity for the lowly and the poor;
　　the lives of the poor he shall save.　R.

Practice of Faith

This twelfth day of Christmas, was called the festival of lights in ancient times. We rejoice because, just as a star led the Magi to Christ, we have been guided by faith to the same destination. Scripture scholars believe the Magi would have come from Iran or Iraq—so we realize anew that Christ came to unite the world in love, peace, and mutual respect. Bless your home today, asking for those qualities to fill every heart during the coming year. Use chalk to mark the lintel of the front door: 20+C+M+B+08. The letters represent the names tradition gave to the Magi: Caspar, Melchior, and Balthazar. They also stand for *Christus mansionem benedicat*—May Christ bless this home. Process through every room, bearing candles. Sing carols, especially "We Three Kings" and "The Twelve Days of Christmas." Then have a candlelit feast!

Scripture Insights

The good news on the feast of the Epiphany is stated in Paul's letter to the Ephesians and dramatized in today's Gospel. Through Jesus Christ, God has revealed that both Jews and Gentiles are now invited into a relationship of covenant love with God.

The hope that all nations would come to know God through the Israelites and their covenant relationship with God appeared in the Old Testament prophets' message hundreds of years before this hope was fulfilled in Jesus Christ. Today's passage from Isaiah offered this hope to the exiles who returned to the holy land after the Babylonian exile (587–537).

The exiles had already suffered greatly and continued to suffer as they tried to rebuild their temple. The prophet who wrote today's reading is often referred to as third Isaiah. (The book of Isaiah contains the prophecies of three prophets who lived at different times.) He acknowledges the suffering of the people when he says, "See, darkness covers the earth, / and thick clouds cover the peoples. . . ." However, their suffering is not without hope and purpose. God will do something new and wonderful through the Israelites. Through them other nations will come to know God. Matthew, in teaching the significance of Jesus' role in salvation history as it was understood after the Resurrection, alludes to today's reading from Isaiah. He pictures Magi from the east, bearing gifts of gold, frankincense, and myrrh, following a star until they find "the newborn king of the Jews." When they do find Jesus, they recognize his divinity: "They prostrated themselves and did him homage." So do we.

• Isaiah's images of light give hope to the exiles. What specific words convey those hopeful light images?

• In what ways has Christ been light to you recently?

• In what ways is Christ a light to the nations?

READING I   *Isaiah 42:1—4, 6—7*

Thus says the LORD:
Here is my servant whom I uphold,
    my chosen one with whom I am pleased,
upon whom I have put my spirit;
    he shall bring forth justice to the nations,
not crying out, not shouting,
    not making his voice heard in the street.
A bruised reed he shall not break,
    and a smoldering wick he shall
        not quench,
until he establishes justice on the earth;
    the coastlands will wait for his teaching.

I, the LORD, have called you
    for the victory of justice,
I have grasped you by the hand;
I formed you, and set you
    as a covenant of the people,
    a light for the nations,
to open the eyes of the blind,
    to bring out prisoners from confinement,
    and from the dungeon,
        those who live in darkness.

READING II   *Acts 10:34—38*

Peter proceeded to speak to those gathered in the house of Cornelius, saying: "In truth, I see that God shows no partiality. Rather, in every nation whoever fears him and acts uprightly is acceptable to him. You know the word that he sent to the Israelites as he proclaimed peace through Jesus Christ, who is Lord of all, what has happened all over Judea, beginning in Galilee after the baptism that John preached, how God anointed Jesus of Nazareth with the Holy Spirit and power. He went about doing good and healing all those oppressed by the devil, for God was with him."

GOSPEL   *Matthew 3:13—17*

Jesus came from Galilee to John at the Jordan to be baptized by him. John tried to prevent him, saying, "I need to be baptized by you, and yet you are coming to me?" Jesus said to him in reply, "Allow it now, for thus it is fitting for us to fulfill all righteousness." Then he allowed him. After Jesus was baptized, he came up from the water and behold, the heavens were opened for him, and he saw the Spirit of God descending like a dove and coming upon him. And a voice came from the heavens, saying, "This is my beloved Son, with whom I am well pleased."

Practice of Prayer

Psalm 29:1–2, 3–4, 3, 9–10 (11b)
R. The Lord will bless his people with peace.

Give to the LORD, you sons of God,
    give to the LORD glory and praise,
Give to the LORD the glory due his name;
    adore the LORD in holy attire. R.

The voice of the LORD is over the waters,
    the LORD, over vast waters.
The voice of the LORD is mighty;
    the voice of the LORD is majestic. R.

The God of glory thunders,
    and in his temple all say, "Glory!"
The LORD is enthroned above the flood;
    the LORD is enthroned as king forever. R.

Practice of Faith

Most everyone knows on what day they were born. But do you know the day you were born into life with Christ and the Christian community? If not, make this the day that you locate and display the baptismal certificates of each person in your household. This is a day to celebrate!: In the sacrament of Baptism we, like Jesus, are affirmed as beloved of the Father. For Jesus, as for each of us, this realization has life-changing consequences! Parents, recount for your children your joyful memories of their baptismal days. You might also talk about the godparents you chose. What qualities did you prize in the faith of those adults that you hoped they would pass on to your children? In Europe it was customary for children to be taken to visit their godparents on this day. If godparents live nearby, you might invite them over for a festive meal.

Scripture Insights

The Gospels took their present form well after the Resurrection. In the light of the Passion, death, and Resurrection, many mysteries had to be explained. The central one was, Who is Jesus Christ? If Jesus were truly God's beloved Son, would God have let him die a and shameful death on a cross? As Matthew tells the story of Jesus' baptism, he responds to these questions.

In the story, we learn that Jesus is God's own beloved Son from the heavenly voice and from the Spirit of God descending on Jesus like a dove. Notice that the voice from heaven alludes to the words from Isaiah: "Thus says the LORD: / Here is my servant whom I uphold, / my chosen one with whom I am pleased, / upon whom I have put my spirit."

This passage dates to the Israelites' exile in Babylon. They were suffering terribly, wondering if they were still God's people. The prophet, called second Isaiah (the second of three whose prophesies make up the book of Isaiah), assures the exiles that God still loves them and that their suffering is not in vain. In this passage, the suffering servant represents the nation Israel. Through Israel's suffering, second Isaiah teaches, other nations will come to know God. The early Church used the suffering servant songs to explore the mystery and meaning of Jesus' suffering.

By alluding to these songs Matthew foreshadows Jesus' suffering and reminds his audience that neither Israel's nor Jesus' suffering was in vain. The crucifixion does not contradict God's love for his Son.

◆ What verses in Isaiah seem to describe Jesus? Which would be especially helpful to the original audience, the Israelites?

◆ How do you understand the purpose of Jesus' baptism? Your own Baptism?

◆ How have you found meaning and purpose in suffering—your own or that of others?

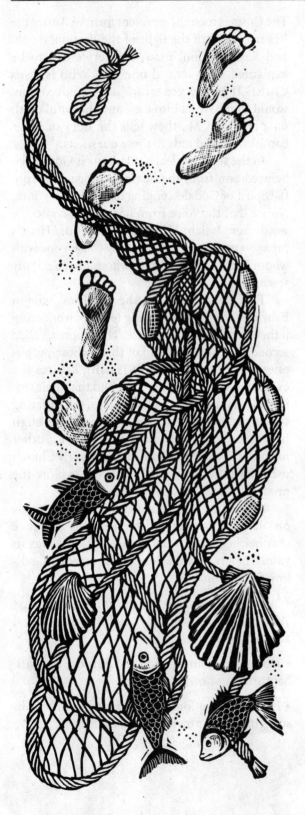

Prayer before Reading the Word

Not to the wise and powerful of this world,
O God of all blessedness,
but to those who are poor in spirit
do you reveal in Jesus
the righteousness of your kingdom.

Gathered here,
like the disciples on the mountain,
we long to listen as Jesus,
        the teacher, speaks.
By the power of his word
refashion our lives
in the pattern of the Beatitudes.

We ask this through our Lord
        Jesus Christ, your Son,
who lives and reigns with you
in the unity of the Holy Spirit,
one God, for ever and ever.

Prayer after Reading the Word

God of all the nations,
we proclaim your wisdom and your power
in the mystery of Christ's cross.

We have heard Christ's call
and it compels us to follow.
Let the truth of the Gospel
break the yoke of our selfishness.
Let the cross draw us and all people
to the joy of salvation.

We ask this through our Lord
        Jesus Christ, your Son,
who lives and reigns with you
in the unity of the Holy Spirit,
one God for ever and ever. Amen.

Weekday Readings

January 14: *1 Samuel 1:1–8; Mark 1:14–20*
January 15: *1 Samuel 1:9–20; Mark 1:21–28*
January 16: *1 Samuel 3:1–10, 19–20; Mark 1:29–39*
January 17: *1 Samuel 4:1–11; Mark 1:40–45*
January 18: *1 Samuel 8:4–7, 10–22a; Mark 2:1–12*
January 19: *1 Samuel 9:1–4, 17–19; 10:1a; Mark 2:13–17*

January 21: *1 Samuel 15:16–23; Mark 2:18–22*
January 22: *1 Samuel 16:1–13; Mark 2:23–28*
January 23: *1 Samuel 17:32–33, 37, 40–51; Mark 3:1–6*
January 24: *1 Samuel 18:6–9; 19:1–7; Mark 3:7–12*
January 25: Feast of the Conversion of Saint Paul
    Acts 22:3–16; Mark 16:15–18
January 26: *2 Timothy 1:1–8; Mark 3:20–21*

January 28: *2 Samuel 5:1–7, 10; Mark 3:22–30*
January 29: *2 Samuel 6:12b–15, 17–19; Mark 3:31–35*
January 30: *2 Samuel 7:4–17; Mark 4:1–20*
January 31: *2 Samuel 7:18–19, 24–29; Mark 4:21–25*
February 1: *2 Samuel 11:1–4a, 5–10a, 13–17; Mark 4:26–34*
February 2: Feast of the Presentation of the Lord
    Malachi 3:1–4; Hebrews 2:14–18; Luke 2:22–40

February 4: *2 Samuel 15:13–14, 30; 16:5–13; Mark 5:1–20*
February 5: *2 Samuel 18:9–10, 14b, 24–25a, 30–19:3;
    Mark 5:21–43*

READING I   *Isaiah 49:3, 5—6*

The LORD said to me: You are my servant,
    Israel, through whom I show my glory.
Now the LORD has spoken
    who formed me as his servant
        from the womb,
that Jacob may be brought back to him
    and Israel gathered to him;
and I am made glorious in the sight
        of the Lord,
    and my God is now my strength!
It is too little, the LORD says,
        for you to be my servant,
    to raise up the tribes of Jacob,
    and restore the survivors of Israel;
I will make you a light to the nations,
    that my salvation may reach
        to the ends of the earth.

READING II   *1 Corinthians 1:1—3*

Paul, called to be an apostle of Christ Jesus by the will of God, and Sosthenes our brother, to the church of God that is in Corinth, to you who have been sanctified in Christ Jesus, called to be holy, with all those everywhere who call upon the name of our Lord Jesus Christ, their Lord and ours. Grace to you and peace from God our Father and the Lord Jesus Christ.

GOSPEL   *John 1:29—34*

John the Baptist saw Jesus coming toward him and said, "Behold, the Lamb of God, who takes away the sin of the world. He is the one of whom I said, 'A man is coming after me who ranks ahead of me because he existed before me.' I did not know him, but the reason why I came baptizing with water was that he might be made known to Israel." John testified further, saying, "I saw the Spirit come down like a dove from heaven and remain upon him. I did not know him, but the one who sent me to baptize with water told me, 'On whomever you see the Spirit come down and remain, he is the one who will baptize with the Holy Spirit.' Now I have seen and testified that he is the Son of God."

Practice of Prayer

R. Here am I, Lord; I come to do your will.

I have waited, waited for the LORD,
    and he stooped toward me and heard my cry.
And he put a new song into my mouth,
    a hymn to our God. R.

Sacrifice or offering you wished not,
    but ears open to obedience you gave me.
Holocausts or sin-offerings you sought not;
    then said I, "Behold I come." R.

"In the written scroll it is prescribed for me,
to do your will, O my God, is my delight,
    and your law is within my heart!" R.

I announced your justice in the vast assembly;
    I did not restrain my lips,
        as you, O LORD, know. R.

Practice of Hope

This coming Thursday we will celebrate the feast of the Conversion of Saint Paul, the apostle. As Saul, the persecutor of Christians, he was traveling to Damascus when he experienced the extraordinary presence of the risen Christ speaking to him. The force of the experience knocked him from his horse, struck him temporarily blind, and changed him forever into a great teacher and shaper of the early Church.

Martin Luther King Jr., whom we remember tomorrow, may not have experienced a dramatic conversion like Paul's, but, following Paul's example, he allowed Christ's words to overpower him. As he led the civil rights movement, he put himself in the service of Christ's peace, choosing nonviolent but forceful ways to confront the sin of racism and to pursue justice. May Christ's peace overpower us as well!

Scripture Insights

Last Sunday, we celebrated the feast of the Baptism of the Lord. Today we read the evangelist John's story of Christ's baptism, told from the perspective of John the Baptist. Both versions describe the descent of the Holy Spirit upon Jesus. For John the Baptist, this served as God's confirmation of Jesus, the Son of God, as the one who baptizes with the Holy Spirit.

John the Baptist looms large prominently in the first chapter of John's account, especially in his "testimony" about Jesus (see also John 3:22–30). Through his testimony, John "make[s] straight the way of the Lord" (John 1:23). When Jesus appears to begin his ministry, John fades from the scene (John 1:35–37; 3:30), his mission accomplished. He has "seen and testified" that Jesus is the Son of God, the "Lamb of God who takes away the sin of the world."

Today's first reading, with the exception of the last line, offers a fitting description of the life and ministry of John the Baptist (see Luke 1:5–25, 57–80). John's mission was solely to the Jewish people. Jesus, however, was sent as "a light for the nations"—for the whole world, Gentiles (non-Jews) as well as Jews. We see this throughout Jesus' ministry. (See also the Gospel for the Ascension.) Jesus, the Lamb of God, takes away the sins of the whole world.

The title Lamb of God is significant, for at the end of the fourth Gospel Jesus is put to death at the very time the Passover lambs are slaughtered for the annual commemoration of Israel's Exodus from Egypt. Passing through death into the fullness of life, Jesus poured out his Spirit of Life and Light on all who would believe.

• How is today's Responsorial Psalm 40 applicable to the life and ministry of John the Baptist?

• What titles and descriptions of Jesus are found in John 1? What do they mean to you?

• How can you "witness" to Jesus in your life?

January 27, 2008

READING I   Isaiah 8:23—9:3

First the LORD degraded the land of Zebulun and the land of Naphtali; but in the end he has glorified the seaward road, the land west of the Jordan, the District of the Gentiles.

> Anguish has taken wing, dispelled is darkness:
> for there is no gloom where
> but now there was distress.
> The people who walked in darkness
> have seen a great light;
> upon those who dwelt in the land of gloom
> a light has shone.
> You have brought them abundant joy
> and great rejoicing,
> as they rejoice before you as at the harvest,
> as people make merry when
> dividing spoils.
> For the yoke that burdened them,
> the pole on their shoulder,
> and the rod of their taskmaster
> you have smashed, as on the day
> of Midian.

READING II   1 Corinthians 1:10—13, 17

I urge you, brothers and sisters, in the name of our Lord Jesus Christ, that all of you agree in what you say, and that there be no divisions among you, but that you be united in the same mind and in the same purpose. For it has been reported to me about you, my brothers and sisters, by Chloe's people, that there are rivalries among you. I mean that each of you is saying, "I belong to Paul," or "I belong to Apollos," or "I belong to Cephas," or "I belong to Christ." Is Christ divided? Was Paul crucified for you? Or were you baptized in the name of Paul? For Christ did not send me to baptize but to preach the gospel, and not with the wisdom of human eloquence, so that the cross of Christ might not be emptied of its meaning.

GOSPEL   Matthew 4:12—23

Shorter: Matthew 4:12 –17

When Jesus heard that John had been arrested, he withdrew to Galilee. He left Nazareth and went to live in Capernaum by the sea, in the region of Zebulun and Naphtali, that what had been said through Isaiah the prophet might be fulfilled:

> *Land of Zebulun and*
> *land of Naphtali,*
> *the way to the sea,*
> *beyond the Jordan,*
> *Galilee of the Gentiles,*
> *the people who sit in darkness*
> *have seen a great light,*
> *on those dwelling in a land*
> *overshadowed by death*
> *light has arisen.*

From that time on, Jesus began to preach and say, "Repent, for the kingdom of heaven is at hand."

As he was walking by the Sea of Galilee, he saw two brothers, Simon who is called Peter, and his brother Andrew, casting a net into the sea; they were fishermen. He said to them, "Come after me, and I will make you fishers of men." At once they left their nets and followed him. He walked along from there and saw two other brothers, James, the son of Zebedee, and his brother John. They were in a boat, with their father Zebedee, mending their nets. He called them, and immediately they left their boat and their father and followed him.

He went around all of Galilee, teaching in their synagogues, proclaiming the gospel of the kingdom, and curing every disease and illness among the people.

Practice of Prayer

Psalm 27:1, 4, 13–14 (1a)

R. The Lord is my light and my salvation.

The LORD is my light and my salvation;
  whom should I fear?
The LORD is my life's refuge;
  of whom should I be afraid? R.

One thing I ask of the LORD;
  this I seek:
to dwell in the house of the LORD
  all the days of my life,
that I may gaze on the loveliness of the LORD,
  and contemplate his temple. R.

I believe that I shall see the bounty of the LORD
  in the land of the living.
Wait for the LORD with courage;
  be stouthearted, and wait for the LORD. R.

Practice of Hope

Christ calls us in distinctive ways. For Blessed Alberto Hurtado Cruchaga, who spent much of his childhood in foster care, the memories of insecurity and his formation at a Jesuit secondary school sparked a life of service. He entered the Jesuit order in Santiago, Chile, in 1923, continued his education in Belgium, and was ordained in 1933. Returning to Chile in 1936, he became a professor of religion and of pedagogy, always inspiring his students to work with the poor. He was a leader in youth ministry, served as a spiritual director, and led many retreats. In the 1940s he began to address the needs of homeless young people by founding homes that offered rehabilitation centers, trade schools, and a formation in Christian values. Inspired by the social teaching of the Church, Father Hurtado also wrote and spoke in support of trade unions. He died in 1952 and was beatified in 1994 by Pope John Paul II. Learn more at http://www.vatican.va/news_services/liturgy/saints/ns_lit_doc_20051023_cruchaga_en.html.

Scripture Insights

Today, the Lectionary begins this year's cycle of Sunday Gospel readings from Matthew. Here in chapter four, we are at the beginning of Jesus' ministry. Note that John the Baptist, having been arrested, is no longer on the scene. This, in fact, signals to Jesus that the time for his public ministry is at hand. Accordingly, he "withdrew" (literally, "returned") to Galilee (4:12), the northern part of the country of Israel, known as the land of the Gentiles because of its large non-Jewish population.

At the beginning of his ministry, Jesus moved from Nazareth where he grew up (2:23), to the city of Capernaum, on the shore of the Sea of Galilee (4:13). Matthew sees this move—as he does so many things in the life of Jesus—as a fulfillment of the prophecies of the Hebrew Scriptures (Old Testament). In this case, he cites a relevant text from the prophet Isaiah, which is the passage chosen for today's first reading.

In his historical context (eighth century BC), Isaiah first speaks of the "degradation" or destruction of the land of the northern tribes of Israel by their Assyrian enemies. But even more importantly, he speaks of its subsequent glorification and redemption when these enemies are overcome.

Matthew sees the glorification of this land as the result of the presence of Jesus' shining light. (See in Matthew 17:2 for a fuller glimpse!) In today's scriptures, as Jesus begins his ministry, this light is *dawning*—just beginning to pierce the darkness of the night, the darkness of ignorance of God's plan of salvation for all people—Gentiles as well as Jews. The light grows in brightness as the kingdom of heaven becomes increasingly realized through Jesus' teaching and miracles (4:17).

Jesus calls for "repentance"—a "turning" *to* his Light and *away* from anything that obscures God's salvation. Fittingly, today's Psalm 27 bids us to remember that the Lord is our true light and salvation.

• How do the different tenses of verbs used with reference to light in today's scriptures speak of our own faith experience?

• How is God's Light made manifest?

• What will help us to receive more of God's Light?

February 3, 2008

READING I *Zephaniah 2:3; 3:12–13*

Seek the LORD, all you humble of the earth,
    who have observed his law;
seek justice, seek humility;
    perhaps you may be sheltered
    on the day of the LORD's anger.

But I will leave as a remnant in your midst
    a people humble and lowly,
who shall take refuge in the name of the LORD:
    the remnant of Israel.
They shall do no wrong
    and speak no lies;
nor shall there be found in their mouths
    a deceitful tongue;
they shall pasture and couch their flocks
    with none to disturb them.

READING II *1 Corinthians 1:26–31*

Consider your own calling, brothers and sisters. Not many of you were wise by human standards, not many were powerful, not many were of noble birth. Rather, God chose the foolish of the world to shame the wise, and God chose the weak of the world to shame the strong, and God chose the lowly and despised of the world, those who count for nothing, to reduce to nothing those who are something, so that no human being might boast before God. It is due to him that you are in Christ Jesus, who became for us wisdom from God, as well as righteousness, sanctification, and redemption, so that, as it is written, "Whoever boasts, should boast in the Lord."

GOSPEL *Matthew 5:1–12a*

When Jesus saw the crowds, he went up the mountain, and after he had sat down, his disciples came to him. He began to teach them, saying:

"Blessed are the poor in spirit,
    for theirs is the kingdom of heaven.
Blessed are they who mourn,
    for they will be comforted.
Blessed are the meek,
    for they will inherit the land.
Blessed are they who hunger and
        thirst for righteousness,
    for they will be satisfied.
Blessed are the merciful,
    for they will be shown mercy.
Blessed are the clean of heart,
    for they will see God.
Blessed are the peacemakers,
    for they will be called children of God.
Blessed are they who are persecuted
        for the sake of righteousness,
    for theirs is the kingdom of heaven.
Blessed are you when they
        insult you and persecute you
    and utter every kind of evil
        against you falsely because of me.
Rejoice and be glad, for your reward
    will be great in heaven."

Practice of Prayer

Psalm 146:6–7, 8–9, 9–10 (Matthew 5:3)

R. Blessed are the poor in spirit;
    the kingdom of heaven is theirs!
or: Alleluia.
The LORD God keeps faith forever,
    secures justice for the oppressed,
    gives food to the hungry.
The LORD sets captives free. R.

The LORD gives sight to the blind;
  the LORD raises up
    those who were bowed down.
The LORD loves the just;
  the LORD protects strangers. R.

The fatherless and the widow the LORD sustains,
  but the way of the wicked he thwarts.
The LORD shall reign forever;
  your God, O Zion, through all generations.
    Alleluia. R.

Practice of Charity

"Your most important work may begin after you retire." So says the Ignatian Volunteer Corps (IVC). IVC volunteers are retirees who want to offer their breadth of knowledge and experience to those who need it most, while also deepening their prayer life. IVC is expanding across the nation, with a presence in Los Angeles and several locations each in the East Coast and Midwest. Volunteers serve two days a week for ten months in their own communities in a wide variety of programs. They journal daily and meet with a spiritual conversation partner once a month to consider their experiences in the light of Ignatian spirituality. Since community is a crucial part of the program, they meet frequently with fellow volunteers for prayer and fellowship, and they make three retreats a year. To learn about becoming a volunteer, or to make a donation to this valuable work, contact www.ilvc.org.

Scripture Insights

Today's scriptures set before us the Lord's impending judgment, that "day of the Lord's anger." Our first reading offers us not only a prescription of what to do that we might be "sheltered," but the Lord's promise of preserving the few who are faithful—a "remnant" of his people (twice repeated), through whom and in whom his promises shall be fulfilled. Humility and righteousness (justice) are their most prominent characteristics.

It is striking how many of Jesus' maxims in today's Gospel can be categorized under these two virtues. The second to last verse offers a glimpse of life in Matthew's community: ". . . when they insult you and persecute you . . . ." Matthew wrote for Jewish-Christians, who, because of their belief in Jesus, had been expelled from their synagogues. They suffered greatly—and grieved deeply—because of rejection by their relatives and friends. Nevertheless, they hungered and thirsted for "righteousness"—being in the right relationship with God through fidelity to the Law—as Jesus expounded and expanded it. They had experienced insult, persecution, and slander because of their belief in Jesus. And they knew the response that was required: meekness, mercy, purity of heart. They knew what it meant to be "poor in spirit"—totally dependent on God.

How Matthew's community would have identified with Zephaniah's words about a faithful remnant! Yet, even in their "minority" situation, Jesus assures them: theirs *is* the kingdom of heaven. (Note that the verbs are present tense in both instances!) Yet to come is a great reward in heaven—after the day of God's judgment—when God would fulfill all their needs. (Note the future tense of the verbs in the other verses.)

And what about ourselves, present-day disciples of Jesus? What about our "own calling"? How do we measure up?

May we be led this day to live ever more faithful to Jesus' teaching that we might be truly blessed.

◆ What themes from today's Gospel are found in the second reading?

◆ How do you understand the blessedness Jesus promises?

◆ How are each of Jesus' maxims applicable in your life?

Lent

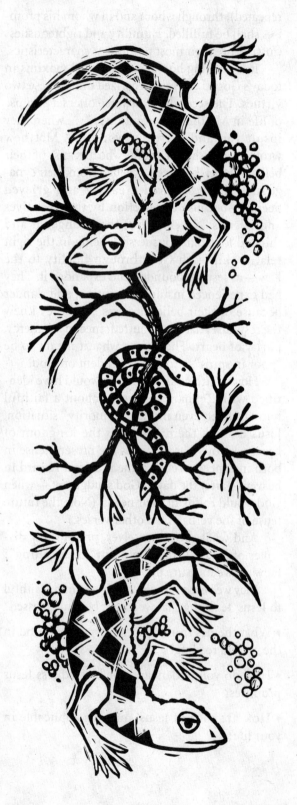

Prayer before Reading the Word

To Abraham and Sarah you called out,
O God of mystery,
inviting them to journey to a land of promise.
To us also you call out,
inviting us to pass through Lent to Easter's glory.
Open our ears, therefore, to listen to Jesus,
the Beloved Son in whom you are well pleased,
so that, embracing the mystery of the cross,
we may come to the holy mountain,
        to immortal life,
and a share in Christ's transfigured glory.

We ask this through our Lord
        Jesus Christ, your Son,
who lives and reigns with you
in the unity of the Holy Spirit,
one God for ever and ever. Amen.

Prayer after Reading the Word

O God, the living fountain of new life,
to the human race, parched with thirst,
you offer the living water of grace
that springs up from the rock,
our Savior Jesus Christ.

Grant your people the gift of the Spirit,
that we may learn to profess our faith
with courage and conviction
and announce with joy
the wonders of your saving love.

We ask this through our Lord
        Jesus Christ, your Son,
who lives and reigns with you
in the unity of the Holy Spirit,
one God for ever and ever. Amen.

Weekday Readings

February 6: Ash Wednesday
Joel 2:12–18; 2 Corinthians 5:20—6:2;
Matthew 6:1–6, 16–18
February 7: *Deuteronomy 30:15–20; Luke 9:22–25*
February 8: *Isaiah 58:1–9a; Matthew 9:14–15*
February 9: *Isaiah 58:9b–14; Luke 5:27–32*

February 11: *Leviticus 19:1–2, 11–18; Matthew 25:31–46*
February 12: *Isaiah 55:10–11; Matthew 6:7–15*
February 13: *Jonah 3:1–10; Luke 11:29–32*
February 14: *Esther C:12, 14–16, 23–25; Matthew 7:7–12*
February 15: *Ezekiel 18:21–28; Matthew 5:20–26*
February 16: *Deuteronomy 26:16–19; Matthew 5:43–48*

February 18: *Daniel 9:4b–10; Luke 6:36–38*
February 19: *Isaiah 1:10, 16–20; Matthew 23:1–12*
February 20: *Jeremiah 18:18–20; Matthew 20:17–28*
February 21: *Jeremiah 17:5–10; Luke 16:19–31*
February 22: Feast of the Chair of Saint Peter
1 Peter 5:1–4; Matthew 16:13–19
February 23: *Micah 7:14–15, 18–20; Luke 15:1–3, 11–32*

February 25: *2 Kings 5:1–15b; Luke 4:24–30*
February 26: *Daniel 3:25, 34–43; Matthew 18:21–35*
February 27: *Deuteronomy 4:1, 5–9; Matthew 5:17–19*
February 28: *Jeremiah 7:23–28; Luke 11:14–23*
February 29: *Hosea 14:2–10; Mark 12:28–34*
March 1: *Hosea 6:1–6; Luke 18:9–14*

March 3: *Isaiah 65:17–21; John 4:43–54*
March 4: *Ezekiel 47:1–9, 12; John 5:1–16*
March 5: *Isaiah 49:8–15; John 5:17–30*
March 6: *Exodus 32:7–14; John 5:31–47*
March 7: *Wisdom 2:1a, 12–22; John 7:1–2, 10, 25–30*
March 8: *Jeremiah 11:18–20; John 7:40–53*

March 10: *Deuteronomy 13:1–9, 15–17, 19–30, 33–62;*
John 8:1–11
March 11: *Numbers 21:4–9; John 8:21–30*
March 12: *Deuteronomy 3:14–20, 91–92, 95; John 8:31–42*
March 13: *Genesis 17:3–9; John 8:51–59*
March 14: *Jeremiah 20:10–13; John 10:31–42*

March 15: Solemnity of Saint Joseph
2 Samuel 7:4–5a, 12–14a, 16; Romans 4:13, 16–18, 22;
Matthew 1:16, 18–21, 24a

March 17: *Isaiah 42:1–7; John 12:1–11*
March 18: *Isaiah 49:1–6; John 13:21–33, 36–38*
March 19: *Isaiah 50:4–9a; Matthew 26:14–25*

READING I *Genesis 2:7—9; 3:1—7*

The LORD God formed man out of the clay of the ground and blew into his nostrils the breath of life, and so man became a living being.

Then the LORD God planted a garden in Eden, in the east, and placed there the man whom he had formed. Out of the ground the LORD God made various trees grow that were delightful to look at and good for food, with the tree of life in the middle of the garden and the tree of the knowledge of good and evil.

Now the serpent was the most cunning of all the animals that the Lord God had made. The serpent asked the woman, "Did God really tell you not to eat from any of the trees in the garden?" The woman answered the serpent: "We may eat of the fruit of the trees in the garden; it is only about the fruit of the tree in the middle of the garden that God said, 'You shall not eat it or even touch it, lest you die.'" But the serpent said to the woman: "You certainly will not die! No, God knows well that the moment you eat of it your eyes will be opened and you will be like gods who know what is good and what is evil." The woman saw that the tree was good for food, pleasing to the eyes, and desirable for gaining wisdom. So she took some of its fruit and ate it; and she also gave some to her husband, who was with her, and he ate it. Then the eyes of both of them were opened, and they realized that they were naked; so they sewed fig leaves together and made loincloths for themselves.

READING II *Romans 5:12, 17—19*

Longer: Romans 5:12 –19

Brothers and sisters:

Through one man sin entered the world, and through sin, death, and thus death came to all men, inasmuch as all sinned.

For if, by the transgression of the one, death came to reign through that one, how much more will those who receive the abundance of grace and of the gift of justification come to reign in life through the one Jesus Christ. In conclusion, just as through one transgression condemnation came upon all, so, through one righteous act, acquittal and life came to all. For just as through the disobedience of the one man the many were made sinners, so, through the obedience of the one, the many will be made righteous.

GOSPEL *Matthew 4:1—11*

At that time Jesus was led by the Spirit into the desert to be tempted by the devil. He fasted for forty days and forty nights, and afterwards he was hungry. The tempter approached and said to him, "If you are the Son of God, command that these stones become loaves of bread." He said in reply, "It is written:

> One does not live on bread alone,
>   but on every word that comes forth
>   from the mouth of God."

Then the devil took him to the holy city, and made him stand on the parapet of the temple, and said to him, "If you are the Son of God, throw yourself down. For it is written:

> He will command his angels concerning you
>   and with their hands they will support you,
> lest you dash your foot against a stone."

Jesus answered him, "Again it is written,

> You shall not put the Lord,
>   your God, to the test."

Then the devil took him up to a very high mountain, and showed him all the kingdoms of the world in their magnificence, and he said to him, "All these I shall give to you, if you will prostrate yourself and worship me." At this, Jesus said to him, "Get away, Satan! It is written:

> The Lord, your God, shall you worship
>   and him alone shall you serve."

Then the devil left him and, behold, angels came and ministered to him.

Practice of Prayer

Psalm 51:3—4, 5—6, 12—13, 17 (see 3a)
R. Be merciful, O Lord, for we have sinned.

Have mercy on me, O God, in your goodness;
    in the greatness of your compassion
        wipe out my offense.
Thoroughly wash me from my guilt
    and of my sin cleanse me. R.

For I acknowledge my offense,
    and my sin is before me always:
"Against you only have I sinned,
    and done what is evil in your sight." R.

A clean heart create for me, O God,
    and a steadfast spirit renew within me.
Cast me not out from your presence,
    and your Holy Spirit take not from me. R.

Give me back the joy of your salvation,
    and a willing spirit sustain in me.
O Lord, open my lips,
    and my mouth shall proclaim
        your praise. R.

Practice of Faith

Three journeys. Two different responses to God. One choice.

Adam and Eve fall to the temptation to trust their own knowledge and judgment rather than God's. In doing so they set themselves up for a journey that takes them away from the garden and eternal life with God.

In the Gospel, Jesus journeys with the The Spirit into the desert, where he faces the temptation to take physical and spiritual matters into his own hands. But Jesus places his trust in God for everything he needs and sends the devil away.

We make the third journey. Lent invites us to move closer to God by trusting that God's will is the path to our peace. New life awaits.

Scripture Insights

In the Genesis reading, the man and woman succumb to temptation; in the Gospel reading, Jesus overcomes it. By looking carefully at these stories we can learn about the source of temptation and how we might find strength to overcome it.

The story of the man and woman in the garden probes the mysteries of sin and suffering through signs and symbols. In the garden, God, the creator and protector, has planted trees for the couple and established a moral order: he gives permission to eat the fruit of nearly everything in the garden; only the tree of the knowledge of good and evil is forbidden. God explains that the order exists for the couple's well-being. But the serpent, a symbol for temptation, convinces the woman to think that God's order only keeps them from becoming more like God.

The woman allows herself to be convinced and eats from the tree of knowledge as does Adam. The result is shame and broken relationships: they hide their nakedness, hide from God, and blame one another. Sin brings suffering.

Jesus, on the other hand, can resist temptation because he trusts God's love. The devil tries to persuade Jesus to prove he is the Son of God by using his power to feed himself and by testing God's protective love. But Jesus is completely secure in his loving relationship with God. He doesn't have to prove anything; he knows that God's order, God's will in his life, is for his good and everyone else's.

The more we trust God's love and the wisdom of his ways, the more we will be able to overcome the temptation to sin.

◆ What assurance did the man, woman, and Jesus have of God's love? How did they learn of it?

◆ What assurances do you have? How have they come to you?

◆ Once we recognize our sin, how does the psalm teach us what to do?

February 17, 2008

READING I   *Genesis 12:1—4a*

The LORD said to Abram: "Go forth from the land of your kinsfolk and from your father's house to a land that I will show you.

"I will make of you a great nation,
 and I will bless you;
I will make your name great,
 so that you will be a blessing.
I will bless those who bless you
 and curse those who curse you.
All the communities of the earth
 shall find blessing in you."

Abram went as the LORD directed him.

READING II   *2 Timothy 1:8b—10*

Beloved:

Bear your share of hardship for the gospel with the strength that comes from God.

He saved us and called us to a holy life, not according to our works but according to his own design and the grace bestowed on us in Christ Jesus before time began, but now made manifest through the appearance of our savior Christ Jesus, who destroyed death and brought life and immortality to light through the gospel.

GOSPEL   *Matthew 17:1—9*

Jesus took Peter, James, and John his brother, and led them up a high mountain by themselves. And he was transfigured before them; his face shone like the sun and his clothes became white as light. And behold, Moses and Elijah appeared to them, conversing with him. Then Peter said to Jesus in reply, "Lord, it is good that we are here. If you wish, I will make three tents here, one for you, one for Moses, and one for Elijah." While he was still speaking, behold, a bright cloud cast a shadow over them, then from the cloud came a voice that said, "This is my beloved Son, with whom I am well pleased; listen to him."

When the disciples heard this, they fell prostrate and were very much afraid. But Jesus came and touched them, saying, "Rise, and do not be afraid." And when the disciples raised their eyes, they saw no one else but Jesus alone.

As they were coming down from the mountain, Jesus charged them, "Do not tell the vision to anyone until the Son of Man has been raised from the dead."

Practice of Prayer

Psalm 33:4—5, 18—19, 20, 22 (22)

R. Lord, let your mercy be on us,
      as we place our trust in you.

Upright is the word of the LORD,
      and all his works are trustworthy.
He loves justice and right;
      of the kindness of the LORD
            the earth is full.   R.

See, the eyes of the LORD are upon
            those who fear him,
      upon those who hope for his kindness,
to deliver them from death
      and preserve them in spite of famine.   R.

Our soul waits for the LORD,
      who is our help and our shield.
May your kindness, O LORD, be upon us
      who have put our hope in you.   R.

Practice of Hope

In the crush of work and family responsibilities, of social obligations and pleasures, quiet time for listening to the Holy Spirit often gets pushed aside. In today's Gospel, the Spirit led Jesus into the desert. If we haven't felt the Spirit leading us into the desert (and that wouldn't be surprising in the din of our lives!) or we haven't had the freedom to respond when we did feel the pull, perhaps we need to schedule it for ourselves. Make an appointment with the desert!

Retreat centers provide a welcoming, quiet space away from your life. They offer a variety of lengths and types of retreats, and some offer spiritual direction. Whatever type of retreat you can arrange, write it in your appointment book, savor it when it comes, reflect on it when it's past, and make another appointment. Find a directory of Catholic retreat centers at http://www.catholiclinks.org/retirosunitedstates.htm.

Scripture Insights

In every age there are conflicting voices clamoring for our attention. In Jesus' time religious sects in Judaism, such as the Pharisees and the Sadducees, disputed each other. In our age there are disagreements among Christians, among political parties, and between the values of our Church and our culture. To whom should we listen?

In today's Gospel, Matthew is teaching his primarily Jewish audience that they should listen to Jesus. When Jesus takes Peter, James, and John up the mountain, he is "transfigured" before them. That is, his glowing clothes and face show his divinity. Moses and Elijah, who represent the Law and the prophets, are with Jesus. As at Jesus' baptism, a voice from heaven identifies him as God's "beloved Son with whom I am well pleased." However, the voice goes on to say, "Listen to him."

Peter doesn't understand what's happening. He asks if he should build tents for Jesus, Moses, and Elijah. But after the voice from heaven speaks, Moses and Elijah have disappeared, for they have not come to "tent," or to dwell with the people again. "They saw no one else but Jesus alone."

As they come down from the mountain, Jesus tells the disciples to tell no one of the vision until he had "risen from the dead." Why would Jesus give such a direction? Perhaps Jesus knew that the apostles did not yet understand the significance of what they had witnessed. Only after the Resurrection would they understand well enough to teach others.

During Lent, we too need to withdraw to a private place with Jesus and listen to him. Only when we listen carefully can we be faithful witnesses to Jesus Christ.

• What specific details does Matthew include in his story to teach his readers to listen to Jesus?

• What clamoring voices in our culture are competing for your attention?

• How is the call of Abram in the first reading similar to or different from the call we disciples have received in the second reading?

• What private time could you arrange to have with Jesus this Lent?

READING I   Exodus 17:3–7

In those days, in their thirst for water, the people grumbled against Moses, saying, "Why did you ever make us leave Egypt? Was it just to have us die here of thirst with our children and our livestock?" So Moses cried out to the LORD, "What shall I do with this people? A little more and they will stone me!" The LORD answered Moses, "Go over there in front of the people, along with some of the elders of Israel, holding in your hand, as you go, the staff with which you struck the river. I will be standing there in front of you on the rock in Horeb. Strike the rock, and the water will flow from it for the people to drink." This Moses did, in the presence of the elders of Israel. The place was called Massah and Meribah, because the Israelites quarreled there and tested the LORD, saying, "Is the LORD in our midst or not?"

READING II   Romans 5:1–2, 5–8

Brothers and sisters:

Since we have been justified by faith, we have peace with God through our Lord Jesus Christ, through whom we have gained access by faith to this grace in which we stand, and we boast in hope of the glory of God.

And hope does not disappoint, because the love of God has been poured out into our hearts through the Holy Spirit who has been given to us. For Christ, while we were still helpless, died at the appointed time for the ungodly. Indeed, only with difficulty does one die for a just person, though perhaps for a good person one might even find courage to die. But God proves his love for us in that while we were still sinners Christ died for us.

GOSPEL   John 4:5–15, 19b–26, 39a, 40–42

Longer: John 4:5–42

Jesus came to a town of Samaria called Sychar, near the plot of land that Jacob had given to his son Joseph. Jacob's well was there. Jesus, tired from his journey, sat down there at the well. It was about noon.

A woman of Samaria came to draw water. Jesus said to her, "Give me a drink." His disciples had gone into the town to buy food. The Samaritan woman said to him, "How can you, a Jew, ask me, a Samaritan woman, for a drink?"—For Jews use nothing in common with Samaritans.—Jesus answered and said to her, "If you knew the gift of God and who is saying to you, 'Give me a drink,' you would have asked him and he would have given you living water." The woman said to him, "Sir, you do not even have a bucket and the cistern is deep; where then can you get this living water? Are you greater than our father Jacob, who gave us this cistern and drank from it himself with his children and his flocks?" Jesus answered and said to her, "Everyone who drinks this water will be thirsty again; but whoever drinks the water I shall give will never thirst; the water I shall give will become in him a spring of water welling up to eternal life." The woman said to him, "Sir, give me this water, so that I may not be thirsty or have to keep coming here to draw water.

"I can see that you are a prophet. Our ancestors worshiped on this mountain; but you people say that the place to worship is in Jerusalem." Jesus said to her, "Believe me, woman, the hour is coming when you will worship the Father neither on this mountain nor in Jerusalem. You people worship what you do not understand; we worship what we understand, because salvation is from the Jews. But the hour is coming, and is now here, when true worshipers will worship the Father in Spirit and truth; and indeed the Father seeks such people to worship him. God is Spirit, and those who worship him must worship in Spirit and truth." The woman said to him, "I know that the Messiah is coming, the one called the Christ; when he comes, he will tell us everything." Jesus said to her, "I am he, the one who is speaking with you."

Many of the Samaritans of that town began to believe in him. When the Samaritans came to him, they invited him to stay with them; and he stayed there two days. Many more began to believe in him because of his word, and they said to the woman, "We no longer believe because of your word; for we have heard for ourselves, and we know that this is truly the savior of the world."

Practice of Prayer

Psalm 95:1—2, 6—7, 8—9 (8)

R. If today you hear his voice,
  harden not your hearts.

Come, let us sing joyfully to the LORD;
  let us acclaim the Rock of our salvation.
Let us come into his presence with thanksgiving;
  let us joyfully sing psalms to him.   R.

Come, let us bow down in worship;
  let us kneel before the LORD who made us.
For he is our God,
  and we are the people he shepherds,
    the flock he guides.   R.

Oh, that today you would hear his voice:
  "Harden not your hearts as at Meribah,
    as in the day of Massah in the desert,
where your fathers tempted me;
  they tested me though
    they had seen my works."   R.

Practice of Hope

When a group of volunteers sponsored by Catholic Charities went to New Orleans to help homeowners gut their storm-damaged homes after Hurricane Katrina, they found that hope flourished. The chaos resulting when flood waters covered 80 percent of the city brought racism and injustice to the surface, but it also provided an opportunity for something new to grow in their place. "Good will come from this," the volunteers heard over and over again, to their amazement.

The Samaritan woman was amazed by what Jesus revealed about her life and thirsted for the hope that his "living water" promises. How is that "living water" refreshing your life?

Scripture Insights

For what do you thirst? One thing for which we all thirst is loving relationships—with God and with others. The woman in today's Gospel must have been looking for love in all the wrong places, for, as Jesus says in the longer version of this reading, she has had five husbands, and the man she is with now is not her husband. She comes to the well at noon, not in the cool of the morning when most people would come. Perhaps she, a sinner, wants to avoid meeting the other women of the town.

Jesus loves sinners. He sees this woman by herself, and strikes up a conversation with her, "Give me a drink." Jesus is ignoring a number of taboos. Normally a Jew would not have asked a Samaritan woman for a drink since Samaritans were considered to be unclean.

As the conversation continues it becomes evident that Jesus knows the woman's past. Yet he has not the slightest desire to avoid or punish her. Rather, he longs to welcome her in love. He tells the woman that he wants to give her "living water," that is, baptism. He reveals to her his identity as the Christ. The woman is responding to Jesus' unconditional love when she goes back to the town and tells others about her own personal experience with Jesus.

Jesus is the revelation of God's love. As Paul tells us in today's reading from Romans, God loves us first even though we are sinners. We do not earn God's love: "But God proves his love for us in that while we were still sinners Christ died for us."

During Lent we remember that in order to be in loving relationship with God and others we must respond to God's love by turning away from sin.

• What things in today's Gospel illustrate God's love at work?

• Who has brought God's love into your life, even when you felt God could not love you?

• If you were to tell others about your experience of Jesus, what stories would you tell?

READING I   1 Samuel 16:1b, 6—7, 10—13a

The LORD said to Samuel: "Fill your horn with oil, and be on your way. I am sending you to Jesse of Bethlehem, for I have chosen my king from among his sons."

As Jesse and his sons came to the sacrifice, Samuel looked at Eliab and thought, "Surely the LORD's anointed is here before him." But the LORD said to Samuel: "Do not judge from his appearance or from his lofty stature, because I have rejected him. Not as man sees does God see, because man sees the appearance but the LORD looks into the heart." In the same way Jesse presented seven sons before Samuel, but Samuel said to Jesse, "The LORD has not chosen any one of these." Then Samuel asked Jesse, "Are these all the sons you have?" Jesse replied, "There is still the youngest, who is tending the sheep." Samuel said to Jesse, "Send for him; we will not begin the sacrificial banquet until he arrives here." Jesse sent and had the young man brought to them. He was ruddy, a youth handsome to behold and making a splendid appearance. The LORD said, "There—anoint him, for this is the one!" Then Samuel, with the horn of oil in hand, anointed David in the presence of his brothers; and from that day on, the spirit of the LORD rushed upon David.

READING II   Ephesians 5:8—14

Brothers and sisters:

You were once darkness, but now you are light in the Lord. Live as children of light, for light produces every kind of goodness and righteousness and truth. Try to learn what is pleasing to the Lord. Take no part in the fruitless works of darkness; rather expose them, for it is shameful even to mention the things done by them in secret; but everything exposed by the light becomes visible, for everything that becomes visible is light. Therefore, it says:

> "Awake, O sleeper,
> and arise from the dead,
> and Christ will give you light."

GOSPEL   John 9:1, 6—9, 13—17, 34—38

Longer: John 9:1–41

As Jesus passed by he saw a man blind from birth. He spat on the ground and made clay with the saliva, and smeared the clay on his eyes, and said to him, "Go wash in the Pool of Siloam"—which means Sent—. So he went and washed, and came back able to see.

His neighbors and those who had seen him earlier as a beggar said, "Isn't this the one who used to sit and beg?" Some said, "It is," but others said, "No, he just looks like him." He said, "I am."

They brought the one who was once blind to the Pharisees. Now Jesus had made clay and opened his eyes on a sabbath. So then the Pharisees also asked him how he was able to see. He said to them, "He put clay on my eyes, and I washed, and now I can see." So some of the Pharisees said, "This man is not from God, because he does not keep the sabbath." But others said, "How can a sinful man do such signs?" And there was a division among them. So they said to the blind man again, "What do you have to say about him, since he opened your eyes?" He said, "He is a prophet."

They answered and said to him, "You were born totally in sin, and are you trying to teach us?" Then they threw him out.

When Jesus heard that they had thrown him out, he found him and said, "Do you believe in the Son of Man?" He answered and said, "Who is he, sir, that I may believe in him?" Jesus said to him, "You have seen him, the one speaking with you is he." He said, "I do believe, Lord," and he worshiped him.

Practice of Prayer

Psalm 23:1—3a, 3b—4, 5, 6 (1)

R. The Lord is my shepherd;
  there is nothing I shall want.

The LORD is my shepherd; I shall not want.
  In verdant pastures he gives me repose;
beside restful waters he leads me;
  he refreshes my soul. R.

He guides me in right paths
  for his name's sake.
Even though I walk in the dark valley
  I fear no evil; for you are at my side
with your rod and your staff
  that give me courage. R.

You spread the table before me
  in the sight of my foes;
you anoint my head with oil;
  my cup overflows. R.

Only goodness and kindness follow me
  all the days of my life;
and I shall dwell in the house of the LORD
  for years to come. R.

Practice of Charity

Scotomas aren't something that people usually talk about—because most people don't know they have them. Scotomas are visual defects, blind spots in our visual field. Sometimes we have blind spots in our thinking too—things we overlook or just don't see because of the way we think.

The man at the center of today's Gospel regains his sight, but isn't able to see Jesus for who he is right away. That comes into focus slowly. As his faith grows, his view changes and his world is transformed. He doesn't just see Jesus; he sees the Light, which allows him to see even more. In the end it is the people around him who are blind because they refuse to see and believe.

Are there people around us that we either cannot or will not see? How would the world change for them—and for us—if we could?

Scripture Insights

Today's Gospel tells us the story of Jesus giving sight to a blind man—not only physical sight but also spiritual *ins*ight. As the story begins, Jesus sees a blind man, and without the blind man even asking, Jesus heals his blindness. All he had to do to gain his sight was to follow Jesus' direction to "'wash in the Pool of Siloam,' which means Sent." The man washed, and when he returned he could see.

If this story were only about physical healing it could have ended with the man now able to see. However, it doesn't end there. Rather, through incremental steps we watch the man gain spiritual insight. When asked how he can now see, the man recounts his experience: a man called Jesus healed him. When pressed by some Pharisees to say more about this man, the once blind man concludes, "He is a prophet."

The Pharisees do not believe Jesus is a prophet because he is not legalistic in his interpretation of the Law. They tell the once blind man that Jesus is a sinner. The man refuses to be persuaded, insisting that Jesus must be from God or he would not have had the power to heal.

Later Jesus asks the man, "Do you believe in the Son of Man?" The man is open to Jesus' words. So Jesus reveals himself to the man. The man says, "'I do believe, Lord,' and he worshiped him."

We are like this man. Even though we were born blind we have washed in the pool (Baptism) and have been sent. Jesus is our Light. If we open ourselves to Jesus' presence, Jesus' word in our lives, we will be able to see more and more: Jesus is truly a man, and even more than a prophet from God—the Word made flesh. We, too, adore.

◆ What phrases in the story capture each step toward full belief that the once blind man takes?

◆ Do you feel "sent" by virtue of your Baptism? Explain.

◆ What ideas about your sight and insight do the first and second readings contribute?

March 9, 2008

READING I *Ezekiel 37:12—14*

Thus says the Lord GOD:

O my people, I will open your graves and have you rise from them, and bring you back to the land of Israel. Then you shall know that I am the LORD, when I open your graves and have you rise from them, O my people! I will put my spirit in you that you may live, and I will settle you upon your land; thus you shall know that I am the LORD. I have promised, and I will do it, says the LORD.

READING II *Romans 8:8—11*

Brothers and sisters:

Those who are in the flesh cannot please God. But you are not in the flesh; on the contrary, you are in the spirit, if only the Spirit of God dwells in you. Whoever does not have the Spirit of Christ does not belong to him. But if Christ is in you, although the body is dead because of sin, the spirit is alive because of righteousness. If the Spirit of the one who raised Jesus from the dead dwells in you, the one who raised Christ from the dead will give life to your mortal bodies also, through his Spirit dwelling in you.

GOSPEL *John 11:3—7, 17, 20—27, 33ᵇ—45*

Longer: John 11:1–45

The sisters of Lazarus sent word to Jesus, saying, "Master, the one you love is ill." When Jesus heard this he said, "This illness is not to end in death, but is for the glory of God, that the Son of God may be glorified through it." Now Jesus loved Martha and her sister and Lazarus. So when he heard that he was ill, he remained for two days in the place where he was. Then after this he said to his disciples, "Let us go back to Judea."

When Jesus arrived, he found that Lazarus had already been in the tomb for four days. When Martha heard that Jesus was coming, she went to meet him; but Mary sat at home. Martha said to Jesus, "Lord, if you had been here, my brother would not have died. But even now I know that whatever you ask of God, God will give you." Jesus said to her, "Your brother will rise." Martha said, "I know he will rise, in the resurrection on the last day." Jesus told her, "I am the resurrection and the life; whoever believes in me, even if he dies, will live, and everyone who lives and believes in me will never die. Do you believe this?" She said to him, "Yes, Lord. I have come to believe that you are the Christ, the Son of God, the one who is coming into the world."

He became perturbed and deeply troubled, and said, "Where have you laid him?" They said to him, "Sir, come and see." And Jesus wept. So the Jews said, "See how he loved him." But some of them said, "Could not the one who opened the eyes of the blind man have done something so that this man would not have died?"

So Jesus, perturbed again, came to the tomb. It was a cave, and a stone lay across it. Jesus said, "Take away the stone." Martha, the dead man's sister, said to him, "Lord, by now there will be a stench; he has been dead for four days." Jesus said to her, "Did I not tell you that if you believe you will see the glory of God?" So they took away the stone. And Jesus raised his eyes and said, "Father, I thank you for hearing me. I know that you always hear me; but because of the crowd here I have said this, that they may believe that you sent me." And when he had said this, he cried out in a loud voice, "Lazarus, come out!" The dead man came out, tied hand and foot with burial bands, and his face was wrapped in a cloth. So Jesus said to them, "Untie him and let him go."

Now many of the Jews who had come to Mary and seen what he had done began to believe in him.

Practice of Prayer

Psalm 130:1–2, 3–4, 5–6, 7–8 (7)

R. With the Lord there is mercy
     and fullness of redemption.

Out of the depths I cry to you, O LORD;
     LORD, hear my voice!
Let your ears be attentive
     to my voice in supplication.   R.

If you, O LORD, mark iniquities,
     LORD, who can stand?
But with you is forgiveness,
     that you may be revered.   R.

I trust in the LORD;
     my soul trusts in his word.
More than sentinels wait for the dawn,
     let Israel wait for the LORD.   R.

For with the LORD is kindness
     and with him is plenteous redemption;
and he will redeem Israel
     from all their iniquities.   R.

Practice of Faith

In his book *Tuesdays with Morrie* Mitch Albom describes the experience of a former professor who is dying of amyotrophic lateral sclerosis or Lou Gehrig's disease. As his condition worsens, Morrie Schwartz finds himself weeping while watching or reading the news. "Now that I'm suffering, I feel closer to people who suffer than I ever did before," he says. "I feel their anguish as if it were my own."

In his Apostolic Letter *Salvific Suffering* (http://www.vatican.va/holy_father/john_paul_ii/apost_letters/documents/hf_jp-ii_apl_11021984_salvifici-doloris_en.html), John Paul II observes that Jesus stayed close to human suffering, feeling it keenly, healing and comforting, and finally taking it on himself in order to redeem us.

At the death of Lazarus, Jesus weeps.

We too can weep for the suffering of others, pray for them, and be the compassionate presence of Christ in their anguish.

Scripture Insights

In Jesus' time the Jewish people were divided on the issue of life after death. The Pharisees believed; the Sadducees did not. The idea of life after death had entered Jewish thought only two hundred years earlier.

The Ezekiel reading dates from the Babylonian exile (587 BC–537 BC). When Ezekiel says that God will "open your graves and have you rise from them," he is offering the exiles hope that the people will return to the holy land. He is not speaking of individual resurrection. However, Christians interpret Ezekiel's message of hope as an image of resurrection. Jesus rose from the dead. We hope, we expect, not only to die with Jesus, but to rise with him. Both New Testament readings help us to ponder this Good News.

John tells the story of Jesus raising Lazarus to life. Jesus tells Martha, "whoever believes in me, even if he dies, will live. . . ." We see Jesus' compassion for human sorrow and his dramatic demonstration of his saving power over death. Paul is teaching the Romans the same Good News, that "the one who raised Christ from the dead will give life to your mortal bodies also, through his Spirit dwelling in you."

In the Gospel reading, Martha and Mary say to Jesus, "Lord, if you had been here, my brother would not have died." As we prepare for Easter we remember that because the risen Christ truly is with us we will not die, but like him, we will have eternal life.

◆ Ezekiel and Matthew both present vivid stories. What particular words and images stand out for you and what effect do they have on you?

◆ How does the promise of resurrection affect the way you live your life? view your death?

◆ How does your belief in the communion of saints affect how you experience the presence of loved ones no longer on earth?

READING I   *Isaiah 50:4–7*

The Lord God has given me
    a well-trained tongue,
that I might know how to speak to the weary
    a word that will rouse them.
Morning after morning
    he opens my ear that I may hear;
and I have not rebelled,
    have not turned back.
I gave my back to those who beat me,
    my cheeks to those who plucked
        my beard;
my face I did not shield
    from buffets and spitting.

The Lord God is my help,
    therefore I am not disgraced;
I have set my face like flint,
    knowing that I shall not be put to shame.

READING II   *Philippians 2:6–11*

Christ Jesus, though he was in the form of God,
    did not regard equality with God
    something to be grasped.
Rather, he emptied himself,
    taking the form of a slave,
    coming in human likeness;
    and found human in appearance,
    he humbled himself,
    becoming obedient to the point of death,
    even death on a cross.
Because of this, God greatly exalted him
    and bestowed on him the name
    which is above every name,
    that at the name of Jesus
    every knee should bend,
    of those in heaven and on earth
        and under the earth,
    and every tongue confess that
    Jesus Christ is Lord,
    to the glory of God the Father.

GOSPEL Matthew 26:14—27:66

Shorter: Matthew 27:11–54

One of the Twelve, who was called Judas Iscariot, went to the chief priests and said, "What are you willing to give me if I hand him over to you?" They paid him thirty pieces of silver, and from that time on he looked for an opportunity to hand him over.

On the first day of the Feast of Unleavened Bread, the disciples approached Jesus and said, "Where do you want us to prepare for you to eat the Passover?" He said, "Go into the city to a certain man and tell him, 'The teacher says, "My appointed time draws near; in your house I shall celebrate the Passover with my disciples."'" The disciples then did as Jesus had ordered, and prepared the Passover.

When it was evening, he reclined at table with the Twelve. And while they were eating, he said, "Amen, I say to you, one of you will betray me." Deeply distressed at this, they began to say to him one after another, "Surely it is not I, Lord?" He said in reply, "He who has dipped his hand into the dish with me is the one who will betray me. The Son of Man indeed goes, as it is written of him, but woe to that man by whom the Son of Man is betrayed. It would be better for that man if he had never been born." Then Judas, his betrayer, said in reply, "Surely it is not I, Rabbi?" He answered, "You have said so."

While they were eating, Jesus took bread, said the blessing, broke it, and giving it to his disciples said, "Take and eat; this is my body." Then he took a cup, gave thanks, and gave it to them, saying, "Drink from it, all of you, for this is my blood of the covenant, which will be shed on behalf of many for the forgiveness of sins. I tell you, from now on I shall not drink this fruit of the vine until the day when I drink it with you new in the kingdom of my Father." Then, after singing a hymn, they went out to the Mount of Olives.

Then Jesus said to them, "This night all of you will have your faith in me shaken, for it is written:

I will strike the shepherd,
and the sheep of the flock
will be dispersed;

but after I have been raised up, I shall go before you to Galilee." Peter said to him in reply, "Though all may have their faith in you shaken, mine will never be." Jesus said to him, "Amen, I say to you, this very night before the cock crows, you will deny me three times." Peter said to him, "Even though I should have to die with you, I will not deny you." And all the disciples spoke likewise.

Then Jesus came with them to a place called Gethsemane, and he said to his disciples, "Sit here while I go over there and pray." He took along Peter and the two sons of Zebedee, and began to feel sorrow and distress. Then he said to them, "My soul is sorrowful even to death. Remain here and keep watch with me." He advanced a little and fell prostrate in prayer, saying, "My Father, if it is possible, let this cup pass from me; yet, not as I will, but as you will." When he returned to his disciples he found them asleep. He said to Peter, "So you could not keep watch with me for one hour? Watch and pray that you may not undergo the test. The spirit is willing, but the flesh is weak." Withdrawing a second time, he prayed again, "My Father, if it is not possible that this cup pass without my drinking it, your will be done!" Then he returned once more and found them asleep, for they could not keep their eyes open. He left them and withdrew again and prayed a third time, saying the same thing again. Then he returned to his disciples and said to them, "Are you still sleeping and taking your rest? Behold, the hour is at hand when the Son of Man is to be handed over to sinners. Get up, let us go. Look, my betrayer is at hand."

While he was still speaking, Judas, one of the Twelve, arrived, accompanied by a large crowd, with swords and clubs, who had come from the chief priests and the elders of the people. His betrayer had arranged a sign with them, saying, "The man I shall kiss is the one; arrest him." Immediately he went over to Jesus and said, "Hail, Rabbi!" and he kissed him. Jesus answered him, "Friend, do what you have come for." Then stepping forward they laid hands on Jesus and arrested him. And behold, one of those who accompanied Jesus put his hand to his sword, drew it, and struck the high priest's servant, cutting off his ear. Then Jesus said to him, "Put your sword back into its sheath, for all who take the sword will perish by the sword. Do you think that I cannot call upon my Father and he will not provide me at this moment with more than twelve legions of angels? But then how would the Scriptures be fulfilled which say that it must come to pass in this way?" At that hour Jesus said to the crowds, "Have you come out as against a robber, with swords and clubs to seize me? Day after day I sat teaching in the temple area, yet you did not arrest me. But all this has come to pass that the writings of the prophets may be fulfilled." Then all the disciples left him and fled.

Those who had arrested Jesus led him away to Caiaphas the high priest, where the scribes and the elders were assembled.

Peter was following him at a distance as far as the high priest's courtyard, and going inside he sat down with the servants to see the outcome. The chief priests and the entire Sanhedrin kept trying to obtain false testimony against Jesus in order to put him to death, but they found none, though many false witnesses came forward. Finally two came forward who stated, "This man said, 'I can destroy the temple of God and within three days rebuild it.'" The high priest rose and addressed him, "Have you no answer? What are these men testifying against you?" But Jesus was silent. Then the high priest said to him, "I order you to tell us under oath before the living God whether you are the Christ, the Son of God." Jesus said to him in reply, "You have said so. But I tell you: / From now on you will see 'the Son of Man / seated at the right hand of the Power' / and 'coming on the clouds of heaven.'" Then the high priest tore his robes and said, "He has blasphemed! What further need have we of witnesses? You have now heard the blasphemy; what is your opinion?" They said in reply, "He deserves to die!" Then they spat in his face and struck him, while some slapped him, saying, "Prophesy for us, Christ: who is it that struck you?"

Now Peter was sitting outside in the courtyard. One of the maids came over to him and said, "You too were with Jesus the Galilean." But he denied it in front of everyone, saying, "I do not know what you are talking about!" As he went out to the gate, another girl saw him and said to those who were there, "This man was with Jesus the Nazorean." Again he denied it with an oath, "I do not know the man!" A little later the bystanders came over and said to Peter, "Surely you too are one of them; even your speech gives you away." At that he began to curse and to swear, "I do not know the man." And immediately a cock crowed. Then Peter remembered the words that Jesus had spoken: "Before the cock crows you will deny me three times." He went out and began to weep bitterly.

When it was morning, all the chief priests and the elders of the people took counsel against Jesus to put him to death. They bound him, led him away, and handed him over to Pilate, the governor.

Then Judas, his betrayer, seeing that Jesus had been condemned, deeply regretted what he had done. He returned the thirty pieces of silver to the chief priests and elders, saying, "I have sinned in betraying innocent blood." They said, "What is that to us? Look to it yourself." Flinging the money into the temple, he departed and went off and hanged himself. The chief priests gathered up the money, but said, "It is not lawful to deposit this in the temple treasury, for it is the price of blood." After consultation, they used it to buy the potter's field as a burial place for foreigners. That is why that field even today is called the Field of Blood. Then was fulfilled what had been said through Jeremiah the prophet, *And they took the thirty pieces of silver, the value of a man with a price on his head, a price set by some of the Israelites, and they paid it out for the potter's field just as the Lord had commanded me.*

Now Jesus stood before the governor, who questioned him, "Are you the king of the Jews?" Jesus said, "You say so." And when he was accused by the chief priests and elders, he made no answer. Then Pilate said to him, "Do you not hear how many things they are testifying against you?" But he did not answer him one word, so that the governor was greatly amazed.

Now on the occasion of the feast the governor was accustomed to release to the crowd one prisoner whom they wished. And at that time they had a notorious prisoner called Barabbas. So when they had assembled, Pilate said to them, "Which one do you want me to release to you, Barabbas, or Jesus called Christ?" For he knew that it was out of envy that they had handed him over.

While he was still seated on the bench, his wife sent him a message, "Have nothing to do with that righteous man. I suffered much in a dream today because of him." The chief priests and the elders persuaded the crowds to ask for Barabbas but to destroy Jesus. The governor said to them in reply, "Which of the two do you want me to release to you?" They answered, "Barabbas!" Pilate said to them, "Then what shall I do with Jesus called Christ?" They all said, "Let him be crucified!" But he said, "Why? What evil has he done?" They only shouted the louder, "Let him be crucified!" When Pilate saw that he was not succeeding at all, but that a riot was breaking out instead, he took water and washed his hands in the sight of the crowd, saying, "I am innocent of this man's blood. Look to it yourselves." And the whole people said in reply, "His blood be upon us and upon our children." Then he released Barabbas to them, but after he had Jesus scourged, he handed him over to be crucified.

Then the soldiers of the governor took Jesus inside the praetorium and gathered the whole cohort around him. They stripped off his clothes and threw a scarlet military cloak about him. Weaving a crown out of thorns, they placed it on his head, and a reed in his right hand. And kneeling before him, they mocked him, saying, "Hail, King of the Jews!" They spat upon him and took the reed and kept striking him on the head. And when they had mocked him, they stripped him of the cloak, dressed him in his own clothes, and led him off to crucify him.

As they were going out, they met a Cyrenian named Simon; this man they pressed into service to carry his cross.

And when they came to a place called Golgotha—which means Place of the Skull—, they gave Jesus wine to drink mixed with gall. But when he had tasted it, he refused to drink. After they had crucified him, they divided his garments by casting lots; then they sat down and kept watch over him there. And they placed over his head the written charge against him: This is Jesus, the King of the Jews. Two revolutionaries were crucified with him, one on his right and the other on his left. Those passing by reviled him, shaking their heads and saying, "You who would destroy the temple and rebuild it in three days, save yourself, if you are the Son of God, and come down from the cross!" Likewise the chief priests with the scribes and elders mocked him and said, "He saved others; he cannot save himself. So he is the king of Israel! Let him come down from the cross now, and we will believe in him. He trusted in God; let him deliver him now if he wants him. For he said, 'I am the Son of God.'" The revolutionaries who were crucified with him also kept abusing him in the same way.

From noon onward, darkness came over the whole land until three in the afternoon. And about three o'clock Jesus cried out in a loud voice, *"Eli, Eli, lema sabachthani?"* which means, "My

God, my God, why have you forsaken me?" Some of the bystanders who heard it said, "This one is calling for Elijah." Immediately one of them ran to get a sponge; he soaked it in wine, and putting it on a reed, gave it to him to drink. But the rest said, "Wait, let us see if Elijah comes to save him." But Jesus cried out again in a loud voice, and gave up his spirit.

And behold, the veil of the sanctuary was torn in two from top to bottom. The earth quaked, rocks were split, tombs were opened, and the bodies of many saints who had fallen asleep were raised. And coming forth from their tombs after his resurrection, they entered the holy city and appeared to many. The centurion and the men with him who were keeping watch over Jesus feared greatly when they saw the earthquake and all that was happening, and they said, "Truly, this was the Son of God!" There were many women there, looking on from a distance, who had followed Jesus from Galilee, ministering to him. Among them were Mary Magdalene and Mary the mother of James and Joseph, and the mother of the sons of Zebedee.

When it was evening, there came a rich man from Arimathea named Joseph, who was himself a disciple of Jesus. He went to Pilate and asked for the body of Jesus; then Pilate ordered it to be handed over. Taking the body, Joseph wrapped it in clean linen and laid it in his new tomb that he had hewn in the rock. Then he rolled a huge stone across the entrance to the tomb and departed. But Mary Magdalene and the other Mary remained sitting there, facing the tomb.

The next day, the one following the day of preparation, the chief priests and the Pharisees gathered before Pilate and said, "Sir, we remember that this impostor while still alive said, 'After three days I will be raised up.' Give orders, then, that the grave be secured until the third day, lest his disciples come and steal him and say to the people, 'He has been raised from the dead.' This last imposture would be worse than the first." Pilate said to them, "The guard is yours; go, secure it as best you can." So they went and secured the tomb by fixing a seal to the stone and setting the guard.

Practice of Prayer

Psalm 22:8—9, 17—18, 19—20, 23—24 (2a)

R. My God, my God,
　　why have you abandoned me?

All who see me scoff at me;
　　they mock me with parted lips,
　　　　they wag their heads:
"He relied on the LORD; let him deliver him,
　　let him rescue him, if he loves him." R.

Indeed, many dogs surround me,
　　a pack of evildoers closes in upon me;
They have pierced my hands and my feet;
　　I can count all my bones. R.

They divide my garments among them,
　　and for my vesture they cast lots.
But you, O LORD, be not far from me;
　　O my help, hasten to aid me. R.

I will proclaim your name to my brethren;
　　in the midst of the assembly I will praise you:
"You who fear the LORD, praise him;
　　all you descendants of Jacob,
　　　　give glory to him;
　　revere him, all you descendants
　　　　of Israel!" R.

Scripture Insights

It is sometimes hard to meditate on the crucifixion because it is just too painful. For Matthew's primarily Jewish audience, Jesus' death was also shameful. Jewish law put a curse on anyone who died on a tree (Deuteronomy 21:22–23). As Matthew tells the story of Jesus' crucifixion, he is responding to a question on the mind of his audience: If Jesus really were God's beloved Son, would God have allowed Jesus to die such an ignominious death?

In response to this question, as Matthew tells the story of Jesus' crucifixion, he emphasizes both that God is with Jesus and that Jesus is innocent. How do we know what Matthew emphasizes? We can tell Matthew's special interests by comparing his account to Mark's, which is Matthew's source. When Matthew adds something to the story as it appears in his source, he does so to respond to the needs of his particular audience.

Matthew stresses that God is with Jesus by stating that the events occurring in Jesus' life are fulfilling the words of the prophets. This is to say that God's purposes are being fulfilled. Jesus' innocence is supported by Pilate's wife's dream and by having Pilate wash his hands of the guilt of condemning an innocent man.

Matthew also refutes the charge that, rather than rising from the dead, Jesus' body was stolen by his disciples so that they could claim a resurrection. The author assures us that guards were posted at the tomb.

Like Mark, Matthew relates Jesus' last words: "My God, my God, why have you forsaken me?" But this is not to say that God did forsake Jesus. It is to picture Jesus praying the psalm that we read today, a psalm of lament that ends with a firm faith in God's saving power.

• What details in the first and second readings support Matthew's portrayal of Jesus as innocent and beloved by God?

• Do you find it difficult to meditate on the Passion? Explain.

• Have you ever felt God's apparent absence? What happened?

Holy Thursday brings the end to the Forty Days of Lent, which make up the season of anticipation of the great Three Days. Composed of prayer, alms-giving, fasting, and the preparation of the catechumens for Baptism, the season of Lent is now brought to a close and the Three Days begin as we approach the liturgy of Holy Thursday evening. As those to be initiated into the Church have prepared themselves for their entrance into the fullness of life, so have we been awakening in our hearts, minds, and bodies to our own entrances into the life of Christ, experienced in the life of the Church.

The Three Days, this Easter Triduum (Latin for "three days"), is the center, the core, of the entire year for Christians. These days mark the mystery around which our entire lives are played out. Adults in the community are invited to plan ahead so that the whole time from Thursday night until Easter Sunday is free of social engagements, free of entertainment, and free of meals except for the simplest nourishment. We measure these days—indeed, our very salvation in the life of God—in step with the catechumens themselves; our own rebirths are revitalized as we participate in their initiation rites and as we have supported them along the way.

We are asked to fast on Good Friday and to continue fasting, if possible, all through Holy Saturday as strictly as we can so that we come to the Easter Vigil hungry and full of excitement, parched and longing to feel the sacred water of the font on our skin. Good Friday and Holy Saturday are days of paring down distractions so that we may be free for prayer and anticipation, for reflection, preparation, and silence. The Church is getting ready for the Great Night of the Easter Vigil.

As one who has been initiated into the Church, as one whose life has been wedded to this community gathered at the table, you should anticipate the Triduum with concentration and vigor. With you, the whole Church knows that our presence for the liturgies of the Triduum is not just an invitation. Everyone is needed. We "pull out all the stops" for these days. As human persons wedded to humanity by the joys and travails of life and grafted onto the body of the Church by the sanctifying waters of Baptism, we lead the new members into new life in this community of faith.

To this end, the Three Days are seen not as three liturgies distinct from one another but as one movement. These days have been connected intimately and liturgically from the early days of the Christian Church. As a member of this community, you should be personally committed to preparing for and anticipating the Triduum and its culmination in the Vigil of the Great Night, Holy Saturday.

The Church proclaims the direction of the Triduum by the opening antiphon of Holy Thursday, which comes from Paul's letter to the Galatians (6:14). With this verse the Church sets a spiritual environment into which we as committed Christians enter the Triduum:

> We should glory in the cross of our Lord Jesus Christ, for he is our salvation, our life and resurrection; through him we are saved and made free.

HOLY THURSDAY

On Thursday evening we enter into this Triduum together. Whether presider, baker, lector, preacher, wine maker, greeter, altar server, minister of the Eucharist, decorator, or person in the remote corner in the last pew of the church, we begin, as always, by hearkening to the word of God. These are the scriptures for the liturgy of Holy Thursday:

Exodus 12:1–8, 11–14
Ancient instructions for the meal of the Passover.

1 Corinthians 11:23–26
Eat the bread and drink the cup until the return of the Lord.

John 13:1–15
Jesus washes the feet of the disciples.

Then we, like Jesus, do something strange: We wash feet. Jesus gave us this image of what the Church is supposed to look like, feel like, act like. Our position—whether as washer or washed, servant or served—is a difficult one for us to take. Yet we learn from the discomfort, from the awkwardness.

Then we celebrate the Eucharist. Because it is connected to the other liturgies of the Triduum on Good Friday and Holy Saturday night, the evening liturgy of Holy Thursday has no ending. Whether we stay to pray awhile or leave, we are now in the quiet, peace, and glory of the Triduum.

GOOD FRIDAY

We gather quietly in community on Friday and again listen to the word of God:

Isaiah 52:13—53:12
The servant of the Lord was crushed for our sins.

Hebrews 4:14–16; 5:7–9
The Son of God learned obedience through his suffering.

John 18:1—19:42
The Passion of Jesus Christ.

After the homily, we pray at length for all the world's needs: for the Church; for the Pope, the clergy and all the baptized; for those preparing for initiation; for the unity of Christians; for Jews; for non-Christians; for atheists; for all in public office; and for those in special need.

Then there is another once-a-year event: The holy cross is held up in our midst and we come forward one by one to do reverence with a kiss, bow, or genuflection. This communal reverence of an instrument of torture recalls the painful price, in the past and today, of salvation, the way in which our redemption is wrought, the stripes and humiliation of Jesus Christ that bring direction and life back to a humanity that is lost and dead. During the veneration of the cross, we sing not only of the sorrow but of the glory of the cross by which we have been saved.

Again, we bring to mind the words of Paul: "The cross of Jesus Christ . . . our salvation, our life and resurrection; through him we are saved and made free."

We continue in fasting and prayer and vigil, in rest and quiet, through Saturday. This Saturday for us is God's rest at the end of creation. It is Christ's repose in the tomb. It is Christ's visit with the dead.

EASTER VIGIL

Hungry now, pared down to basics, lightheaded from vigilance and full of excitement, we committed members of the Church, the already baptized, gather in darkness and light a new fire. From this blaze we light a great candle that will make this night bright for us and will burn throughout the Easter season.

We hearken again to the word of God with some of the most powerful narratives and proclamations of our tradition:

Genesis 1:1—2:2
Creation of the world.

Genesis 22:1–18
The sacrifice of Isaac.

Exodus 14:15—15:1
The crossing of the Red Sea.

Isaiah 54:5–14
You will not be afraid.

Isaiah 55:1–11
Come, come to the water.

Baruch 3:9–15, 32—4:4
The shining light.

Ezekiel 36:16–28
The Lord says: I will sprinkle water.

Romans 6:3–11
United with him in death.

Mark 16:1–7
Jesus has been raised up.

After the readings, we pray to all our saints to stand with us as we go to the font and bless the waters. The chosen of all times and all places attend to what is about to take place. The catechumens renounce evil, profess the faith of the Church, and are baptized and anointed.

All of us renew our Baptism. For us these are the moments when death and life meet, when we reject evil and give our promises to God. All of this is in the communion of the Church. So together we go to the table and celebrate the Easter Eucharist.

Easter

Prayer before Reading the Word

God of all creation,
whose mighty power raised Jesus from the dead,
be present to this community of disciples
whom you have called to the hope
of a glorious inheritance among the saints.

As we hear the word that brings salvation,
make our hearts burn within us
that we may recognize Christ crucified and risen,
who opens our hearts to
　　　　understand the scriptures,
who is made known to us in the
　　　　breaking of the bread,
and who lives and reigns with you
in the unity of the Holy Spirit,
one God for ever and ever. Amen.

Prayer after Reading the Word

O God of Easter glory,
gather your baptized people
around the teaching of the apostles,
devoted to the life we share in the Church,
devoted to the breaking of the bread.

Make us so embrace the name of Christ,
that we glorify you in the world
and bear witness to your word
made known to us by Jesus,
our Passover and our peace,
who lives and reigns with you
in the unity of the Holy Spirit,
one God for ever and ever. Amen.

Weekday Readings

March 24: Solemnity of Monday in the Octave of Easter
  Acts 2:14, 22–23; Matthew 28:8–15
March 25: Solemnity of Tuesday in the Octave of Easter
  Acts 2:36–41; John 20:11–18
March 26: Solemnity of Wednesday in the Octave of Easter
  Acts 3:1–10; Luke 24:13–35
March 27: Solemnity of Thursday in the Octave of Easter
  Acts 3:11–26; Luke 24:35–48
March 28: Solemnity of Friday in the Octave of Easter
  Acts 4:1–12; John 21:1–14
March 29: Solemnity of Saturday in the Octave of Easter
  Acts 4:13–21; Mark 16:9–15

March 31: Solemnity of the Annunciation of the Lord
  Isaiah 7:10–14; 8:10; Hebrews 10:4–10; Luke 1:26–38
April 1: *Acts 4:32–37; John 3:7b–15*
April 2: *Acts 5:17–26; John 3:16–21*
April 3: *Acts 5:27–33; John 3:31–36*
April 4: *Acts 5:34–42; John 6:1–15*
April 5: *Acts 6:1–7; John 6:16–21*

April 7: *Acts 6:8–15; John 6:22–29*
April 8: *Acts 7:51—8:1a; John 6:30–35*
April 9: *Acts 8:1b–8; John 6:35–40*
April 10: *Acts 8:26–40; John 6:44–51*
April 11: *Acts 9:1–20; John 6:52–59*
April 12: *Acts 9:31–42; John 6:60–69*

April 14: *Acts 11:1–18; John 10:11–18*
April 15: *Acts 11:19–26; John 10:22–30*
April 16: *Acts 12:24—13:5a; John 12:44–50*
April 17: *Acts 13:13–25; John 13:16–20*
April 18: *Acts 13:26–33; John 14:1–6*
April 19: *Acts 13:44–52; John 14:7–14*

April 21: *Acts 14:5–18; John 14:21–26*
April 22: *Acts 14:19–28; John 14:27–31a*
April 23: *Acts 15:1–6; John 15:1–8*
April 24: *Acts 15:7–21; John 15:9–11*
April 25: Feast of Saint Mark
  1 Peter 5:5b–14; Mark 16:15–20
April 26: *Acts 16:1–10; John 15:18–21*

April 28: *Acts 16:11–15; John 15:26—16:4a*
April 29: *Acts 16:22–34; John 16:5–11*
April 30: *Acts 17:15, 22—18:1; John 16:12–15*
May 1: Solemnity of the Ascension of the Lord (In some regions, transferred to Seventh Sunday of Easter)
  Acts 1:1–11; Ephesians 1:17–23; Matthew 28:16–20
May 2: *Acts 18:9–18; John 16:20–23*
May 3: Feast of Saint Philip and Saint James
  1 Corinthians 15:1–8; John 14:6–14

May 5: *Acts 19:1–8 ; John 16:29–33*
May 6: *Acts 20:17–27; John 17:1–11a*
May 7: *Acts 20:28–38; John 17:11b–19*
May 8: *Acts 22:30; 23:6–11; John 17:20–26*
May 9: *Acts 25:13b–21; John 21:15–19*
May 10: *Acts 28:16–20, 30–31; John 21:20–25*

READING I   Acts 10:34a, 37—43

Peter proceeded to speak and said: "You know what has happened all over Judea, beginning in Galilee after the baptism that John preached, how God anointed Jesus of Nazareth with the Holy Spirit and power. He went about doing good and healing all those oppressed by the devil, for God was with him. We are witnesses of all that he did both in the country of the Jews and in Jerusalem. They put him to death by hanging him on a tree. This man God raised on the third day and granted that he be visible, not to all the people, but to us, the witnesses chosen by God in advance, who ate and drank with him after he rose from the dead. He commissioned us to preach to the people and testify that he is the one appointed by God as judge of the living and the dead. To him all the prophets bear witness, that everyone who believes in him will receive forgiveness of sins through his name."

READING II   Colossians 3:1—4

Alternate: 1 Corinthians 5:6b–8

Brothers and sisters:

If then you were raised with Christ, seek what is above, where Christ is seated at the right hand of God. Think of what is above, not of what is on earth. For you have died, and your life is hidden with Christ in God. When Christ your life appears, then you too will appear with him in glory.

GOSPEL   John 20:1—9

On the first day of the week, Mary of Magdala came to the tomb early in the morning, while it was still dark, and saw the stone removed from the tomb. So she ran and went to Simon Peter and to the other disciple whom Jesus loved, and told them, "They have taken the Lord from the tomb, and we don't know where they put him." So Peter and the other disciple went out and came to the tomb. They both ran, but the other disciple ran faster than Peter and arrived at the tomb first; he bent down and saw the burial cloths there, but did not go in. When Simon Peter arrived after him, he went into the tomb and saw the burial cloths there, and the cloth that had covered his head, not with the burial cloths but rolled up in a separate place. Then the other disciple also went in, the one who had arrived at the tomb first, and he saw and believed. For they did not yet understand the Scripture that he had to rise from the dead.

Practice of Prayer

R. This is the day the Lord has made;
    let us rejoice and be glad.
or: Alleluia.

Give thanks to the LORD, for he is good,
    for his mercy endures forever.
Let the house of Israel say,
    "His mercy endures forever." R.

"The right hand of the LORD
    has struck with power;
    the right hand of the LORD is exalted."
I shall not die, but live,
    and declare the works of the LORD. R.

The stone which the builders rejected
    has become the cornerstone.
By the LORD has this been done;
    it is wonderful in our eyes. R.

Practice of Hope

How do you spell hope? If you live in a developing country where fresh drinking water is scarce, you might spell it NCCW and CRS. The National Council of Catholic Women and Catholic Relief Services have been working together to ensure that communities around the world have "Water for Life." This joint effort provides resources that enable people to build water systems that give them access to safe, clean water. "Water for Life" has the added benefit of creating jobs.

At the Easter Vigil this weekend, thousands of children and adults also will place their hope in water—the waters of Baptism. This water creates jobs, too. Having received new life in Christ, we are called to carry on his work of caring for all who thirst for love, righteousness, and the basic necessities of life. CRS can offer you many ways to be part of that work at www.crs.org.

Scripture Insights

On Easter Sunday we celebrate the core event of Christianity, the Resurrection of Jesus from the dead. Of course no Gospel account describes the Resurrection itself. Testimony about this mystery is presented through stories: empty tomb stories, appearance stories, and commissioning stories. Today we read an empty tomb story from the Gospel according to John.

A mysterious character appears in this Gospel account—the beloved disciple. This unnamed person appears only in John, during the accounts of the Passion, death, and Resurrection.

Both he and Peter run to the tomb, but the beloved disciple runs faster and arrives first. He respectfully waits for Peter so that Peter is the first to enter the tomb. Both men see the same thing: the burial cloths alone in the empty space. However, John tells us clearly that only the beloved disciple "saw and believed." (Mary of Magdala had concluded that the body had been stolen.) So the beloved disciple is the first to believe in the Resurrection. He alone believes before hearing about any of the post-Resurrection appearances.

John's account of the Gospel was written late in the first century, well after the expected time of the Second Coming, and John's audience is asking, "Where is Christ?" John wants to help these late first-century Christians believe in the presence of the risen Christ even if they cannot physically see and touch him. By picturing the beloved disciple as the first to the tomb and the first to believe, John is teaching his audience, and us, that a close, loving relationship with Jesus Christ opens the heart to faith. Nothing is more important than love.

We, too, are disciples whom Jesus loves. We, too, believe that Christ is alive.

◆ From the first reading, what do we learn about how Peter later became a believing witness of the Resurrection?

◆ If faith grows most easily in a loving relationship with Christ, how might we deepen that relationship?

◆ Today's readings show us that the people close to Jesus each came to believe in the Resurrection in different ways. What hindered or helped them? What has hindered or helped you?

March 30, 2008

READING I   Acts 2:42—47

They devoted themselves to the teaching of the apostles and to the communal life, to the breaking of bread and to the prayers. Awe came upon everyone, and many wonders and signs were done through the apostles. All who believed were together and had all things in common; they would sell their property and possessions and divide them among all according to each one's need. Every day they devoted themselves to meeting together in the temple area and to breaking bread in their homes. They ate their meals with exultation and sincerity of heart, praising God and enjoying favor with all the people. And every day the Lord added to their number those who were being saved.

READING II   1 Peter 1:3—9

Blessed be the God and Father of our Lord Jesus Christ, who in his great mercy gave us a new birth to a living hope through the resurrection of Jesus Christ from the dead, to an inheritance that is imperishable, undefiled, and unfading, kept in heaven for you who by the power of God are safeguarded through faith, to a salvation that is ready to be revealed in the final time. In this you rejoice, although now for a little while you may have to suffer through various trials, so that the genuineness of your faith, more precious than gold that is perishable even though tested by fire, may prove to be for praise, glory, and honor at the revelation of Jesus Christ. Although you have not seen him you love him; even though you do not see him now yet believe in him, you rejoice with an indescribable and glorious joy, as you attain the goal of your faith, the salvation of your souls.

GOSPEL   John 20:19—31

On the evening of that first day of the week, when the doors were locked, where the disciples were, for fear of the Jews, Jesus came and stood in their midst and said to them, "Peace be with you." When he had said this, he showed them his hands and his side. The disciples rejoiced when they saw the Lord. Jesus said to them again, "Peace be with you. As the Father has sent me, so I send you." And when he had said this, he breathed on them and said to them, "Receive the Holy Spirit. Whose sins you forgive are forgiven them, and whose sins you retain are retained."

Thomas, called Didymus, one of the Twelve, was not with them when Jesus came. So the other disciples said to him, "We have seen the Lord." But he said to them, "Unless I see the mark of the nails in his hands and put my finger into the nailmarks and put my hand into his side, I will not believe."

Now a week later his disciples were again inside and Thomas was with them. Jesus came, although the doors were locked, and stood in their midst and said, "Peace be with you." Then he said to Thomas, "Put your finger here and see my hands, and bring your hand and put it into my side, and do not be unbelieving, but believe." Thomas answered and said to him, "My Lord and my God!" Jesus said to him, "Have you come to believe because you have seen me? Blessed are those who have not seen and have believed."

Now, Jesus did many other signs in the presence of his disciples that are not written in this book. But these are written that you may come to believe that Jesus is the Christ, the Son of God, and that through this belief you may have life in his name.

Practice of Prayer

Psalm 118:2—4, 13—15, 22—24 (1)

R. Give thanks to the Lord, for he is good,
    his love is everlasting.
or: Alleluia.

Let the house of Israel say,
    "His mercy endures forever."
Let the house of Aaron say,
    "His mercy endures forever."
Let those who fear the LORD say,
    "His mercy endures forever." R.

I was hard pressed and was falling,
    but the LORD helped me.
My strength and my courage is the LORD,
    and he has been my savior.
The joyful shout of victory
    in the tents of the just: R.

The stone which the builders rejected
    has become the cornerstone.
By the LORD has this been done;
    it is wonderful in our eyes.
This is the day the LORD has made;
    let us be glad and rejoice in it. R.

Practice of Hope

Thomas's doubt is well known, and some would write him off for it. But Jesus, in his mercy and love, gave Thomas everything he needed to believe. Also in today's Gospel reading, Jesus gave to the disciples the power to forgive sins, to extend mercy in his name. Paul also speaks of mercy today, and the first reading describes a community bathed in the peace that springs from forgiveness.

On April 30, 2000, Pope John Paul II instituted the feast of Divine Mercy, to be celebrated each year on the Second Sunday of Easter. On this day, the Church ponders and celebrates the great mercy described in the readings. Many parishes will gather this afternoon for special prayers; many of the faithful will celebrate the sacrament of Penance and be encouraged to forgive others. Read more about Divine Mercy Sunday on the Vatican Web site: http://www.vatican.va/roman_ curia/tribunals/apost_penit/documents/rc_trib_ appen_doc_20020629_decree-ii_en.html.

Scripture Insights

John is writing his Gospel account to people living at the end of the first century, long after Jesus' expected return. They might well be saying, "Unless I personally experience a post-Resurrection appearance, or unless I see Jesus come on the clouds of heaven, I will not believe."

This post-Resurrection appearance story shows Jesus commissioning the disciples: "As the Father has sent me, so I send you." In John's account, the disciples receive the Spirit on "the evening of the first day of the week," that is, on the very evening of the Resurrection. Jesus gives the disciples not only the mission to carry on his work but the power to accomplish that mission.

Thomas is not with the others when Jesus appears, nor will he believe that they have seen the Lord. Thomas is like John's audience and, perhaps, like us.

Although Jesus is not pictured as being visibly present when Thomas expresses his doubt, he is there nevertheless. We know this because when Jesus appears again, he invites Thomas to do the very thing Thomas said he would have to do in order to believe. Thomas does not respond by touching Jesus' wounds but by adoring him.

Jesus' words to Thomas are John's words to his end-of-the-century audience and to us: "Have you come to believe because you have seen me? Blessed are those who have not seen and have believed." Jesus is just as present to us as he was to his original disciples. He calls us to a deeper trust so that we do not need to touch him, as Thomas did, in order to know he is present and to adore him.

◆ What details in John's account show Jesus' desire that his disciples, John's audience, and we also, believe in his Resurrection?

◆ What do you need to see in order to believe?

◆ What do Jesus' words, "As the Father has sent me, so I send you," mean to you?

READING I   Acts 2:14, 22—33

Then Peter stood up with the Eleven, raised his voice, and proclaimed: "You who are Jews, indeed all of you staying in Jerusalem. Let this be known to you, and listen to my words. You who are Israelites, hear these words. Jesus the Nazarene was a man commended to you by God with mighty deeds, wonders, and signs, which God worked through him in your midst, as you yourselves know. This man, delivered up by the set plan and foreknowledge of God, you killed, using lawless men to crucify him. But God raised him up, releasing him from the throes of death, because it was impossible for him to be held by it. For David says of him:

I saw the Lord ever before me,
> *with him at my right hand*
> > *I shall not be disturbed.*
Therefore my heart has been glad
> *and my tongue has exulted;*
> *my flesh, too, will dwell in hope,*
because you will not abandon
> *my soul to the netherworld,*
> *nor will you suffer your holy one*
> > *to see corruption.*
You have made known to me the paths of life;
> *you will fill me with joy in your presence.*

"My brothers, one can confidently say to you about the patriarch David that he died and was buried, and his tomb is in our midst to this day. But since he was a prophet and knew that God had sworn an oath to him that he would set one of his descendants upon his throne, he foresaw and spoke of the resurrection of the Christ, that neither was he abandoned to the netherworld nor did his flesh see corruption. God raised this Jesus; of this we are all witnesses. Exalted at the right hand of God, he received the promise of the Holy Spirit from the Father and poured him forth, as you see and hear."

READING II   1 Peter 1:17—21

Beloved:

If you invoke as Father him who judges impartially according to each one's works, conduct yourselves with reverence during the time of your sojourning, realizing that you were ransomed from your futile conduct, handed on by your ancestors, not with perishable things like silver or gold but with the precious blood of Christ as of a spotless unblemished lamb.

He was known before the foundation of the world but revealed in the final time for you, who through him believe in God who raised him from the dead and gave him glory, so that your faith and hope are in God.

GOSPEL   Luke 24:13—35

That very day, the first day of the week, two of Jesus' disciples were going to a village seven miles from Jerusalem called Emmaus, and they were conversing about all the things that had occurred. And it happened that while they were conversing and debating, Jesus himself drew near and walked with them, but their eyes were prevented from recognizing him. He asked them, "What are you discussing as you walk along?" They stopped, looking downcast. One of them, named Cleopas, said to him in reply, "Are you the only visitor to Jerusalem who does not know of the things that have taken place there in these days?" And he replied to them, "What sort of things?" They said to him, "The things that happened to Jesus the Nazarene, who was a prophet mighty in deed and word before God and all the people, how our chief priests and rulers both handed him over to a sentence of death and crucified him. But we were hoping that he would be the one to redeem Israel; and besides all this, it is now the third day since this took place. Some women from our group, however, have astounded us: they were at the tomb early in the morning and did not find his body; they came back and reported that they had indeed seen a vision of angels who announced that he was alive. Then some of those with us went to the tomb and found things just as the women had described, but him they did not see." And he said to them, "Oh, how foolish you are! How slow of heart to believe all that the prophets spoke! Was it not necessary that the Christ should suffer these things and enter into his glory?" Then beginning with Moses and all the prophets, he interpreted to them what referred to him in all the Scriptures. As they approached the village to which they were going, he gave the impression that he was going on farther. But they urged him, "Stay with us, for it is nearly evening and the day is almost over." So he went in to stay with them. And it happened that, while he was with them at table, he took bread, said the blessing, broke it, and gave it to them. With that their eyes were opened and they recognized him, but he vanished from their sight. Then they said to each other, "Were not our hearts burning within us while he spoke to us on the way and opened the Scriptures to us?" So they set out at once and returned to Jerusalem where they found gathered together the eleven and those with them who were saying, "The Lord has truly been raised and has appeared to Simon!" Then the two recounted what had taken place on the way and how he was made known to them in the breaking of bread.

Practice of Charity

Life. Love. Blessing. Bread sustains us, brings us together, and offers us comfort. Is it any wonder that the source of all life and love and blessing should make himself known in the breaking of bread?

While it is not actually food, the monetary donation called Saint Anthony Bread presents a wonderful way to bring new life and give comfort to those in need. A Franciscan tradition dating to the thirteenth century, Saint Anthony Bread is a gift made in honor of Saint Anthony of Padua or in thanksgiving for blessings received. The Franciscan Friars of Cincinnati, who run Saint Anthony Shrine there, note that all of this "bread" is used in their work among the poor.

To learn more about this beloved saint or the ministries of the Franciscan Friars, visit www.stanthony.org/donate/stanthonybread.asp.

One element the post-Resurrection appearance stories often share is that even those who know and love Jesus, at first fail to recognize him. We see this in today's story of the disciples on the road to Emmaus.

Although the disciples were talking about Jesus as they walked along, when Jesus joined them, "their eyes were prevented from recognizing him." Even when Jesus "interpreted to them what referred to him in all the scriptures," they still did not recognize him. Only when they stop for the night and are breaking bread together do they realize that the risen Christ is, and has been, in their midst.

We cannot fail to recognize the eucharistic language that Luke uses to describe this scene. While Jesus "was with them at table, he took bread, said the blessing, broke it, and gave it to them." We too recognize Jesus' presence in the breaking of the bread. However, this story encourages us to recognize the risen Christ in other places as well.

Like the two disciples in today's Gospel reading, we are disciples walking along life's road. Like them, we may be unaware that Jesus is actually walking with us. We may not see him in the stranger we meet on the way, or hear him in the living word of scripture. May our recognition of Jesus in the breaking of the bread open our eyes, as it did the disciples', so that we recognize the risen Christ in all the places he is truly present and accompanying us on our journey.

• In what ways were the disciples closed to Jesus in this story? In what ways were they opened?

• Where in your experience are you most open and most closed to the presence of the risen Christ?

• How could you open yourself to see Christ where you have not seen him before?

• In the first reading, how does Peter use a psalm to open the minds of his audience to the Resurrection of Christ?

READING I   Acts 2:1, 4a, 36—41

Then Peter stood up with the Eleven, raised his voice, and proclaimed: "Let the whole house of Israel know for certain that God has made both Lord and Christ, this Jesus whom you crucified."

Now when they heard this, they were cut to the heart, and they asked Peter and the other apostles, "What are we to do, my brothers?" Peter said to them, "Repent and be baptized, every one of you, in the name of Jesus Christ for the forgiveness of your sins; and you will receive the gift of the Holy Spirit. For the promise is made to you and to your children and to all those far off, whomever the Lord our God will call." He testified with many other arguments, and was exhorting them, "Save yourselves from this corrupt generation." Those who accepted his message were baptized, and about three thousand persons were added that day.

READING II   1 Peter 2:20b—25

Beloved:

If you are patient when you suffer for doing what is good, this is a grace before God. For to this you have been called, because Christ also suffered for you, leaving you an example that you should follow in his footsteps. *He committed no sin, and no deceit was found in his mouth.*

When he was insulted, he returned no insult; when he suffered, he did not threaten; instead, he handed himself over to the one who judges justly. He himself bore our sins in his body upon the cross, so that, free from sin, we might live for righteousness. By his wounds you have been healed. For you had gone astray like sheep, but you have now returned to the shepherd and guardian of your souls.

GOSPEL   John 10:1—10

Jesus said:

"Amen, amen, I say to you, whoever does not enter a sheepfold through the gate but climbs over elsewhere is a thief and a robber. But whoever enters through the gate is the shepherd of the sheep. The gatekeeper opens it for him, and the sheep hear his voice, as the shepherd calls his own sheep by name and leads them out. When he has driven out all his own, he walks ahead of them, and the sheep follow him, because they recognize his voice. But they will not follow a stranger; they will run away from him, because they do not recognize the voice of strangers." Although Jesus used this figure of speech, the Pharisees did not realize what he was trying to tell them.

So Jesus said again, "Amen, amen, I say to you, I am the gate for the sheep. All who came before me are thieves and robbers, but the sheep did not listen to them. I am the gate. Whoever enters through me will be saved, and will come in and go out and find pasture. A thief comes only to steal and slaughter and destroy; I came so that they might have life and have it more abundantly."

Practice of Prayer

Psalm 23:1—3a, 3b—4, 5, 6 (1)

R. The Lord is my shepherd;
    there is nothing I shall want.
or: Alleluia.

The LORD is my shepherd; I shall not want.
    In verdant pastures he gives me repose;
beside restful waters he leads me;
    he refreshes my soul.   R.

He guides me in right paths
    for his name's sake.
Even though I walk in the dark valley
    I fear no evil; for you are at my side,
with your rod and your staff
    that give me courage.   R.

You spread the table before me
    in the sight of my foes;
you anoint my head with oil;
    my cup overflows.   R.

Only goodness and kindness follow me
    all the days of my life;
and I shall dwell in the house of the LORD
    for years to come.   R.

Practice of Faith

In recent years, the film *The Chronicles of Narnia: The Lion, the Witch and the Wardrobe* has brought C. S. Lewis's marvelous tale of sacrifice and redemption to a new generation. It tells of how young Edmund chooses to follow the beautiful White Witch, Jadis, and believe all of her empty promises to give him what he thinks will make him happy. The choice he faces isn't so different from the choice we are asked to make every day. Many people claim leadership roles in our lives, but who do we follow and why?

Today's readings assure us that there is one voice that will never fail, one call that will lead us to verdant pastures, restful waters, and abundant life. Edmund was offered Turkish Delight, but we are offered something infinitely more precious if we are willing to recognize and follow the one who makes it all possible.

Scripture Insights

In today's readings, we hear how our Savior forgives and heals us through his life, Passion, death, and Resurrection. In the reading from Acts, Peter tells his fellow Israelites that "the promise is made to you and to your children and to all those far off." We are "those far off," both because we are Gentiles and because we live two thousand years after Peter. What has the Lord promised us?

Peter tells us, "Repent and be baptized . . . in the name of Jesus Christ for the forgiveness of your sins; and you will receive the gift of the Holy Spirit." Repentance is essential preparation for receiving the Spirit. Naming our sins and sincerely repenting is not a futile, depressing exercise, but a healthful and healing one. As we read in the letter of Peter, we repent not in order to receive punishment, but to be forgiven, to be healed, to be freed from sin: "By his wounds you have been healed." We are not called to a life of remorse where nothing can be set right. Rather, Jesus came that we "might have life and have it more abundantly." Those who repent and are baptized receive the Holy Spirit—a crucial gift for disciples. As Christians we receive not only forgiveness for our sins but the power to act differently in the future, to model ourselves after Jesus, and grow in holiness. As 1 Peter says, Christ left us "an example that you should follow in his footsteps." The power to avoid sin in the future comes from the Spirit dwelling within us.

It is true that we have all gone astray like sheep. However, Christ, the Good Shepherd, has not only called us, but healed us and given us the power to walk in his way. This is good news indeed!

• According to Jesus' description of the Good Shepherd, what things will he do, as our Savior, to care for us?

• How have you experienced repentance? What has it done for you?

• When have you felt the connection between repentance and the Spirit working in your life?

READING I   Acts 6:1—7

As the number of disciples continued to grow, the Hellenists complained against the Hebrews because their widows were being neglected in the daily distribution. So the Twelve called together the community of the disciples and said, "It is not right for us to neglect the word of God to serve at table. Brothers, select from among you seven reputable men, filled with the Spirit and wisdom, whom we shall appoint to this task, whereas we shall devote ourselves to prayer and to the ministry of the word." The proposal was acceptable to the whole community, so they chose Stephen, a man filled with faith and the Holy Spirit, also Philip, Prochorus, Nicanor, Timon, Parmenas, and Nicholas of Antioch, a convert to Judaism. They presented these men to the apostles who prayed and laid hands on them. The word of God continued to spread, and the number of the disciples in Jerusalem increased greatly; even a large group of priests were becoming obedient to the faith.

READING II   1 Peter 2:4—9

Beloved:

Come to him, a living stone, rejected by human beings but chosen and precious in the sight of God, and, like living stones, let yourselves be built into a spiritual house to be a holy priesthood to offer spiritual sacrifices acceptable to God through Jesus Christ.

For it says in Scripture:

> Behold, I am laying a stone in Zion,
> a cornerstone,
>   chosen and precious,
> and whoever believes in it
>   shall not be put to shame.

Therefore, its value is for you who have faith, but for those without faith:

> The stone that the builders rejected
> has become the cornerstone,

and

> A stone that will make people stumble,
> and a rock that will make them fall.

They stumble by disobeying the word, as is their destiny.

You are "a chosen race, a royal priesthood, a holy nation, a people of his own, so that you may announce the praises" of him who called you out of darkness into his wonderful light.

GOSPEL   John 14:1—12

Jesus said to his disciples:

"Do not let your hearts be troubled. You have faith in God; have faith also in me. In my Father's house there are many dwelling places. If there were not, would I have told you that I am going to prepare a place for you? And if I go and prepare a place for you, I will come back again and take you to myself, so that where I am you also may be. Where I am going you know the way." Thomas said to him, "Master, we do not know where you are going; how can we know the way?" Jesus said to him, "I am the way and the truth and the life. No one comes to the Father except through me. If you know me, then you will also know my Father. From now on you do know him and have seen him." Philip said to him, "Master, show us the Father, and that will be enough for us." Jesus said to him, "Have I been with you for so long a time and you still do not know me, Philip? Whoever has seen me has seen the Father. How can you say, 'Show us the Father'? Do you not believe that I am in the Father and the Father is in me? The words that I speak to you I do not speak on my own. The Father who dwells in me is doing his works. Believe me that I am in the Father and the Father is in me, or else, believe because of the works themselves. Amen, amen, I say to you, whoever believes in me will do the works that I do, and will do greater ones than these, because I am going to the Father."

Practice of Prayer

Psalm 33:1–2, 4–5, 18–19 (22)

R. Lord, let your mercy be on us,
    as we place our trust in you.
or: Alleluia.

Exult, you just, in the LORD;
    praise from the upright is fitting.
Give thanks to the LORD on the harp;
    with the ten-stringed lyre
        chant his praises. R.

Upright is the word of the LORD,
    and all his works are trustworthy.
He loves justice and right;
    of the kindness of the LORD
        the earth is full. R.

See, the eyes of the LORD are upon
        those who fear him,
    upon those who hope for his kindness,
to deliver them from death
    and preserve them in spite of famine. R.

Practice of Hope

A young woman I've never met helped me to make chocolate chip oatmeal cookies last weekend. The mix I used was "lovingly handmade" by Celena, a participant in the Women's Bean Project. This Denver-based nonprofit organization seeks to help women break the cycle of poverty and unemployment by teaching them job readiness and life skills. Most of the women have no high school diplomas, and many are single mothers with a history of incarceration or substance abuse. They know what chronic unemployment is. By assembling the various cookie, bread, bean soup, bean and salsa mixes of the Women's Bean Project, they also get to know who they are and what they're capable of.

To help someone see that she is "chosen and precious in the sight of God," visit www.womensbeanproject.com or call (303) 292-1919.

Scripture Insights

On the Fifth Sunday of Easter we read part of a long theological discourse that John pictures Jesus giving at his last meal with the disciples before his death. Jesus encourages the disciples to have faith in him: "You have faith in God; have faith also in me." To have faith in Jesus, the disciples (including us) need to know who Jesus is. Today's passage probes the mystery of Jesus' identity by discussing his relationship with God the Father. Through the dialogue, we learn that Jesus and the Father are one.

We see that unity between Father and Son throughout the discourse in Jesus' "I am" statements, one of which appears in today's reading. "I am the way and the truth and the life," says Jesus. Upon hearing the Son say "I am," readers would remember God, who, at the burning bush, revealed his name to be I AM WHO AM.

We are pressed to consider the mystery of Jesus' identity even further when Thomas and Philip both fail to understand what Jesus is telling them. In response, Jesus makes two intriguing statements: "If you know me, then you will also know my Father" and "Do you not believe that I am in the Father and the Father is in me?" To know Jesus is to know the Father.

We too are called to have faith in Jesus. If we do, we will know that the risen Christ is present, be empowered to carry on his work, and be united with the Father.

• Which statements in this discourse are most powerful for you at expressing the bond between the Father and the Son? Which words describe where Jesus' disciples stand in relation to them?

• How is Jesus "the way, the truth and the life" for you?

• How are you personally carrying on Jesus' work?

• How might we be "like living stones . . . built into a spiritual house" (second reading)?

READING I   *Acts 8:5—8, 14—17*

Philip went down to the city of Samaria and proclaimed the Christ to them. With one accord, the crowds paid attention to what was said by Philip when they heard it and saw the signs he was doing. For unclean spirits, crying out in a loud voice, came out of many possessed people, and many paralyzed or crippled people were cured. There was great joy in that city.

Now when the apostles in Jerusalem heard that Samaria had accepted the word of God, they sent them Peter and John, who went down and prayed for them, that they might receive the Holy Spirit, for it had not yet fallen upon any of them; they had only been baptized in the name of the Lord Jesus. Then they laid hands on them and they received the Holy Spirit.

READING II   *1 Peter 3:15—18*

Beloved:

Sanctify Christ as Lord in your hearts. Always be ready to give an explanation to anyone who asks you for a reason for your hope, but do it with gentleness and reverence, keeping your conscience clear, so that, when you are maligned, those who defame your good conduct in Christ may themselves be put to shame. For it is better to suffer for doing good, if that be the will of God, than for doing evil.

For Christ also suffered for sins once, the righteous for the sake of the unrighteous, that he might lead you to God. Put to death in the flesh, he was brought to life in the Spirit.

GOSPEL   *John 14:15—21*

Jesus said to his disciples:

"If you love me, you will keep my commandments. And I will ask the Father, and he will give you another Advocate to be with you always, the Spirit of truth, whom the world cannot accept, because it neither sees nor knows him. But you know him, because he remains with you, and will be in you. I will not leave you orphans; I will come to you. In a little while the world will no longer see me, but you will see me, because I live and you will live. On that day you will realize that I am in my Father and you are in me and I in you. Whoever has my commandments and observes them is the one who loves me. And whoever loves me will be loved by my Father, and I will love him and reveal myself to him."

Practice of Prayer

Psalm 66:1—3, 4—5, 6—7, 16, 20 (1)

R. Let all the earth cry out to God with joy.
or: Alleluia.

Shout joyfully to God, all the earth,
    sing praise to the glory of his name;
    proclaim his glorious praise.
Say to God, "How tremendous
      are your deeds!"   R.

"Let all on earth worship and sing praise to you,
    sing praise to your name!"
Come and see the works of God,
    his tremendous deeds among
      the children of Adam.   R.

He has changed the sea into dry land;
    through the river they passed on foot;
    therefore let us rejoice in him.
He rules by his might forever.   R.

Hear now, all you who fear God,
    while I declare what he has done for me.
Blessed be God who refused me not
    my prayer or his kindness!   R.

Practice of Hope

The first reading generally points to the Gospel in some way. This week is a rare exception—the first reading is a fulfillment of what Jesus will promise us in John's account of the Gospel. The community of believers has made prayer their source of strength and is doing what Jesus asked, and so Samaria is a city of joy.

Following hurricanes Katrina and Rita in 2005, Baton Rouge, Louisiana, was not a city of joy. Lives were destroyed as countless homes, businesses, and churches were left in ruins. In the face of so much loss, the diocese of Baton Rouge launched a stewardship campaign. Instead of seeking money, however, they sought prayer. Through One Church One Community, those who suffered had powerful advocates around the country and were never truly alone. Leaning on Jesus, they built hope, knowing that hope would get the rest of the work done.

Scripture Insights

In John's account of the Gospel, at the Last Supper Jesus promises his disciples, "I will not leave you orphans; I will come to you. In a little while the world will no longer see me, but you will see me, because I live and you will live."

As you read these words, remember the situation of John's audience at the end of the first century—they have lived well past the expected time of the Second Coming. John is trying to help them see that Jesus did indeed return soon as he promised—in his post-Resurrection appearances—and that he has never left.

Jesus' promise to the disciples that in a little while he will come to them is fulfilled when Jesus appears to the disciples on the evening of the first day of the week, that is, Easter evening. "Jesus came and stood in their midst and said to them, 'Peace be with you.' . . .The disciples rejoiced when they saw the Lord" (John 20:19—20).

In today's Gospel reading, Jesus also promises the disciples that he will ask the Father to send them "another Advocate to be with you always, the Spirit of truth." This promise was also fulfilled on the first Easter evening appearance to the disciples, where "he breathed on them and said to them, 'Receive the holy Spirit'" (John 20:22).

John wants his fellow Christians to realize that the risen Christ is already present to them, and that the Spirit dwells within them. Because the risen Christ is also present to us, and his Spirit dwells within us, we stand ready to respond to today's words in the letter of Peter: "Always be ready to give an explanation to anyone who asks you for a reason for your hope." Our hope rests in Jesus Christ, the Son of God, who has risen from the dead.

• In the Gospel reading, what is the difference between the way the world sees and the way disciples are learning to see?

• Who in your community needs a word of hope?

• What hope do you have to offer?

READING I   *Acts 1:1—11*

In the first book, Theophilus, I dealt with all that Jesus did and taught until the day he was taken up, after giving instructions through the Holy Spirit to the apostles whom he had chosen. He presented himself alive to them by many proofs after he had suffered, appearing to them during forty days and speaking about the kingdom of God. While meeting with them, he enjoined them not to depart from Jerusalem, but to wait for "the promise of the Father about which you have heard me speak; for John baptized with water, but in a few days you will be baptized with the Holy Spirit."

When they had gathered together they asked him, "Lord, are you at this time going to restore the kingdom to Israel?" He answered them, "It is not for you to know the times or seasons that the Father has established by his own authority. But you will receive power when the Holy Spirit comes upon you, and you will be my witnesses in Jerusalem, throughout Judea and Samaria, and to the ends of the earth." When he had said this, as they were looking on, he was lifted up, and a cloud took him from their sight. While they were looking intently at the sky as he was going, suddenly two men dressed in white garments stood beside them. They said, "Men of Galilee, why are you standing there looking at the sky? This Jesus who has been taken up from you into heaven will return in the same way as you have seen him going into heaven."

READING II   *Ephesians 1:17—23*

Brothers and sisters:

May the God of our Lord Jesus Christ, the Father of glory, give you a Spirit of wisdom and revelation resulting in knowledge of him. May the eyes of your hearts be enlightened, that you may know what is the hope that belongs to his call, what are the riches of glory in his inheritance among the holy ones, and what is the surpassing greatness of his power for us who believe, in accord with the exercise of his great might, which he worked in Christ, raising him from the dead and seating him at his right hand in the heavens, far above every principality, authority, power, and dominion, and every name that is named not only in this age but also in the one to come. And he put all things beneath his feet and gave him as head over all things to the church, which is his body, the fullness of the one who fills all things in every way.

GOSPEL   *Matthew 28:16—20*

The eleven disciples went to Galilee, to the mountain to which Jesus had ordered them. When they saw him, they worshiped, but they doubted. Then Jesus approached and said to them, "All power in heaven and on earth has been given to me. Go, therefore, and make disciples of all nations, baptizing them in the name of the Father, and of the Son, and of the Holy Spirit, teaching them to observe all that I have commanded you. And behold, I am with you always, until the end of the age."

Practice of Prayer

Psalm 47:2—3, 6—7, 8—9 (6)

R. God mounts his throne to shouts of joy:
    a blare of trumpets for the Lord.
or: Alleluia.

All you peoples, clap your hands,
    shout to God with cries of gladness.
For the Lord, the Most High, the awesome,
    is the great king over all the earth.   R.

God mounts his throne amid shouts of joy;
　　the LORD, amid trumpet blasts.
Sing praise to God, sing praise;
　　sing praise to our king, sing praise. R.

For king of all the earth is God;
　　sing hymns of praise.
God reigns over the nations,
　　God sits upon his holy throne. R.

Practice of Faith

Before Jesus returns to his heavenly home, he entrusts everything in his earthly home to his disciples with this commission: "Go, therefore, and make disciples of all nations." While he made the "what" of their commission pretty plain, Jesus left the "how" up to his followers. That is a question that continues to occupy people of good will to this day.

While Jesus probably didn't have watermelon in mind as an evangelization tool, one pastoral administrator at a Catholic parish in northwest Kansas found that cold slices of the popular fruit opened doors in the neighborhood on a hot summer day. By taking the refreshment to neighbors, she laid the foundation for relationship and dialogue that makes Jesus' commission possible.

This week, look for simple ways to build up the kingdom of God. It doesn't have to be difficult to bear fruit.

Scripture Insights

As Matthew concludes his Gospel narrative, Jesus orders the 11 disciples to go to a mountain in Galilee. In Luke's account, however, the apostles are instructed to stay in Jerusalem. This and other differences among the four Gospel narratives show that their writers were more concerned about teaching theology than history. Events certainly do lie behind their stories, but each Gospel writer shapes his story to teach the significance of those events to his particular audience.

Luke, who is writing to Gentiles, structures both his Gospel account and his other book, Acts, around Jerusalem. From Jerusalem the word will go out. Jesus tells the apostles, "You will be my witnesses in Jerusalem, throughout Judea, and Samaria, and to the ends of the earth."

Matthew, on the other hand, addresses fellow Jews who want to understand the relationship between Jesus and their two-thousand-year tradition of covenant love with God. In Matthew, Jesus appears to the disciples on a mountain because it was on a mountain that God revealed himself to Moses and from which Moses taught the commandments. Jesus tells the 11 that God has given him all power (all authority). The disciples must now teach what Jesus commanded.

Jesus then commissions the disciples to "make disciples of all nations." Matthew ends his story with Jesus saying, "I will be with you always, until the end of the age."

On this solemnity of the Ascension, in addition to Luke's image of Jesus disappearing in a cloud, we hear Matthew focusing on the victorious conclusion of Jesus' mission on earth and the beginning of Jesus' disciples carrying on that mission. As disciples who have been commissioned by our Baptism to carry on Jesus' mission, we know that the risen Christ is and will always be with us, until the end of the age.

◆ Besides the setting (Jerusalem vs. the mountain) what other differences can you name between Luke's and Matthew's stories?

◆ As disciples trying to carry out Jesus' mission, what things in today's three readings do you find reassuring?

◆ How do you reconcile Jesus being "in heaven" and yet "with" you?

May 4, 2008

READING I   Acts 1:12—14

After Jesus had been taken up to heaven the apostles returned to Jerusalem from the mount called Olivet, which is near Jerusalem, a sabbath day's journey away.

When they entered the city they went to the upper room where they were staying, Peter and John and James and Andrew, Philip and Thomas, Bartholomew and Matthew, James son of Alphaeus, Simon the Zealot, and Judas son of James. All these devoted themselves with one accord to prayer, together with some women, and Mary the mother of Jesus, and his brothers.

READING II   1 Peter 4:13—16

Beloved:

Rejoice to the extent that you share in the sufferings of Christ, so that when his glory is revealed you may also rejoice exultantly. If you are insulted for the name of Christ, blessed are you, for the Spirit of glory and of God rests upon you. But let no one among you be made to suffer as a murderer, a thief, an evildoer, or as an intriguer. But whoever is made to suffer as a Christian should not be ashamed but glorify God because of the name.

GOSPEL   John 17:1—11a

Jesus raised his eyes to heaven and said,

"Father, the hour has come. Give glory to your son, so that your son may glorify you, just as you gave him authority over all people, so that your son may give eternal life to all you gave him. Now this is eternal life, that they should know you, the only true God, and the one whom you sent, Jesus Christ. I glorified you on earth by accomplishing the work that you gave me to do. Now glorify me, Father, with you, with the glory that I had with you before the world began.

"I revealed your name to those whom you gave me out of the world. They belonged to you, and you gave them to me, and they have kept your word. Now they know that everything you gave me is from you, because the words you gave to me I have given to them, and they accepted them and truly understood that I came from you, and they have believed that you sent me. I pray for them. I do not pray for the world but for the ones you have given me, because they are yours, and everything of mine is yours and everything of yours is mine, and I have been glorified in them. And now I will no longer be in the world, but they are in the world, while I am coming to you."

Practice of Prayer

Psalm 27:1, 4, 7—8 (13)

R. I believe that I shall see the good things
    of the Lord in the land of the living.
or: Alleluia.

The Lord is my light and my salvation;
    whom should I fear?
The Lord is my life's refuge;
    of whom should I be afraid?   R.

One thing I ask of the Lord;
    this I seek:
to dwell in the house of the Lord
    all the days of my life,
that I may gaze on the loveliness of the Lord
    and contemplate his temple.   R.

Hear, O Lord, the sound of my call;
    have pity on me, and answer me.
Of you my heart speaks; you my glance seeks.   R.

Practice of Hope

Perhaps you've seen unsolicited stock tips sent by fax or e-mail. This one was particularly arresting: Reporting on a discredited arthritis medication, it advised investors "How You Can Turn Pain into Profit." This "killer opportunity" could only be seized by forgetting about arthritis sufferers and concentrating on self.

But that doesn't constitute profit, or rather blessing, where Jesus is concerned. Today's readings make a connection between sharing in the suffering of Christ and sharing in his eternal life with God.

Prayer is an essential part of turning pain into blessing. For many who are chronically ill or living with disabilities, CUSA fosters that link. Through this apostolate, groups of about eight people encourage one another through prayers, letters, and e-mail. Each group has a leader and spiritual adviser and takes on a unique character by adopting a patron saint, motto, and intention. The goal remains the same, however: "We find a purpose in suffering." To learn more about CUSA, visit www.cusan.org./index.htm.

Scripture Insights

In today's Gospel reading, John shows Jesus praying to his Father, asking that his glory, that is, his divinity, become visible. As he does throughout his Gospel narrative, John presents Jesus to us as a divine person.

At the time John was writing, those Jews who believed in the divinity of Jesus were being expelled from the synagogue by those Jews who did not. Because Jews were exempt from the Roman law requiring everyone to participate in emperor worship, those expelled from the synagogue lost that status. Of course, honoring the emperor as a god would be against the conscience of a Christian as well as a Jew, so expulsion from the synagogue resulted in the persecution of Jewish Christians. Under these circumstances, some were tempted to acknowledge Jesus as a great teacher, but to deny his divinity in order to avoid persecution. John stresses that believing in Jesus' divinity is essential for disciples.

During Jesus' prayer, he refers to "the glory that I had with you before the world began." This recalls the very beginning of John's account of the Gospel where Jesus is presented as the Word that existed before all of creation: " . . . and the Word was with God, / and the Word was God."

Jesus wants his glory to become visible so that he can give eternal life. He says, "Now this is eternal life, that they should know you, the only true God, and the one whom you sent, Jesus Christ." John is reminding his fellow Jews, who truly understood that Jesus had come from the Father, to remain faithful in their witness to the true identity of Jesus Christ. We must be faithful witnesses too.

◆ What specific words and phrases in Jesus' prayer point to his divine nature?

◆ Have you ever felt afraid to witness to your beliefs about Jesus? What would have helped you?

◆ In the first reading, how do you explain the actions of the apostles and the women in the upper room?

◆ How do the words in the second reading strike you? Is this a hard teaching? a comfort? a mystery?

May 11, 2008

READING I   Acts 2:1—11

When the time for Pentecost was fulfilled, they were all in one place together. And suddenly there came from the sky a noise like a strong driving wind, and it filled the entire house in which they were. Then there appeared to them tongues as of fire, which parted and came to rest on each one of them. And they were all filled with the Holy Spirit and began to speak in different tongues, as the Spirit enabled them to proclaim.

Now there were devout Jews from every nation under heaven staying in Jerusalem. At this sound, they gathered in a large crowd, but they were confused because each one heard them speaking in his own language. They were astounded, and in amazement they asked, "Are not all these people who are speaking Galileans? Then how does each of us hear them in his native language? We are Parthians, Medes, and Elamites, inhabitants of Mesopotamia, Judea and Cappadocia, Pontus and Asia, Phrygia and Pamphylia, Egypt and the districts of Libya near Cyrene, as well as travelers from Rome, both Jews and converts to Judaism, Cretans and Arabs, yet we hear them speaking in our own tongues of the mighty acts of God."

READING II   1 Corinthians 12:3—7, 12—13

Brothers and sisters:

No one can say, "Jesus is Lord," except by the Holy Spirit.

There are different kinds of spiritual gifts but the same Spirit; there are different forms of service but the same Lord; there are different workings but the same God who produces all of them in everyone. To each individual the manifestation of the Spirit is given for some benefit.

As a body is one though it has many parts, and all the parts of the body, though many, are one body, so also Christ. For in one Spirit we were all baptized into one body, whether Jews or Greeks, slaves or free persons, and we were all given to drink of one Spirit.

GOSPEL   John 20:19—23

On the evening of that first day of the week, when the doors were locked, where the disciples were, for fear of the Jews, Jesus came and stood in their midst and said to them, "Peace be with you." When he had said this, he showed them his hands and his side. The disciples rejoiced when they saw the Lord. Jesus said to them again, "Peace be with you. As the Father has sent me, so I send you." And when he had said this, he breathed on them and said to them, "Receive the Holy Spirit. Whose sins you forgive are forgiven them, and whose sins you retain are retained."

Practice of Prayer

Psalm 104:1, 24, 29—30, 29, 31, 34 (see 10)

R. Lord, send out your Spirit,
    and renew the face of the earth.
or: Alleluia.

Bless the LORD, O my soul!
    O LORD, my God, you are great indeed!
How manifold are your works, O LORD!
    the earth is full of your creatures.   R.

May the glory of the L
ORD endure forever;
    may the L
ORD, be glad in his works!
Pleasing to him be my theme;
    I will be glad in the L
ORD. R.

If you take away their breath, they perish
    and return to their dust.
When you send forth your spirit, they are created,
    and you renew the face of the earth. R.

Practice of Hope

How we pray and talk about God indicates our relationship with God and one another. All too often, however, that which should unite us divides us in dramatic ways. Fearing that to be true in their corner of the world, the Sisters of St. Benedict of St. Mary's Monastery in Rock Island, Illinois, invited Muslim and Christian women to come together for a series of dialogues about prayer, ritual, family, and life. Peace doesn't start by raising arms, they said, but by raising hands in greeting at the grocery store and on the street. Being able to hear and understand one another was the first step.

If you are interested in learning about Islamic-Catholic relations and perhaps participating in interreligious dialogue, see the many resources from the Office for Ecumenical and Interreligious Affairs on the Web site of the United States Conference of Catholic Bishops, http://www.usccb.org/seia/islam.shtml.

Scripture Insights

On Pentecost Sunday we celebrate the coming of the Spirit into the Church and into our individual lives. Though we celebrate it as a single event, it is a never-ending event. The Spirit has come, is coming, and will come.

Our reading from Acts pictures the coming of the Spirit to the disciples as they wait in Jerusalem, according to Jesus' instructions. Not only the apostles, but other disciples had been waiting as well, including "some women, and Mary the mother of Jesus" (Acts 1:14).

The Spirit comes "like a strong driving wind" and "tongues of fire." Wind and fire are traditional scripture images for the presence of God. The tongues of fire do not rest just on a few chosen leaders but on "each one of them. And they were all filled with the Holy Spirit." Luke shows us the Spirit's effect—the speaking in tongues and the amazement of onlookers. Through the power of the Spirit, the Gospel would be preached to the whole world.

In the Gospel reading from John, the Spirit is given to the Church "on the evening of that first day of the week." This is the occasion on which Jesus fulfills the promises he made to the disciples just before he died—that they would see him again and that the Advocate would come. (See the Sixth Sunday of Easter.)

In John, the giving of the Spirit is part of the disciples' commissioning: "As the Father has sent me, so I send you." The disciples will not only teach the Good News, but will make it possible for people to experience the forgiveness of sins. Forgiveness of sins is, of course, the effect of Baptism. And the Church has instituted the sacrament of Penance for the forgiveness of sins after Baptism. Having received the Holy Spirit at our Baptism and Confirmation, we know that the Spirit lives in us, yet we want to deepen our awareness and understanding. On Pentecost we, like the disciples gathered in Jerusalem, pray, "Come, holy Spirit. Come."

♦ In what details do Luke (the Acts passage) and John (the Gospel) differ when they describe the coming of the Spirit?

♦ How do you interpret the tongues of fire resting on each person?

♦ How have you experienced the Spirit?

Ordinary Time, Summer

Prayer before Reading the Word

God, sower of the seed,
we marvel at how your word accomplishes
the purpose for which you sent it forth:
how few of the seeds you sow take root,
yet how spectacular their abundant yield.

Make us good soil, ready to receive what you sow,
that we may hear the word and understand it,
bear fruit and yield a hundredfold.

We ask this through our Lord
    Jesus Christ, your Son,
who lives and reigns with you
in the unity of the Holy Spirit,
one God for ever and ever. Amen.

Prayer after Reading the Word

To us, sinners and yet disciples,
O Lord of the harvest,
you entrust a share in the mission of Jesus,
who sent the Twelve to proclaim the Good News
and to bear witness without fear.

With your love forever sheltering
    and surrounding us,
may we proclaim from the housetops
the Gospel we have heard
and acknowledge openly before all
the one whom we confess as Lord,
Jesus Christ, your Son, who lives
    and reigns with you
in the unity of the Holy Spirit,
one God for ever and ever. Amen.

Weekday Readings

May 12: *James 1:1–11; Mark 8:11–13*
May 13: *James 1:12–18; Mark 8:14–21*
May 14: Feast of Saint Matthias
   Acts 1:15–17; 20–26; John 15:9–17
May 15: *James 2:1–9; Mark 8:27–33*
May 16: *James 2:14–24; Mark 8:34—9:1*
May 17: *James 3:1–10; Mark 9:2–13*

May 19: *James 3:13–18; Mark 9:14–29*
May 20: *James 4:1–10; Mark 9:30–37*
May 21: *James 4:13–17; Mark 9:38–40*
May 22: *James 5:1–6; Mark 9:41–50*
May 23: *James 5:9–12; Mark 10:1–12*
May 24: *James 5:13–20; Mark 10:13–16*

May 26: *1 Peter 1:3–9; Mark 10:17–27*
May 27: *1 Peter 1:10–16; Mark 10:28–31*
May 28: *1 Peter 1:18–25; Mark 10:32–45*
May 29: *1 Peter 2:2–5, 9–12; Mark 10:46–52*
May 30: Solemnity of the Most Sacred Heart of Jesus
   Deuteronomy 7:6–11; 1 John 4:7–16; Matthew 11:25–30
May 31: Feast of the Visitation of the Blessed Virgin Mary
   Zephania 3:14–18a; Luke 1:39–56

June 2: *2 Peter 1:2–7; Mark 12:1–12*
June 3: *2 Peter 3:12–15a, 17–18; Mark 12:13–17*
June 4: *2 Timothy 1:1–3, 6–12; Mark 12:18–27*
June 5: *2 Timothy 2:8–15; Mark 12:28–34*
June 6: *2 Timothy 3:10–17; Mark 12:35–37*
June 7: *2 Timothy 4:1–8; Mark 12:38–44*

June 9: *1 Kings 17:1–6; Matthew 5:1–12*
June 10: *1 Kings 17:7–16; Matthew 5:13–16*
June 11: *Acts 11:21b–26; 13:1–3; Matthew 5:17–19*
June 12: *1 Kings 18:41–46; Matthew 5:20–26*
June 13: *1 Kings 19:9a, 11–16; Mathew 5:27–32*
June 14: *1 Kings 19:19–21; Matthew 5:33–37*

June 16: *1 Kings 21:1–16; Matthew 5:38–42*
June 17: *1 Kings 21:17–29; Matthew 5:43–48*
June 18: *2 Kings 2:1, 6–14; Matthew 6:1–6, 16–18*
June 19: *Sirach 48:1–14; Matthew 6:7–15*
June 20: *2 Kings 11:1–4, 9–18, 20; Matthew 6:19–23*
June 21: *2 Chronicles 24:17–25; Matthew 6:24–34*

June 23: *2 Kings 17:5–8, 13–15a, 18; Matthew 7:1–5*
June 24: Solemnity of the Nativity of John the Baptist
   Isaiah 49:1–6; Acts 13:22–26; Luke 1:57–66, 80
June 25: *2 Kings 22:8–13; 23:1–3; Matthew 7:15–20*
June 26: *2 Kings 24:8–17; Matthew 7:21–29*
June 27: *2 Kings 25:1–12; Matthew 8:1–4*
June 28: *Lamentations 2:2, 10–14, 18–19; Matthew 8:5–17*

June 30: *Amos 2:6–10, 13–16; Matthew 8:18–22*
July 1: *Amos 3:1–8; 4:11–12; Matthew 8:23–27*
July 2: *Amos 5:14–15, 21–24; Matthew 8:28–34*
July 3: Feast of Saint Thomas
   Ephesians 2:19–22; John 20:24–29

July 4: *Amos 8:4–6, 9–12; Matthew 9:9–13*
July 5: *Amos 9:11–15; Matthew 9:14–17*

July 7: *Hosea 2:16, 17b–18, 21–22; Matthew 9:18–26*
July 8: *Hosea 8:4–7, 11–13; Matthew 9:32–38*
July 9: *Hosea 10:1–3, 7–8, 12; Matthew 10:1–7*
July 10: *Hosea 11:1–4, 8c–9; Matthew 10:7–15*
July 11: *Hosea 14:2–10; Matthew 10:16–23*
July 12: *Isaiah 6:1–8; Matthew 10:24–33*

July 14: *Isaiah 1:10–17; Matthew 10:34—11:1*
July 15: *Isaiah 7:1–9; Matthew 11:20–24*
July 16: *Isaiah 10:5–7, 13b–16; Matthew 11:25–27*
July 17: *Isaiah 26:7–9, 12, 16–19; Matthew 11:28–30*
July 18: *Isaiah 38:1–6, 21–22, 7–8; Matthew 12:1–8*
July 19: *Micah 2:1–5; Matthew 12:14–21*

July 21: *Micah 6:1–4, 6–8; Matthew 12:38–42*
July 22: *Micah 7:14–15, 18–20; John 20:1–2, 11–18*
July 23: *Jeremiah 1:1, 4–10; Matthew 13:1–9*
July 24: *Jeremiah 2:1–3, 7–8, 12–13; Matthew 13:10–17*
July 25: Feast of Saint James
   2 Corinthians 4:7–15; Matthew 20:20–28
July 26: *Jeremiah 7:1–11; Matthew 13:24–30*

July 28: *Jeremiah 13:1–11; Matthew 13:31–35*
July 29: *Jeremiah 14:17–22; John 11:19–27*
July 30: *Jeremiah 15:10, 16–21; Matthew 13:44–46*
July 31: *Jeremiah 18:1–6; Matthew 13:47–53*
August 1: *Jeremiah 26:1–9; Matthew 13:54–58*
August 2: *Jeremiah 26:11–16, 24; Matthew 14:1–12*

August 4: *Jeremiah 28:1–17; Matthew 14:22–36*
August 5: *Jeremiah 30:1–2, 12–15, 18–22; Matthew 14:22–36*
August 6: Feast of the Transfiguration of the Lord
   Daniel 7:9–10, 13–14; 2 Peter 1:16–19; Matthew 17:1–9
August 7: *Jeremiah 31:31–34; Matthew 16:13–23*
August 8: *Nahum 2:1, 3; 3:1–3, 6–7; Matthew 16:24–28*
August 9: *Hebrews 1:12—2:4; Matthew 17:14–20*

August 11: *Ezekiel 1:2–5, 24–28c; Matthew 17:22–27*
August 12: *Ezekiel 2:8—3:4; Matthew 18:1–5, 10, 12–14*
August 13: *Ezekiel 9:1–7; 10:18–22; Matthew 18:15–20*
August 14: *Ezekiel 12:1–2; Matthew 18:21—19:1*
August 15 Solemnity of the Assumption of the Blessed Virgin Mary
   Revelation 11:19a; 12:1–6a, 10ab;
   1 Corinthians 15:20–27; Luke 1:39–56
August 16: *Ezekiel 18:1–10, 13b, 30–32; Matthew 19:13–15*

August 18: *Ezekiel 24:15–24; Matthew 19:16–22*
August 19: *Ezekiel 28:1–10; Matthew 19:23–30*
August 20: *Ezekiel 34:1–11; Matthew 20:1–16*
August 21: *Ezekiel 36:23–28; Matthew 22:1–14*
August 22: *Ezekiel 37:1–14; Matthew 22:34–40*
August 23: *Ezekiel 43:1–7ab; Matthew 23:1–12*

May 18, 2008

READING I   Exodus 34:4b—6, 8—9

Early in the morning Moses went up Mount Sinai as the Lord had commanded him, taking along the two stone tablets.

Having come down in a cloud, the Lord stood with Moses there and proclaimed his name, "Lord." Thus the Lord passed before him and cried out, "The Lord, the Lord, a merciful and gracious God, slow to anger and rich in kindness and fidelity." Moses at once bowed down to the ground in worship. Then he said, "If I find favor with you, O Lord, do come along in our company. This is indeed a stiff-necked people; yet pardon our wickedness and sins, and receive us as your own."

READING II   2 Corinthians 13:11—13

Brothers and sisters, rejoice. Mend your ways, encourage one another, agree with one another, live in peace, and the God of love and peace will be with you. Greet one another with a holy kiss. All the holy ones greet you.

The grace of the Lord Jesus Christ and the love of God and the fellowship of the Holy Spirit be with all of you.

GOSPEL   John 3:16—18

God so loved the world that he gave his only Son, so that everyone who believes in him might not perish but might have eternal life. For God did not send his Son into the world to condemn the world, but that the world might be saved through him. Whoever believes in him will not be condemned, but whoever does not believe has already been condemned, because he has not believed in the name of the only Son of God.

Practice of Prayer

R. Glory and praise for ever!

Blessed are you, O Lord, the God of our fathers,
    praiseworthy and exalted above all forever;
And blessed is your holy and glorious name,
    praiseworthy and exalted
        above all for all ages. R.

Blessed are you in the temple of your holy glory,
    praiseworthy and glorious
        above all forever. R.

Blessed are you on the throne of your kingdom,
    praiseworthy and exalted
        above all forever. R.

Blessed are you who look into the depths
    from your throne upon the cherubim,
    praiseworthy and exalted
        above all forever. R.

Practice of Charity

Grace. Love. Fellowship. These are qualities attributed to the three divine persons of the Holy Trinity in today's reading from 2 Corinthians. Surely the Holy Trinity was present in the Amish response to a school shooting that took place in Lancaster County, Pennsylvania, in October 2006. A gunman broke into the West Nickel Mines Amish School, killed five girls, and wounded five more before turning the gun on himself. After burying their own daughters, members of the Amish community reached out to the gunman's family, attending his funeral and offering words of forgiveness and support. Though most people could not have responded so generously, all people of faith would recognize the grace at work in the love and fellowship they offered. May the grace of the Lord Jesus Christ and the love of God and the fellowship of the Holy Spirit be with all of you.

Scripture Insights

The formal doctrine of the Trinity, which we celebrate today but profess every Sunday in our Creed, developed later than did our biblical texts. However, we certainly find the roots for our belief in scripture. Today's reading from 2 Corinthians is a prime example. Paul offers the Corinthians a blessing, one which is familiar to us because we still use it in our own liturgies.

In today's first reading God reveals himself to Moses as "merciful and gracious, . . . slow to anger and rich in kindness and fidelity." Moses invites this gracious God to "come along in our company." The people are stiff-necked and sinful. They need to better know this God of love.

When Moses invited God to "come along in our company" he never envisioned the extent to which God would go to do just that. As John tells us in today's reading, "God so loved the world that he gave his only Son, so that everyone who believes in him might not perish but might have eternal life." As we know from last week's readings on Pentecost, Jesus, in turn, sent the Spirit to dwell with us. Through the Spirit, God continues to "come along in our company."

We have come to know our one God through the manifestation of three persons: Father, Son, and Holy Spirit. Our triune God continues to "come along in our company."

◆ What does Paul tell the Corinthians to do so that the "God of love and peace will be with you"?

◆ In the first reading, we learn much about God's nature, both from what God tells Moses about himself and from the drama of the scene—especially Moses' reaction. Looking carefully at the details, what would be your impressions if you were standing with Moses?

◆ Do you more often pray to one person of the Trinity than another? If so, do you know why?

◆ Are you always comfortable with the idea that God is always coming along in your company? Why or why not?

May 25, 2008

READING I   Deuteronomy 8:2—3, 14b—16a

Moses said to the people:

"Remember how for forty years now the LORD, your God, has directed all your journeying in the desert, so as to test you by affliction and find out whether or not it was your intention to keep his commandments. He therefore let you be afflicted with hunger, and then fed you with manna, a food unknown to you and your fathers, in order to show you that not by bread alone does one live, but by every word that comes forth from the mouth of the LORD.

"Do not forget the LORD, your God, who brought you out of the land of Egypt, that place of slavery; who guided you through the vast and terrible desert with its saraph serpents and scorpions, its parched and waterless ground; who brought forth water for you from the flinty rock and fed you in the desert with manna, a food unknown to your fathers."

READING II   1 Corinthians 10:16—17

Brothers and sisters:

The cup of blessing that we bless, is it not a participation in the blood of Christ? The bread that we break, is it not a participation in the body of Christ? Because the loaf of bread is one, we, though many, are one body, for we all partake of the one loaf.

GOSPEL   John 6:51—58

Jesus said to the Jewish crowds:

"I am the living bread that came down from heaven; whoever eats this bread will live forever; and the bread that I will give is my flesh for the life of the world."

The Jews quarreled among themselves, saying, "How can this man give us his flesh to eat?" Jesus said to them, "Amen, amen, I say to you, unless you eat the flesh of the Son of Man and drink his blood, you do not have life within you. Whoever eats my flesh and drinks my blood has eternal life, and I will raise him on the last day. For my flesh is true food, and my blood is true drink. Whoever eats my flesh and drinks my blood remains in me and I in him. Just as the living Father sent me and I have life because of the Father, so also the one who feeds on me will have life because of me. This is the bread that came down from heaven. Unlike your ancestors who ate and still died, whoever eats this bread will live forever."

Practice of Prayer

Psalm 147:12–13, 14–15, 19–20 (12)

R. Praise the Lord, Jerusalem.
or: Alleluia.

Glorify the LORD, O Jerusalem;
    praise your God, O Zion.
For he has strengthened the bars of your gates;
    he has blessed your children within you. R.

He has granted peace in your borders;
    with the best of wheat he fills you.
He sends forth his command to the earth;
    swiftly runs his word! R.

He has proclaimed his word to Jacob,
    his statutes and his ordinances to Israel.
He has not done thus for any other nation;
    his ordinances he has not made
        known to them. Alleluia. R.

Practice of Faith

Visitors to St. Christopher's parish in Indianapolis, Indiana, encounter a surprising invitation. It is extended by an interactive sculpture of Christ, who is sitting at a table, breaking bread. In addition to the bronze figure of Jesus, there are places at the table for 12 more. While it was designed to offer opportunities for prayer, the sculpture also gives physical form to Jesus' call to break bread with him. It also reminds us—as do today's readings—that our liturgical celebration is not a passive event. Through the cup that is blessed and the Eucharistic bread we share, we participate in the body of Christ and continue to do so long after Mass is over. Every day we are surrounded by members of the body who hunger for love, for freedom from sin and death, for the Bread of Life. In what ways are we working to bring them to the table? Jesus is waiting.

Scripture Insights

John writes near the end of the first century, teaching his readers truths that Christians understood only after the Resurrection, but he presents them in stories set before the Resurrection. Today John is teaching about Jesus' divinity and about the practice of Eucharist.

When Jesus says, "I am the living bread that came down from heaven," his contemporaries interpret "bread from heaven" to mean the manna that God provided for the Israelites in the desert. But John's audience, catechized in his community, understands that the living bread from heaven is Jesus, the Word that existed before creation, who came from heaven, became flesh, and dwelt among us, as the opening words of John's account of the Gospel proclaim.

John describes Jesus insisting that his followers must eat his flesh and drink his blood. In the story, Jesus' listeners take him literally and are perplexed. But John's readers recognize that he is explaining the significance of their practice of Eucharist. Jesus gives himself to us in Eucharist.

Because Eucharist is truly the body and blood of Christ, those who receive it are united with the risen Christ. Disciples need not wait for the end of human history for Christ's power and presence to be felt in our lives. Christ is present and active in us now, through Eucharist.

In the second reading, Paul teaches that we not only *receive* the body of Christ, we *become* one body in Christ. "We, though many, are one body, for we all partake of the one loaf." Eucharist not only unites us with the risen Christ, but also with each other. Eucharist is true food and drink for our journey into eternal life.

◆ What specific words in the readings express the bond with Christ that Eucharist creates?

◆ In what way do these words capture your experience of Eucharist?

◆ How might you deepen your experience of Eucharist?

READING I   Deuteronomy 11:18, 26—28, 32

Moses told the people,
"Take these words of mine into
    your heart and soul.
Bind them at your wrist as a sign,
    and let them be a pendant on your forehead.

"I set before you here, this day,
    a blessing and a curse:
a blessing for obeying the commandments
    of the LORD, your God,
which I enjoin on you today;
a curse if you do not obey the commandments
    of the LORD, your God,
but turn aside from the way
    I ordain for you today,
to follow other gods, whom you
    have not known.
Be carful to observe all the
    statutes and decrees
that I set before you today."

READING II   Romans 3:21—25, 28

Brothers and sisters,
Now the righteousness of God has been
    manifested apart from the law,
    though testified to by the law
    and the prophets,
    the righteousness of God
        through faith in Jesus Christ
    for all who believe.
For there is no distinction;
    all have sinned and are deprived
        of the glory of God.
They are justified freely by his grace
    through the redemption in Christ Jesus,
    whom God set forth as an expiation,
    through faith, by his blood.
For we consider that a person is justified by faith
    apart from works of the law.

GOSPEL   Matthew 7:21—27

Jesus said to his disciples:
"Not everyone who says to me, 'Lord, Lord,'
    will enter the kingdom of heaven,
    but only the one who does the
        will of my Father in heaven.
Many will say to me on that day,
    'Lord, Lord, did we not
        prophesy in your name?
Did we not drive out demons in your name?
Did we not do mighty deeds in your name?'
Then I will declare to them solemnly,
    'I never knew you. Depart from me,
        you evildoers.'

"Everyone who listens to these words
        of mine and acts on them
    will be like a wise man who
        built his house on rock.
The rain fell, the floods came,
    and the winds blew and buffeted the house.
But it did not collapse; it had been
        set solidly on rock.
And everyone who listens to these words of mine
        but does not act on them
    will be like a fool who built his house on sand.
The rain fell, the floods came,
    and the winds blew and buffeted the house.
And it collapsed and was completely ruined."

Practice of Prayer

Psalm 31:2—3, 3—4, 17, 25 (3b)

R. Lord, be my rock of safety.

In you, O Lord, I take refuge;
    let me never be put to shame.
In your justice rescue me,
    incline your ear to me,
      make haste to deliver me!

Be my rock of refuge,
    a stronghold to give me safety.
You are my rock and my fortress;
    for your name's sake you will
      lead and guide me.

Let your face shine upon your servant;
    save me in your kindness.
Take courage and be stouthearted,
    all you who hope in the Lord.

Practice of Faith

Thomas Merton is considered to be a great spiritual leader of modern times and yet one of his most popular reflections talks about being out of control and unsure of just about everything. Perhaps that is why it is so popular. In "Thoughts in Solitude," the Trappist monk and author admits: "My Lord God, I have no idea where I am going . . . and the fact that I think I am following your will does not mean I am actually doing so. But I believe the desire to please you does in fact please you. And I hope that I have that desire in all that I am doing." Merton knew that having the right answers and doing the right things aren't enough. It is faithfulness that means everything to our God, who has never failed to keep faith with us. With that faithfulness and trust, anything is possible—even eternal life. To learn more about Thomas Merton, visit www.merton.org.

Scripture Insights

Hearing and doing are two inseparable elements for the one who would belong to God. Not merely doing good works—no matter how good. Not merely listening, untouched, in one ear and out the other. But rather, taking God's words into one's heart and soul (Deuteronomy 11:18), into the very depths and totality of one's being—and acting on them.

In the book of Deuteronomy, Moses instructs the people as they are about to enter the Promised Land: "Now, Israel, hear the statutes and decrees which I am teaching you to observe, that you may live and may enter in and take possession of the land which the Lord . . . is giving you (Deuteronomy 4:1; see also 11:27).

In today's Gospel reading, Jesus teaches the people what is required of those who would enter the Promised Land of God's kingdom. Note that today's passage is the conclusion of the Sermon on the Mount discourse (Matthew 5–7), where Jesus, portrayed as a "new Moses," has explained what fidelity to God's Law requires.

It is not enough to call on the Lord's name or to speak or act in the name of the Lord. Rather, one's whole being, heart and mind and soul, must be conformed to the will of the Father as made known in the teaching, the commands, the demands of Jesus.

In order to be formed according to that teaching, we must first of all come as one among the crowds to *listen* to that word. Then, like supple clay in the hands of a potter, we must allow ourselves to be shaped according to the teaching of God's Son. If we come and listen, and act accordingly to his word, we will build our house on that rock who is Christ, our God. He alone is our rock of safety.

♦ How would you explain the "blessing" for obedience to God's commandments?

♦ How do we allow the word to form us deeply?

♦ Which is the most challenging command for you to act on at this time? Why?

June 8, 2008

READING I *Hosea 6:3—6*

In their affliction, people will say:
"Let us know, let us strive to know the LORD;
    as certain as the dawn is his coming,
    and his judgment shines forth
        like the light of day!
He will come to us like the rain,
    like spring rain that waters the earth."

What can I do with you, Ephraim?
    What can I do with you, Judah?
Your piety is like a morning cloud,
    like the dew that early passes away.
For this reason I smote them
        through the prophets,
    I slew them by the words of my mouth;
for it is love that I desire, not sacrifice,
    and knowledge of God rather
        than holocausts.

READING II *Romans 4:18—25*

Brothers and sisters:

Abraham believed, hoping against hope, that he would become "the father of many nations," according to what was said, "Thus shall your descendants be." He did not weaken in faith when he considered his own body as already dead—for he was almost a hundred years old—and the dead womb of Sarah. He did not doubt God's promise in unbelief; rather, he was strengthened by faith and gave glory to God and was fully convinced that what he had promised he was also able to do. That is why *it was credited to him as righteousness.* But it was not for him alone that it was written that *it was credited to him;* it was also for us, to whom it will be credited, who believe in the one who raised Jesus our Lord from the dead, who was handed over for our transgressions and was raised for our justification.

GOSPEL *Matthew 9:9—13*

As Jesus passed on from there, he saw a man named Matthew sitting at the customs post. He said to him, "Follow me." And he got up and followed him. While he was at table in his house, many tax collectors and sinners came and sat with Jesus and his disciples. The Pharisees saw this and said to his disciples, "Why does your teacher eat with tax collectors and sinners?" He heard this and said, "Those who are well do not need a physician, but the sick do. Go and learn the meaning of the words, 'I desire mercy, not sacrifice.' I did not come to call the righteous but sinners."

Practice of Prayer

Psalm 50:1, 8, 12—13, 14—15 (23b)

R. To the upright I will show
    the saving power of God.

God the LORD has spoken and
    summoned the earth,
   from the rising of the sun to its setting.
"Not for your sacrifices do I rebuke you,
   for your holocausts are before me always." R.

"If I were hungry, I would not tell you,
   for mine are the world and its fullness.
Do I eat the flesh of strong bulls,
   or is the blood of goats my drink?" R.

"Offer to God praise as your sacrifice
   and fulfill your vows to the Most High;
then call upon me in time of distress;
   I will rescue you,
    and you shall glorify me." R.

Practice of Charity

The Downtown Chapel in Portland, Oregon, is a parish, a center for service to the needy in the inner city, and a center for spirituality, all supported by the Holy Cross order. Its distinctive charism is the integration of service and spirituality. All volunteers participate in scripture sharing and reflection before service and debriefing afterward. All recipients of service are welcome at parish liturgies and retreats. Some of the retreats offered include sessions for those suffering from depression, Lenten retreats for those preparing to receive sacraments at Easter, and—most distinctive—a day-long "personal poverty retreat" in which participants alternate between serving in the Chapel's many service ministries, learning about the needs of the people they serve, scripture reflection, and faith sharing. They are led to discover their own inner poverty in order to give themselves more authentically in service. To discover more about the many aspects of service and spirituality at the Downtown Chapel, visit http://www.downtownchapel.org.

Scripture Insights

"It is love that I desire, not sacrifice"—so the word of God challenges us today. These words of Hosea were originally addressed to a "pious" people, careful to observe the precepts of the Law when it came to sacrifices of cereals and grain, burnt offerings (holocausts), and ritual purity . . . but who missed the deeper meaning of covenant fidelity which is expressed only by non-judgmental mercy and unconditional love for others. It is this which Jesus manifests in his table-fellowship with tax collectors and sinners. To sit at table with someone, to share a meal, symbolized a bond of acceptance and a willingness to enter into relationship.

The Pharisees, who rigorously observed the letter of the Law, believed that associating with tax collectors (Jews who worked for the Romans and profited from it) and others judged to be "unfaithful" to the Law, would "defile" them. Accordingly, they avoided and disdained them—a far cry from mercy and love.

For Hosea, the "mercy" God desires is rendered by the Hebrew word *hesed*, often translated as "covenant love." This word occurs twice in today's passage: line 9 where it is translated as the people's fleeting "piety" and line 13 as the love that God desires. In the Greek translation of the Old Testament, used by Matthew at the end of today's Gospel reading, the word is translated *eleos* (mercy, compassion). In the Old Testament, mercy is characteristic of God (Exodus 34:6).

Jesus constantly shows this mercy to those who welcome him into their homes and their lives, as did Matthew, the tax collector. It is not the professionally religious who were able to receive Jesus, who judged themselves as being in right relationship with God by virtue of their adherence to the Law, but rather, those who knew their sin and their need for God's mercy. In acknowledging their total dependence on God, they were open to what God alone could give and do for them.

♦ What themes from today's readings are evident in Psalm 50?

♦ What is the relationship between faith and righteousness according to the second reading?

♦ How have you shown or received mercy recently?

READING I   *Exodus 19:2—6a*

In those days, the Israelites came to the desert of Sinai and pitched camp.

While Israel was encamped here in front of the mountain, Moses went up the mountain to God. Then the LORD called to him and said, "Thus shall you say to the house of Jacob; tell the Israelites: You have seen for yourselves how I treated the Egyptians and how I bore you up on eagle wings and brought you here to myself. Therefore, if you hearken to my voice and keep my covenant, you shall be my special possession, dearer to me than all other people, though all the earth is mine. You shall be to me a kingdom of priests, a holy nation."

READING II   *Romans 5:6—11*

Brothers and sisters:

Christ, while we were still helpless, yet died at the appointed time for the ungodly. Indeed, only with difficulty does one die for a just person, though perhaps for a good person one might even find courage to die. But God proves his love for us in that while we were still sinners Christ died for us. How much more then, since we are now justified by his blood, will we be saved through him from the wrath. Indeed, if, while we were enemies, we were reconciled to God through the death of his Son, how much more, once reconciled, will we be saved by his life. Not only that, but we also boast of God through our Lord Jesus Christ, through whom we have now received reconciliation.

GOSPEL   *Matthew 9:36—10:8*

At the sight of the crowds, Jesus' heart was moved with pity for them because they were troubled and abandoned, like sheep without a shepherd. Then he said to his disciples, "The harvest is abundant but the laborers are few; so ask the master of the harvest to send out laborers for his harvest."

Then he summoned his twelve disciples and gave them authority over unclean spirits to drive them out and to cure every disease and every illness. The names of the twelve apostles are these: first, Simon called Peter, and his brother Andrew; James, the son of Zebedee, and his brother John; Philip and Bartholomew, Thomas and Matthew the tax collector; James, the son of Alphaeus, and Thaddeus; Simon from Cana, and Judas Iscariot who betrayed him.

Jesus sent out these twelve after instructing them thus, "Do not go into pagan territory or enter a Samaritan town. Go rather to the lost sheep of the house of Israel. As you go, make this proclamation: 'The kingdom of heaven is at hand.' Cure the sick, raise the dead, cleanse lepers, drive out demons. Without cost you have received; without cost you are to give."

Practice of Prayer

Psalm 100:1—2, 3, 5 (3c)

R. We are his people, the sheep of his flock.

Sing joyfully to the Lord, all you lands;
  serve the Lord with gladness;
  come before him with joyful song.   R.

Know that the Lord is God;
  he made us, his we are;
  his people, the flock he tends.   R.

The Lord is good:
  his kindness endures forever,
  and his faithfulness to all generations.   R.

Practice of Faith

The disciples watched Jesus free people from sickness, demons, and even death, and in today's passage from Matthew he invites them to share his ministry. This reading is often used to encourage men and women to consider a life of service through the priesthood and consecrated life. The Church has long emphasized that everyone has a vocation to serve God and the people of God in some fashion. Many do not feel qualified to take up the mission of Jesus, but Saint Therese of Lisieux proved that great deeds and great learning are not necessary to do great good. Her "little way" consisted of doing whatever she could with love and the utmost trust in Jesus. She never left the Carmelite cloister in France that she entered in 1888, but due to her spiritual and written support for missionaries, she was named patroness of the missions after her canonization in 1925. In what "little way" can you transform the world? You can learn more about the Carmelite order at http://carmelites.org/.

Scripture Insights

Though the pasturing of flocks is not part of everyday experience for most of us, the image of a shepherd caring for his sheep brings deep comfort. Think of Psalm 23 ("The Lord is my shepherd") and John 10 ("I am the good shepherd"). The image of God (Jesus) as shepherd, carefully tending his flock, is prominent in today's readings.

The first reading is situated at the foot of Mount Sinai, just before the giving of the commandments. From their departure from Egypt throughout their desert wanderings, God had carefully "cared" for the people, lifting them up and carrying them, bringing them to a place where he would manifest himself and enter into covenant with them. Although shepherd imagery isn't obvious in this passage, the psalmist's understanding of the guidance and care of God, the "shepherd," bursts forth joyfully in today's responsorial Psalm 100.

In the course of Israel's history, when their kings and rulers were no longer faithful to the covenant, God's flock was misled and scattered. "Woe to the shepherds who mislead and scatter the flock of my pasture, says the Lord" (Jeremiah 23:1). "I myself will look after and tend my sheep" (Ezekiel 34:11).

That is precisely what Jesus is doing in today's Gospel when he sends out the 12 disciples to the "lost sheep of the house of Israel." They will care for the people and proclaim the "kingdom of heaven" (Matthew's expression for the kingdom of God).

Today's scriptures invite us to know ourselves as the sheep of God's pasture and to remember, with thanksgiving, the many manifestations of his providential care. With the Lord as our shepherd, nothing shall we want.

• What specific words in the first reading and the Gospel reading show God's care for us? How does the Gospel fulfill the promise of the first reading?

• In the second reading Paul points to the double action of Christ's care for us: while sinners we are reconciled through Christ's death, and once reconciled we are saved by his life. Have you felt that difference?

• How do you experience God's providential care, God's "shepherding" in your life?

READING I   *Jeremiah 20:10—13*

Jeremiah said:
"I hear the whisperings of many:
    'Terror on every side!
    Denounce! let us denounce him!'
All those who were my friends
    are on the watch for any misstep of mine.
'Perhaps he will be trapped; then we
       can prevail,
    and take our vengeance on him.'
But the LORD is with me,
    like a mighty champion:
my persecutors will stumble,
    they will not triumph.
In their failure they will be put to utter shame,
    to lasting, unforgettable confusion.
O LORD of hosts, you who test the just,
    who probe mind and heart,
let me witness the vengeance you take
      on them,
    for to you I have entrusted my cause.
Sing to the LORD,
    praise the LORD,
for he has rescued the life of the poor
    from the power of the wicked!"

READING II   *Romans 5:12—15*

Brothers and sisters:

Through one man sin entered the world, and through sin, death, and thus death came to all men, inasmuch as all sinned — for up to the time of the law, sin was in the world, though sin is not accounted when there is no law. But death reigned from Adam to Moses, even over those who did not sin after the pattern of the trespass of Adam, who is the type of the one who was to come.

But the gift is not like the transgression. For if by the transgression of the one the many died, how much more did the grace of God and the gracious gift of the one man Jesus Christ overflow for the many.

GOSPEL   *Matthew 10:26—33*

Jesus said to the Twelve:

"Fear no one. Nothing is concealed that will not be revealed, nor secret that will not be known. What I say to you in the darkness, speak in the light; what you hear whispered, proclaim on the housetops. And do not be afraid of those who kill the body but cannot kill the soul; rather, be afraid of the one who can destroy both soul and body in Gehenna. Are not two sparrows sold for a small coin? Yet not one of them falls to the ground without your Father's knowledge. Even all the hairs of your head are counted. So do not be afraid; you are worth more than many sparrows. Everyone who acknowledges me before others I will acknowledge before my heavenly Father. But whoever denies me before others, I will deny before my heavenly Father."

Practice of Prayer

Psalm 69:8–10, 14, 17, 33–35 (14c)

R. Lord, in your great love, answer me.

For your sake I bear insult,
    and shame covers my face.
I have become an outcast to my brothers,
    a stranger to my mother's children,
because zeal for your house consumes me,
        and the insults of those who blaspheme you
            fall upon me. R.

I pray to you, O LORD,
    for the time of your favor, O God!
In your great kindness answer me
    with your constant help.
Answer me, O LORD, for bounteous
        is your kindness;
    in your great mercy turn toward me. R.

"See, you lowly ones, and be glad;
    you who seek God, may your hearts revive!
For the LORD hears the poor,
    and his own who are in bonds he spurns not.
Let the heavens and the earth praise him,
    the seas and whatever moves in them!" R.

Practice of Faith

When was the last time you heard someone proclaim the Good News from the housetops? That may be because people are unsure of what to proclaim. The pastoral staff at the Church of St. Paul in Ham Lake, Minnesota, noticed this and the effect it was having on the children in their religious education program. Determined to help parents reclaim their role as the primary educators of their children, they developed Family Formation. This program moves learning from the parish center to the center of family life by bringing parents to church once a month for some catechesis of their own with the pastor. Equipped with Catholic teaching and lesson plans based on scripture, the *Catechism of the Catholic Church,* and the three-year liturgical cycle, parents share what they have learned with their children over the next three weeks. As families deepen their faith, the parish benefits. To learn about Family Formation, visit www. churchofsaintpaul.com and click on "Formation."

Scripture Insights

The scriptures show that when God's chosen prophets and apostles faithfully carry out their mission, they always encounter suffering. This is especially evident in the life of the prophet Jeremiah, who recounts his painful struggles in five sections of his book known as his Confessions. Today's first reading is from one of them. But something remarkable happens in this passage: though Jeremiah begins by describing a dire situation, he shifts to an expression of confidence that God is with him and will see him through the crisis. What a powerful example for us in our own struggles—to bring them to the Lord with all the details of the misery, the pain, and the confusion we experience—and then to affirm our trust that God is with us and will deliver us!

In the book of Psalms, we find many prayers that do precisely this. Known as the Psalms of Lament or Supplication, they make up nearly one third of the 150 psalms. Today's responsorial psalm follows their pattern: description of personal distress, prayer for deliverance, confidence and thanksgiving for God's help.

Today's Gospel reading comes in the middle of a long instruction Jesus gives to his 12 disciples prior to sending them out on mission. He minces no words about the opposition they will endure. At the same time, he calls them to unshakeable courage: "Do not be afraid . . . you are worth more than many sparrows." What a firm basis for hope he offers us when he promises: "Everyone who acknowledges me before others I will acknowledge before my heavenly Father." May his words of promise be the basis of our courage and hope, whatever we may face in faithfully responding to the mission that is ours.

♦ In the first reading and psalm, which words depict the plight of the sufferer? Which words express the trust and confidence in God?

♦ Drawing on a personal or communal experience of suffering, compose your own psalm of lament.

♦ In what ways can we "acknowledge" Jesus before others?

READING I   Acts 12:1–11

In those days, King Herod laid
      hands upon some members
      of the Church to harm them.
He had James, the brother of John,
      killed by the sword,
    and when he saw that this was
      pleasing to the Jews
he proceeded to arrest Peter also.
—It was the feast of Unleavened Bread.—
He had him taken into custody and put in prison
    under the guard of four squads
      of four soldiers each.
He intended to bring him before
      the people after Passover.
Peter thus was being kept in prison,
    but prayer by the Church was
      fervently being made
    to God on his behalf.

On the very night before Herod
      was to bring him to trial,
Peter, secured by double chains,
was sleeping between two soldiers,
while outside the door guards
      kept watch on the prison.
Suddenly the angel of the Lord stood by him
    and a light shone in the cell.
He tapped Peter on the side and
      awakened him, saying,
    "Get up quickly."
The chains fell from his wrists.
The angel said to him, "Put on your
      belt and your sandals."
He did so.
Then he said to him, "Put on your
      cloak and follow me."
So he followed him out,
    not realizing that what was happening
      through the angel was real;
    he thought he was seeing a vision.
They passed the first guard, then the second,
    and came to the iron gate
      leading out to the city,
    which opened for them by itself.
They emerged and made their way down an alley,
    and suddenly the angel left him.
Then Peter recovered his senses and said,
    "Now I know for certain
    that the Lord sent his angel
    and rescued me from the hand of
    Herod and from all that the Jewish
    people had been expecting."

READING II   2 Timothy 4:6–8, 17–18

I, Paul, am already being poured out like a libation,
    and the time of my departure is at hand.
I have competed well; I have finished the race;
    I have kept the faith.
From now on the crown of
      righteousness awaits me,
    which the Lord, the just judge,
    will award to me on that day,
      and not only to me,
    but to all who have longed for his appearance.

The Lord stood by me and gave me strength,
    so that through me the proclamation
      might be completed
    and all the Gentiles might hear it.
And I was rescued from the lion's mouth.
The Lord will rescue me from every evil threat
    and will bring me safe to his
      heavenly Kingdom.
To him be glory forever and ever. Amen.

GOSPEL   Matthew 16:13–19

When Jesus went into the region of
      Caesarea Philippi
    he asked his disciples,
    "Who do people say that the Son of Man is?"
They replied, "Some say John the Baptist,
      others Elijah,
    still others Jeremiah or one of the prophets."
He said to them, "But who do you say that I am?"
Simon Peter said in reply,
    "You are the Christ, the Son of the living God."
Jesus said to him in reply, "Blessed are you,
      Simon son of Jonah.
For flesh and blood has not revealed this to you,
    but my heavenly Father.

And so I say to you, you are Peter,
  and upon this rock I will build my Church,
  and the gates of the netherworld
    shall not prevail against it.
I will give you the keys to the Kingdom of heaven.
Whatever you bind on earth shall
    be bound in heaven;
  and whatever you loose on earth
    shall be loosed in heaven."

Practice of Prayer

Psalm 34:2—3, 4—5, 6—7, 8—9 (5b)
R. The angel of the Lord will
  rescue those who fear him.

I will bless the LORD at all times;
  his praise shall be ever in my mouth.
Let my soul glory in the LORD;
  the lowly will hear me and be glad.

Glorify the LORD with me,
  let us together extol his name.
I sought the LORD, and he answered me
  and delivered me from all my fears.

Look to him that you may be radiant with joy,
  and your faces may not blush with shame.
When the poor one called out, the LORD heard,
  and from all his distress he saved him.

The angel of the LORD encamps
  around those who fear him, and delivers them.
Taste and see how good the LORD is;
  blessed the man who takes refuge in him.

Practice of Faith

A major problem facing people today is their difficulty forgiving one another. It is significant that Jesus made the power to forgive part of Peter's commission as the leader of the faith community that Jesus had established. Jesus knew that true communion is only possible where charity and forgiveness abound.

Scripture Insights

Today's Gospel reading emphasizes the role of the Church, and of Peter, the rock of her foundation, as "gate-keepers" of the kingdom of heaven, entrusted with its keys. "The gates of the netherworld shall not prevail against it." The "netherworld": in Greek, *Hades;* in Hebrew, *Sheol* is the realm of the dead. Death shall not have power over the kingdom of heaven and those who belong to it.

Iron gates imprison Peter in his heavily guarded cell as the Church prays fervently for him. Luke recounts Peter's miraculous deliverance by the angel of the Lord. The chains fall from his wrists and the prison gates swing open.

Later in life, when both he and Paul were put to death under the Roman emperor Nero, it could seem that the gates of death *had* prevailed. But note Paul's words in the second reading as the time of his "departure" approaches: "The Lord will rescue me from every evil threat and will bring me safe"—through yet another set of gates—"to his heavenly kingdom." This is the ultimate deliverance and true cause for praise and thanksgiving!

How strong Paul's faith! How eager his expectation as his death draws near—knowing that the gates of the netherworld will not prevail and anticipating what awaits him beyond heaven's gates. At times, he desires it fervently. "I long to depart this life and be with Christ, for that is far better" (Philippeans 1:23); ". . . our citizenship is in heaven" (Philemon 3:20—21). What glory awaits us, too, beyond those gates!

◆ What themes and images from today's first two readings are found in Psalm 34?

◆ What is the significance of the various answers to Jesus' question in today's Gospel reading?

◆ How do we "bind" and "loose" one another in daily life?

July 6, 2008

READING I   Zechariah 9:9—10

Thus says the LORD:
Rejoice heartily, O daughter Zion,
    shout for joy, O daughter Jerusalem!
See, your king shall come to you;
    a just savior is he,
meek, and riding on an ass,
    on a colt, the foal of an ass.
He shall banish the chariot from Ephraim,
    and the horse from Jerusalem;
the warrior's bow shall be banished,
    and he shall proclaim peace to the nations.
His dominion shall be from sea to sea,
    and from the River to the ends
        of the earth.

READING II   Romans 8:9, 11—13

Brothers and sisters:

You are not in the flesh; on the contrary, you are in the spirit, if only the Spirit of God dwells in you. Whoever does not have the Spirit of Christ does not belong to him. If the Spirit of the one who raised Jesus from the dead dwells in you, the one who raised Christ from the dead will give life to your mortal bodies also, through his Spirit that dwells in you. Consequently, brothers and sisters, we are not debtors to the flesh, to live according to the flesh. For if you live according to the flesh, you will die, but if by the Spirit you put to death the deeds of the body, you will live.

GOSPEL   Matthew 11:25—30

At that time Jesus exclaimed:

"I give praise to you, Father, Lord of heaven and earth, for although you have hidden these things from the wise and the learned you have revealed them to little ones. Yes, Father, such has been your gracious will. All things have been handed over to me by my Father. No one knows the Son except the Father, and no one knows the Father except the Son and anyone to whom the Son wishes to reveal him.

"Come to me, all you who labor and are burdened, and I will give you rest. Take my yoke upon you and learn from me, for I am meek and humble of heart; and you will find rest for yourselves. For my yoke is easy, and my burden light."

Practice of Prayer

R. I will praise your name for ever,
    my king and my God.
or: Alleluia.

I will extol you, O my God and King,
    and I will bless your name forever and ever.
Every day will I bless you,
    and I will praise your name
        forever and ever.   R.

The LORD is gracious and merciful,
    slow to anger and of great kindness.
The LORD is good to all
    and compassionate toward all his works.   R.

Let all your works give you thanks, O LORD,
    and let your faithful ones bless you.
Let them discourse of the glory of your kingdom
    and speak of your might.   R.

The LORD is faithful in all his words
    and holy in all his works.
The LORD lifts up all who are falling
    and raises up all who are bowed down.   R.

Practice of Faith

This is the time of year when people are either taking vacations or dreaming of them. That includes popes. Despite his many hours of meetings and ministry, Pope John Paul II always made time to go skiing or hiking. Pope Benedict XVI has followed that wise tradition by vacationing in the Italian village of Les Combes each July and visiting Castelgandolfo, long known as the summer residence of the popes. Capuchin Father Raniero Cantalamessa, a preacher of the papal household, once told Vatican Radio that relaxing and having fun are necessary parts of a vacation, but said people should not forget that vacations can also be a time of discovery. "Perhaps the most beautiful meaning of vacation is that of getting back into an intimate, profound contact with the root of our being, with God," he said. Americans are said to forego vacations more than any other nation in the world. Perhaps we're losing more than sleep.

Scripture Insights

"Come to me, all you who labor and are burdened, and I will give you rest." Such inviting words from our Lord, yet how perplexing to hear: "Take my yoke upon you . . ."—another burden? Granted, a yoke is a weight placed upon one's shoulders, but it is also a means of balance.

Jewish tradition spoke of the Law and of wisdom as a yoke (Sirach 6:23–30; 51:26). In Matthew 23:2–4, Jesus decries the teaching of the scribes and Pharisees as a "heavy" burden. What a contrast is Jesus' yoke!

Throughout his account of the Gospel, Matthew depicts Jesus as the new and authoritative lawgiver, who does not abolish the Law, but fulfills it (Matthew 5:17). His teaching provides the means and shows the way to peace and rest. "Learn from me," he invites all would-be disciples.

What must be learned is not only his words of instruction, but the very manner of life he embraced: "I am meek and humble of heart." Meekness and humility are very close in meaning. Meekness connotes a quality of gentleness; humility, a lowliness and mildness of manner that comes across in a most ordinary or common way, as opposed to an arrogant self-exaltation or boastfulness (see Matthew 23:12).

However, what is perhaps most important in Jesus' words is the qualifying phrase "of heart," the very center of one's being, embracing mind and will as well as emotion. His is a meekness and humility that relies not on his own resources, but on those of his heavenly Father. In this, he finds his peace. Learning from Jesus' meekness and humility of heart will likewise result in our deep peace and "rest" (the Greek word *anápausis* conveys the sense of relief and refreshment as well).

Let us take Jesus' words to heart. His yoke will lighten our burden and lead us to peace.

• Matthew cites the beginning of this Zechariah passage at Jesus' entry into Jerusalem (21:1–5). How is Jesus' meekness demonstrated here?

• When have you experienced the heart-felt meekness and humility Jesus describes—in yourself or another?

• How do you experience Jesus' yoke?

READING I   Isaiah 55:10–11

Thus says the LORD:
Just as from the heavens
    the rain and snow come down
and do not return there
        till they have watered the earth,
        making it fertile and fruitful,
giving seed to the one who sows
        and bread to the one who eats,
so shall my word be
        that goes forth from my mouth;
my word shall not return to me void,
        but shall do my will,
        achieving the end for which I sent it.

READING II   Romans 8:18–23

Brothers and sisters:

I consider that the sufferings of this present time are as nothing compared with the glory to be revealed for us. For creation awaits with eager expectation the revelation of the children of God; for creation was made subject to futility, not of its own accord but because of the one who subjected it, in hope that creation itself would be set free from slavery to corruption and share in the glorious freedom of the children of God. We know that all creation is groaning in labor pains even until now; and not only that, but we ourselves, who have the firstfruits of the Spirit, we also groan within ourselves as we wait for adoption, the redemption of our bodies.

GOSPEL   Matthew 13:1–23

Shorter: Matthew 13:1–9

On that day, Jesus went out of the house and sat down by the sea. Such large crowds gathered around him that he got into a boat and sat down, and the whole crowd stood along the shore. And he spoke to them at length in parables, saying: "A sower went out to sow. And as he sowed, some seed fell on the path, and birds came and ate it up. Some fell on rocky ground, where it had little soil. It sprang up at once because the soil was not deep, and when the sun rose it was scorched, and it withered for lack of roots. Some seed fell among thorns, and the thorns grew up and choked it. But some seed fell on rich soil, and produced fruit, a hundred or sixty or thirtyfold. Whoever has ears ought to hear."

The disciples approached him and said, "Why do you speak to them in parables?" He said to them in reply, "Because knowledge of the mysteries of the kingdom of heaven has been granted to you, but to them it has not been granted. To anyone who has, more will be given and he will grow rich; from anyone who has not, even what he has will be taken away. This is why I speak to them in parables, because

they look but do not see and hear
        but do not listen or understand.

Isaiah's prophecy is fulfilled in them, which says:

You shall indeed hear but not understand,
        you shall indeed look but never see.
Gross is the heart of this people,
        they will hardly hear with their ears,
        they have closed their eyes,
        lest they see with their eyes
        and hear with their ears
and understand with their hearts and
                be converted,
        and I heal them.

"But blessed are your eyes, because they see, and your ears, because they hear. Amen, I say to you, many prophets and righteous people longed to see what you see but did not see it, and to hear what you hear but did not hear it.

"Hear then the parable of the sower. The seed sown on the path is the one who hears the word of the kingdom without understanding it, and the evil one comes and steals away what was sown in his heart. The seed sown on rocky ground is the one who hears the word and receives it at once with joy. But he has no root and lasts only for a time. When some tribulation or persecution comes because of the word, he immediately falls away. The seed sown among thorns is the one who hears the word, but then worldly anxiety and the lure of riches choke the word and it bears no fruit. But the seed sown on rich soil is the one who hears the word and understands it, who indeed bears fruit and yields a hundred or sixty or thirtyfold."

Practice of Prayer

Psalm 65:10, 11, 12—13, 14 (Luke 8:8)

R. The seed that falls on good ground
      will yield a fruitful harvest.

You have visited the land and watered it;
    greatly have you enriched it.
God's watercourses are filled;
    you have prepared the grain. R.

Thus have you prepared the land:
      drenching its furrows,
    breaking up its clods,
Softening it with showers,
    blessing its yield. R.

You have crowned the year with your bounty,
    and your paths overflow with a rich harvest;
the untilled meadows overflow with it,
    and rejoicing clothes the hills. R.

The fields are garmented with flocks
    and the valleys blanketed with grain.
    They shout and sing for joy. R.

Practice of Charity

Saint Francis of Assisi advised his community to "preach the Gospel at all times and when necessary use words." The Dominican Sisters of Springfield, Illinois, part of the worldwide Order of Preachers, celebrate this truth regularly. Their Web site shows members "Caught in the Act of Preaching": donating clothes to the poor, preparing the parish bulletin, etc. These "preachers" are making sure that the word of God does not return to him void. Visit www.springfieldop.org.

Scripture Insights

At the beginning of the letter to the Romans, Paul captures the essence of a theology of creation that pervades today's Lectionary texts: "Ever since the creation of the world, [God's] invisible attributes of eternal power and divinity have been able to be understood and perceived in what he has made" (Romans 1:20). Not only does creation manifest the glory of God and God's providential care for all, the rhythms of nature speak to us of how God so orders creation that all is brought to fulfillment according to his plan. This is particularly evident in today's first reading from Isaiah and Psalm 65. Isaiah likens God's word to the life-giving waters of rain and snow, which bring forth a fruitful harvest.

Nature is also used to teach about the human response to God's word in today's Gospel. The shorter form consists of only the parable, a comparison from nature whose meaning must be uncovered by the hearers. This shorter form most probably reflects the parable as told by Jesus. The evangelist and the early Church have added the interpretation after it. Those verses help explain why not all who heard Jesus believed in his word.

Yet another aspect of a theology of creation is heard in today's second reading. Paul leaves no doubt: all creation will be transformed at the end of time.

Today's scriptures make it clear that all of nature speaks of God and his marvelous care for creation. If we are attuned to its wisdom, nature has much to teach us about ourselves.

• Looking carefully at the second reading, how do you see this transformation taking place?

• What types of "fruits" show that God's word has really been heard?

• How does nature speak to you of God?

READING I   *Wisdom 12:13, 16—19*

There is no god besides you
>who have the care of all,
that you need show you have
>not unjustly condemned.
For your might is the source of justice;
>your mastery over all things
>makes you lenient to all.
For you show your might when the perfection
>of your power is disbelieved;
and in those who know you,
>you rebuke temerity.
But though you are master of might,
>you judge with clemency,
and with much lenience you govern us;
>for power, whenever you will, attends you.
And you taught your people, by these deeds,
>that those who are just must be kind;
and you gave your children good ground
>for hope
>that you would permit
>repentance for their sins.

READING II   *Romans 8:26—27*

Brothers and sisters:

The Spirit comes to the aid of our weakness; for we do not know how to pray as we ought, but the Spirit himself intercedes with inexpressible groanings. And the one who searches hearts knows what is the intention of the Spirit, because he intercedes for the holy ones according to God's will.

GOSPEL   *Matthew 13:24—43*

Shorter: Matthew 13:24–30

Jesus proposed another parable to the crowds, saying:

"The kingdom of heaven may be likened to a man who sowed good seed in his field. While everyone was asleep his enemy came and sowed weeds all through the wheat, and then went off. When the crop grew and bore fruit, the weeds appeared as well. The slaves of the householder came to him and said, 'Master, did you not sow good seed in your field? Where have the weeds come from?' He answered, 'An enemy has done this.' His slaves said to him, 'Do you want us to go and pull them up?' He replied, 'No, if you pull up the weeds you might uproot the wheat along with them. Let them grow together until harvest; then at harvest time I will say to the harvesters, "First collect the weeds and tie them in bundles for burning; but gather the wheat into my barn."'"

He proposed another parable to them. "The kingdom of heaven is like a mustard seed that a person took and sowed in a field. It is the smallest of all the seeds, yet when full-grown it is the largest of plants. It becomes a large bush, and the 'birds of the sky come and dwell in its branches.'"

He spoke to them another parable. "The kingdom of heaven is like yeast that a woman took and mixed with three measures of wheat flour until the whole batch was leavened."

All these things Jesus spoke to the crowds in parables. He spoke to them only in parables, to fulfill what had been said through the prophet:

>*I will open my mouth in parables,*
>*I will announce what has lain*
>>*hidden from the foundation*
>>*of the world.*

Then, dismissing the crowds, he went into the house. His disciples approached him and said, "Explain to us the parable of the weeds in the field." He said in reply, "He who sows good seed is the Son of Man, the field is the world, the good seed the children of the kingdom. The weeds are the children of the evil one, and the enemy who sows them is the devil. The harvest is the end of the age, and the harvesters are angels. Just as weeds are collected and burned up with fire, so will it be at the end of the age. The Son of Man will send his angels, and they will collect out of his kingdom all who cause others to sin and all evildoers. They will throw them into the fiery furnace, where there will be wailing and grinding of teeth. Then the righteous will shine like the sun in the kingdom of their Father. Whoever has ears ought to hear."

Practice of Prayer

Psalm 86:5—6, 9—10, 15—16 (5a)

R. Lord, you are good and forgiving.

You, O LORD, are good and forgiving,
>   abounding in kindness
>   to all who call upon you.
Hearken, O LORD, to my prayer
>   and attend to the sound of my pleading.   R.

All the nations you have made shall come
>   and worship you, O LORD,
>   and glorify your name.
For you are great, and you do wondrous deeds;
>   you alone are God.   R.

You, O LORD, are a God merciful and gracious,
>   slow to anger, abounding in
>   kindness and fidelity.
Turn toward me, and have pity on me;
>   give your strength to your servant.   R.

Practice of Charity

Blessed Mother Teresa wasn't a farmer, but she planted plenty of seeds in her time on earth. She sowed seeds of care for the poor and those burdened by disease, seeds of respect for life at all stages, seeds of hope that people all over the world would someday be connected by love and peace. But this doesn't happen without some serious cultivation, said the little woman who tended India's poor with such compassion: "The fruit of silence is prayer, the fruit of prayer is faith, the fruit of faith is love, the fruit of love is service, the fruit of service is peace."

We Americans don't like to be small, but that is often the only way to achieve great things. We grow into them, with the grace of God. Mother Teresa did and she helped us along the way. She proved that one small life can make a world of difference.

Scripture Insights

The author of the first reading, speaking to God, says, "There is no god besides you who have the care of all." God has a love for us so great that it extends even to the gift of his own Spirit. A few verses prior to today's text, the author of the book of Wisdom acclaims: "For you love all things that are and loathe nothing that you have made. . . . you spare all things, because they are yours, O Lord and lover of souls, for your imperishable spirit is in all things" (Wisdom 11:24—12:1). God's desire that we, his weak and fragile human creatures, be one with him and alive in him, is so great, that he gives us something of himself to draw us toward himself and to complete our happiness and well-being.

Throughout his letters, Paul witnesses to the tremendous power of God's Spirit at work within us. The Spirit is the gift with which we are "sealed" or marked in Baptism (Ephesians 1:13). Our bodies are now the dwelling place of the Spirit (1 Corinthians 3:16), who is alive and at work within us, leading us to our Father (Romans 8:14–15). Thanks to the Spirit, our relationship with God is so real and intimate that we call him "Abba" (Romans 8:15), an Aramaic word best rendered as "Daddy," just as Jesus did (Mark 14:36).

It is God's Spirit, alive and pulsing within us, who draws us to our heavenly Father—even in those times when we don't know *how* to pray, for it is the Father's will that we be one with him. What care God shows for us in not leaving us subject to our own limited abilities or conquered by our own weakness and frailty. May we truly know and draw upon the power of his Spirit within us!

◆ What specific words and phrases in today's readings reveal God's caring love for his creatures?

◆ What insights about the kingdom of heaven do we find in the parables in today's Gospel?

◆ How can we better "tap in" to the power of God's Spirit within us?

READING I   *1 Kings 3:5, 7–12*

The LORD appeared to Solomon in a dream at night. God said, "Ask something of me and I will give it to you." Solomon answered: "O LORD, my God, you have made me, your servant, king to succeed my father David; but I am a mere youth, not knowing at all how to act. I serve you in the midst of the people whom you have chosen, a people so vast that it cannot be numbered or counted. Give your servant, therefore, an understanding heart to judge your people and to distinguish right from wrong. For who is able to govern this vast people of yours?"

The LORD was pleased that Solomon made this request. So God said to him: "Because you have asked for this—not for a long life for yourself, nor for riches, nor for the life of your enemies, but for understanding so that you may know what is right—I do as you requested. I give you a heart so wise and understanding that there has never been anyone like you up to now, and after you there will come no one to equal you."

READING II   *Romans 8:28–30*

Brothers and sisters:

We know that all things work for good for those who love God, who are called according to his purpose. For those he foreknew he also predestined to be conformed to the image of his Son, so that he might be the firstborn among many brothers and sisters. And those he predestined he also called; and those he called he also justified; and those he justified he also glorified.

GOSPEL   *Matthew 13:44–52*

Shorter: Matthew 13:44–46

Jesus said to his disciples:

"The kingdom of heaven is like a treasure buried in a field, which a person finds and hides again, and out of joy goes and sells all that he has and buys that field. Again, the kingdom of heaven is like a merchant searching for fine pearls. When he finds a pearl of great price, he goes and sells all that he has and buys it. Again, the kingdom of heaven is like a net thrown into the sea, which collects fish of every kind. When it is full they haul it ashore and sit down to put what is good into buckets. What is bad they throw away. Thus it will be at the end of the age. The angels will go out and separate the wicked from the righteous and throw them into the fiery furnace, where there will be wailing and grinding of teeth.

"Do you understand all these things?" They answered, "Yes." And he replied, "Then every scribe who has been instructed in the kingdom of heaven is like the head of a household who brings from his storeroom both the new and the old."

Practice of Prayer

Psalm 119:57, 72, 76—77, 127—128, 129—130 (97a)

R. Lord, I love your commands.

I have said, O Lord, that my part
    is to keep your words.
The law of your mouth is to me more precious
    than thousands of gold and silver pieces. R.

Let your kindness comfort me
    according to your promise to your servants.
Let your compassion come to me that I may live,
    for your law is my delight. R.

For I love your commands
    more than gold, however fine.
For in all your precepts I go forward;
    every false way I hate. R.

Wonderful are your decrees;
    therefore I observe them.
The revelation of your words sheds light,
    giving understanding to the simple. R.

Practice of Faith

When asked what he was going to preach about one Sunday, a priest in northwest Kansas said that all homilies include three basic thoughts: "Jesus said it. You heard. Go do it." Sounds simple enough, but Catholic parishes have spent years trying to help people understand the importance of the Church's social teaching and how to use it to effect lasting change. According to Jack Jezreel, the founder and executive director of JustFaith, the key is conversion. In partnership with the Catholic Campaign for Human Development, Catholic Charities USA, and Catholic Relief Services, JustFaith fosters that conversion through an extended justice education process that allows people to "grow in their commitment to care for the vulnerable and to become advocates for justice." In addition to the reading and discussion involved, participants pray together and have opportunities for hands-on experiences with the poor. To find out more about how to bring JustFaith to your parish, visit www.justfaith.org.

Scripture Insights

What do you value more than anything else? On what is your heart set? With what are your thoughts most occupied? Your energies most expended? *That* is your treasure.

Treasures are of primary concern in today's scriptures, and three different yet very related ones are presented. In today's first reading, Solomon, son of Israel's great king David, has just begun his reign. While at one of the local shrines offering sacrifice to the Lord, he has the dream recounted in today's text. Note Solomon's humility, his realization of his own neediness. Despite the grandeur that would have been his as king, he recognizes that only God can fulfill that need. He asks for God's *wisdom,* that he might better serve God's people. What selflessness on Solomon's part, to ask not for what would enhance himself, but what would benefit others!

Psalm 119 acclaims the wisdom of God as manifest in the Law or Torah (literally "teaching," understood in the broader sense as referring to the first five books of the Bible). The psalmist recognizes that this is where true wisdom is found and thus acclaims it as more precious than earthly riches.

In a different chapter of Matthew's account of the Gospel than we read today, Jesus is proclaimed as one who came not to abolish the Law, but to fulfill it (5:17–18). In so doing, Jesus sometimes "expands" the Law with new meanings and understandings. Such is the way of the kingdom of heaven he came to proclaim. This kingdom is true treasure, he teaches, more precious than all else and worth any cost. May we honor it in the same way, for where our treasure is, there is our heart.

◆ What can we learn about the kingdom of heaven from the parables in the Gospel reading? How do you interpret Jesus' words about the scribe?

◆ When have you experienced some-one with an understanding heart?

◆ How do we become "conformed" to the image of the Son?

◆ In what way might you re-evaluate what you treasure?

READING I   *Isaiah 55:1—3*

Thus says the LORD:
All you who are thirsty,
    come to the water!
You who have no money,
    come, receive grain and eat;
Come, without paying and without cost,
    drink wine and milk!
Why spend your money for what is not bread;
    your wages for what fails to satisfy?
Heed me, and you shall eat well,
    you shall delight in rich fare.
Come to me heedfully,
    listen, that you may have life.
I will renew with you the everlasting covenant,
    the benefits assured to David.

READING II   *Romans 8:35, 37—39*

Brothers and sisters:

What will separate us from the love of Christ? Will anguish, or distress, or persecution, or famine, or nakedness, or peril, or the sword? No, in all these things we conquer overwhelmingly through him who loved us. For I am convinced that neither death, nor life, nor angels, nor principalities, nor present things, nor future things, nor powers, nor height, nor depth, nor any other creature will be able to separate us from the love of God in Christ Jesus our Lord.

GOSPEL   *Matthew 14:13—21*

When Jesus heard of the death of John the Baptist, he withdrew in a boat to a deserted place by himself. The crowds heard of this and followed him on foot from their towns. When he disembarked and saw the vast crowd, his heart was moved with pity for them, and he cured their sick. When it was evening, the disciples approached him and said, "This is a deserted place and it is already late; dismiss the crowds so that they can go to the villages and buy food for themselves." Jesus said to them, "There is no need for them to go away; give them some food yourselves." But they said to him, "Five loaves and two fish are all we have here." Then he said, "Bring them here to me," and he ordered the crowds to sit down on the grass. Taking the five loaves and the two fish, and looking up to heaven, he said the blessing, broke the loaves, and gave them to the disciples, who in turn gave them to the crowds. They all ate and were satisfied, and they picked up the fragments left over—twelve wicker baskets full. Those who ate were about five thousand men, not counting women and children.

Practice of Prayer

Psalm 145:8—9, 15—16, 17—18 (see 16)

R. The hand of the Lord feeds us;
    he answers all our needs.

The LORD is gracious and merciful,
    slow to anger and of great kindness.
The LORD is good to all
    and compassionate toward all his works. R.

The eyes of all look hopefully to you,
    and you give them their food in due season;
you open your hand
    and satisfy the desire
        of every living thing. R.

The LORD is just in all his ways
    and holy in all his works.
The LORD is near to all who call upon him,
    to all who call upon him in truth. R.

Practice of Charity

This week's scriptures overflow with images of God's abundant love and care for us. We who experience material abundance are called to care for those who have not. Hearing and acting on that call may depend on an experience that awakens us to the need. Catholic Relief Services offers a retreat for youth designed to raise awareness to hunger and create a sense of solidarity with those who suffer. It's called Food Fast and is designed for youngsters 13 to 18 years old. Using the traditional Catholic practices of fasting and prayer, it inspires faith and service. The effects of the retreat are powerful—going beyond the young participants to their families and friends.

On the Food Fast Web site, http://www.foodfast.org/, youth ministers can download free resources for the retreat, find out about other Catholic Relief Services education resources, and connect with other youth ministers engaged in a Food Fast retreat.

Scripture Insights

"What will separate us from the love of Christ?"—absolutely nothing. Indeed, today's scriptures suggest that those things that may seem to separate us are the very things through which we can experience Christ's love.

Throughout scripture, God is revealed as merciful and compassionate. From the earliest days, Israel knew God as one who "witnessed the affliction of my people in Egypt and . . . heard their cry of complaint" (Exodus 3:7). who knows "well what they are suffering," and therefore comes "down to rescue them"

Today's first reading comes at the end of the second part of the book of Isaiah, addressed to the exiles in Babylon. The Jews at that time experienced anguish and distress. They were separated from their homeland and suffered the loss of the temple so sacred to them. Yet it is precisely here in a foreign land that God offers such an insistent invitation: "come" (4 times) and "listen/heed" (3 times), offering "rich fare" and "life" in covenant with him.

Similarly, in today's Gospel, at the sight of the crowds, Jesus' "heart was moved with pity" and he healed and fed them. Had they, like he, heard of the execution—by sword—of John the Baptist?

Anguish, distress, persecution, famine, the sword—these are all forces of destruction that would seem to defeat. Yet, paradoxically, through the love of Christ, we are "more than" victorious in all of these things, for it is here that Christ is moved with pity and feeds and strengthens us. May we never lose heart.

• How is the invitation in today's first reading realized in today's Gospel? In our own lives?

• What is the significance of the way the first reading and Gospel speak about buying our nourishment?

• How can the love of Christ help you be "victorious" in a difficult situation in your life now?

• If the Lord is merciful and loves us, why does it sometimes seem that needs are not met?

READING I 1 Kings 19:9a, 11—13a

At the mountain of God, Horeb, Elijah came to a cave where he took shelter. Then the LORD said to him, "Go outside and stand on the mountain before the LORD; the LORD will be passing by." A strong and heavy wind was rending the mountains and crushing rocks before the LORD—but the LORD was not in the wind. After the wind there was an earthquake—but the LORD was not in the earthquake. After the earthquake there was fire—but the LORD was not in the fire. After the fire there was a tiny whispering sound. When he heard this, Elijah hid his face in his cloak and went and stood at the entrance of the cave.

READING II Romans 9:1—5

Brothers and sisters:

I speak the truth in Christ, I do not lie; my conscience joins with the Holy Spirit in bearing me witness that I have great sorrow and constant anguish in my heart. For I could wish that I myself were accursed and cut off from Christ for the sake of my own people, my kindred according to the flesh. They are Israelites; theirs the adoption, the glory, the covenants, the giving of the law, the worship, and the promises; theirs the patriarchs, and from them, accord-ing to the flesh, is the Christ, who is over all, God blessed forever. Amen.

GOSPEL Matthew 14:22—33

After he had fed the people, Jesus made the disciples get into a boat and precede him to the other side, while he dismissed the crowds. After doing so, he went up on the mountain by himself to pray. When it was evening he was there alone. Meanwhile the boat, already a few miles offshore, was being tossed about by the waves, for the wind was against it. During the fourth watch of the night, he came toward them walking on the sea. When the disciples saw him walking on the sea they were terrified. "It is a ghost," they said, and they cried out in fear. At once Jesus spoke to them, "Take courage, it is I; do not be afraid." Peter said to him in reply, "Lord, if it is you, command me to come to you on the water." He said, "Come." Peter got out of the boat and began to walk on the water toward Jesus. But when he saw how strong the wind was he became frightened; and, beginning to sink, he cried out, "Lord, save me!" Immediately Jesus stretched out his hand and caught Peter, and said to him, "O you of little faith, why did you doubt?" After they got into the boat, the wind died down. Those who were in the boat did him homage, saying, "Truly, you are the Son of God."

Practice of Prayer

Practice of Faith

When people merit recognition for special talents shared or services rendered, we may call them heroes. When they can do no wrong in our eyes, we may even say that they "walk on water." Often this has very little to do with the faith that inspires the passage from Matthew that we hear proclaimed today. That Jesus is able to command the elements and walk on stormy seas is miraculous enough, but Peter's willingness to follow Jesus anywhere is an awesome witness to what faith makes possible. There are many who display the same willingness every day in quiet, unassuming ways. Some of these "hidden heroes" are featured each month on the Web site of the Catholic Church Extension Society, which seeks to build up the Catholic faith in the poor and remote mission areas of the United States. To learn more about these heroes and support the work of the Extension Society, go to www.catholicextension.org.

Scripture Insights

Mountains, deserts, and the sea—three places where people in the Bible often encounter God.

In 1 Kings 19, Elijah, fleeing for his life, is guided by an angel to Horeb (Mt. Sinai). There, like Moses and Israel before him, he encounters God. However, unlike Moses and Israel who experienced God's presence in the thunder, lightning, and volcanic activity (Exodus 19:16–18), Elijah finds God in a "tiny whispering sound"—literally, a tiny sound of quietness or silence. Recognizing God's presence, Elijah hides his face, for according to Exodus 33:20, no one can see God and live. Jesus frequently went to mountains and deserts to find solitude for prayer.

Last week we learned that after hearing of the death of John the Baptist, Jesus came out to a deserted place alone, but was followed by the crowd. In today's Gospel reading, after feeding the crowd, Jesus went up the mountain alone to pray. But the Sea of Galilee becomes the place where he mani-fests his divinity and the disciples recognize him as "truly the Son of God." For many ancient peoples, the sea represented the forces of chaos and destruction. Water covered the earth before creation in Genesis. God led the chosen people safely through the very sea that destroyed the pursuing Egyptian army. Israel's God has complete power over the waters, even to the extent that he "treads upon the crests of the sea" (Job 9:8).

Such is Jesus' power in today's Gospel. Upon seeing it, the disciples, for the first time in Matthew's Gospel narrative, recognized his true identity. May we be so drawn to the places where he is manifest, so alert for his coming, that we too can recognize him.

♦ What are some of the differences between Elijah's encounter with God and Peter's encounter with the Son of God?

♦ Where else in scripture are mountains, deserts, and seas places of encounter with God?

♦ When, where, how have you experienced the presence of God?

READING I   *Isaiah 56:1, 6—7*

Thus says the LORD:
Observe what is right, do what is just;
    for my salvation is about to come,
    my justice, about to be revealed.

The foreigners who join themselves
       to the LORD,
    ministering to him,
loving the name of the LORD,
    and becoming his servants—
all who keep the sabbath free from profanation
    and hold to my covenant,
them I will bring to my holy mountain
    and make joyful in my house of prayer;
their burnt offerings and sacrifices
    will be acceptable on my altar,
for my house shall be called
    a house of prayer for all peoples.

READING II   *Romans 11:13—15, 29—32*

Brothers and sisters:

I am speaking to you Gentiles. Inasmuch as I am the apostle to the Gentiles, I glory in my ministry in order to make my race jealous and thus save some of them. For if their rejection is the reconciliation of the world, what will their acceptance be but life from the dead?

    For the gifts and the call of God are irrevocable. Just as you once disobeyed God but have now received mercy because of their disobedience, so they have now disobeyed in order that, by virtue of the mercy shown to you, they too may now receive mercy. For God delivered all to disobedience, that he might have mercy upon all.

GOSPEL   *Matthew 15:21—28*

At that time, Jesus withdrew to the region of Tyre and Sidon. And behold, a Canaanite woman of that district came and called out, "Have pity on me, Lord, Son of David! My daughter is tormented by a demon." But Jesus did not say a word in answer to her. Jesus' disciples came and asked him, "Send her away, for she keeps calling out after us." He said in reply, "I was sent only to the lost sheep of the house of Israel." But the woman came and did Jesus homage, saying, "Lord, help me." He said in reply, "It is not right to take the food of the children and throw it to the dogs." She said, "Please, Lord, for even the dogs eat the scraps that fall from the table of their masters." Then Jesus said to her in reply, "O woman, great is your faith! Let it be done for you as you wish." And the woman's daughter was healed from that hour.

Practice of Prayer

Psalm 67:2–3, 5, 6, 8 (4)

R. O God, let all the nations praise you!

May God have pity on us and bless us;
  may he let his face shine upon us.
So may your way be known upon earth;
  among all nations, your salvation.   R.

May the nations be glad and exult
  because you rule the peoples in equity;
  the nations on the earth you guide.   R.

May the peoples praise you, O God;
  may all the peoples praise you!
May God bless us,
  and may all the ends of the earth
    fear him!   R.

Practice of Hope

As we read in the scriptures this week about how God expanded his plan for salvation to include foreigners, consider how Gospel values might inform our position on immigration reform in the United States. The Office of Migration and Refugee Policy of the United States Conference of Catholic Bishops maintains a Web site (http: www.usccb.org/mrs/mrp.shtml). Find there an overview of the nation's immigration problems along with an analysis and explanation of the Bishops' advocacy for comprehensive immigration reform. Organized in a question and answer format, it states clearly which legislation the USCCB supports and which it opposes. Especially helpful on the Migration and Refugee Services home Web site are excerpts of relevant Church teachings and scripture.

Scripture Insights

We know that the Old Testament tells the stories of God's dealings with the Israelites, God's chosen people. The New Testament continues in this same vein, portraying Jesus as the Messiah, the fulfillment of all God's promises to the Jewish people. If we think of any inclusion of Gentiles (non-Jews) in God's plan, we probably see it as a later Christian development. But today's readings show that the Gentiles had a role much earlier.

Isaiah wrote shortly after the return of the Jews exiled in Babylon, a return decreed by the Gentile king Cyrus of Persia (see Ezra 1:1–4). When Isaiah speaks for God, saying that the foreigners' sacrifices will be acceptable on his altar, he is including the Gentiles in God's plan of salvation.

As we read in the Romans passage, Paul of Tarsus understood his mission as primarily directed to the Gentiles, and we hear of Gentiles being drawn to Israel's faith in the Acts of the Apostles (the Ethiopian in 8:26–40, and Cornelins in 10:1ff.). In this light, Jesus' hesitation in responding to the Canaanite woman's request can be perplexing. In some instances Jesus says clearly that his mission is focused on Israel. Nevertheless, the Gospel tells of Gentiles who come to him in faith (the Magi in Matthew 2:1–12, and the Roman centurion in 8:5–13), and it is precisely the faith of this Canaanite woman that wins her a hearing. In fact, her "great faith" contrasts with the description of the disciples' "little faith" in Matthew 6:30, 8:26, 14:31, and 16:8.

Significantly, at the end of this Gospel book narrataive, the risen Jesus sends the 11 disciples to "make disciples of all nations" (28:19). Indeed, through the nations' acceptance of the word of the Gospel, the hope of Psalm 67 has been fulfilled. The word went forth from Israel that all nations might praise God's name.

• How does Jesus' response to the woman change in the course of the episode? Why?

• In the second reading, how does the inclusion of the Gentiles in God's plan of salvation affect the "unbelieving" Jews?

• What does God's unconditional acceptance of all peoples say to us about our dealings with those who are not "like" us?

August 24, 2008

READING I *Isaiah 22:19—23*

Thus says the LORD to Shebna,
        master of the palace:
"I will thrust you from your office
        and pull you down from your station.
On that day I will summon my servant
        Eliakim, son of Hilkiah;
I will clothe him with your robe,
        and gird him with your sash,
        and give over to him your authority.
He shall be a father to
        the inhabitants of Jerusalem,
        and to the house of Judah.
I will place the key of the House of
        David on Eliakim's shoulder;
        when he opens, no one shall shut
        when he shuts, no one shall open.
I will fix him like a peg in a sure spot,
        to be a place of honor for his family."

READING II *Romans 11:33—36*

Oh, the depth of the riches and wisdom and
knowledge of God! How inscrutable are his judg-
ments and how unsearchable his ways!

> *For who has known the mind of the Lord*
>   *or who has been his counselor?*
> *Or who has given the Lord anything*
>   *that he may be repaid?*

For from him and through him and for him are
all things. To him be glory forever. Amen.

GOSPEL *Matthew 16:13—20*

Jesus went into the region of Caesarea Philippi and
he asked his disciples, "Who do people say that
the Son of Man is?" They replied, "Some say John
the Baptist, others Elijah, still others Jeremiah or
one of the prophets." He said to them, "But who
do you say that I am?" Simon Peter said in reply,
"You are the Christ, the Son of the living God."
Jesus said to him in reply, "Blessed are you, Simon
son of Jonah. For flesh and blood has not revealed
this to you, but my heavenly Father. And so I say
to you, you are Peter, and upon this rock I will
build my church, and the gates of the netherworld
shall not prevail against it. I will give you the keys
to the kingdom of heaven. Whatever you bind on
earth shall be bound in heaven; and whatever you
loose on earth shall be loosed in heaven." Then
he strictly ordered his disciples to tell no one that
he was the Christ.

Practice of Prayer

Psalm 138:1—2, 2—3, 6, 8 (8bc)

R. Lord, your love is eternal;
      do not forsake the work of your hands.

I will give thanks to you, O LORD,
      with all my heart,
   for you have heard the words of my mouth;
in the presence of the angels
      I will sing your praise;
   I will worship at your holy temple.   R.

I will give thanks to your name,
      because of your kindness and your truth:
when I called, you answered me;
      you built up strength within me.   R.

The LORD is exalted, yet the lowly he sees,
      and the proud he knows from afar.
Your kindness, O LORD, endures forever;
      forsake not the work of your hands.   R.

Practice of Charity

Friday will mark the anniversary of the death of Blessed Edmund Ignatius Rice, teacher of students in poverty-stricken areas and founder of the Irish Christian Brothers. An extraordinary school in Tanzania bears his name and carries on his legacy. Edmund Rice Sinon High School has as its motto "Hope through education." Recent American visitors were struck by the spirit of hospitality extended by the students, who speak excellent English. Many students, male and female, live on campus because of their rigorous academic schedule; often their homes don't have electric lights, hindering nighttime study. Their food is raised on campus, and some students take part in agriculture classes. All students are dedicated and goal oriented. Water, a scarce commodity in Tanzania, became more plentiful recently when a new well was dug. Visit the student-designed Web site, www.edmundrice.habari.co.tz, to learn more about the school or to make a contribution to its scholarship fund.

Scripture Insights

"Oh, the depth of the riches and wisdom and knowledge of God! . . . For who has known the mind of the Lord . . . ?" Paul's words, set at the end of a long reflection on God's call of both Jews and Gentiles to salvation, invite us to reflect on the mysteries of God's ways in our own lives. Surely scripture is the perfect accompaniment to our experience—not necessarily answering our questions, but always drawing us deeper into mystery and awe.

How often, when faced with perplexing circumstances, do we ponder God's words: "my thoughts are not your thoughts, nor are your ways my ways" (Isaiah 55:8)? How often do we take to heart Paul's words: "we know that all things work for good for those who love God, who are called according to his purpose" (Romans 8:28)?

How often, in the face of the scientific and technological advances of our age, do we consider ourselves masters of the universe with little time for reflection—when in fact, our "advanced" knowledge should lead us to greater awe? How often do we step back to rejoice in the universe that surrounds us—the beauty of nature, the intricacies of the human body, the unfolding of the pathways of our own lives? The biblical authors grasped this with a profundity that our own day lacks.

Such awe and reverence must have accompanied Peter's recognition of the Lord's divinity—an awe that pulled him ever deeper into discipleship. Led by the words of scripture, let us this day stop and really *see* the works of the Creator's hand—in the world around us and in all the events and situations of our lives. May we recognize, in the depths of our being, that "from him and through him and for him are all things." With grateful hearts, let us give him glory.

♦ Why does Psalm 138 call humans "the work of your [God's] hands"?

♦ Why does Jesus command the disciples to be silent about his identity?

♦ How can we develop a sense of awe before the works and the ways of the Lord?

Ordinary Time, Autumn

Prayer before Reading the Word

In humility and service, O God,
your Son came among us
to form a community of disciples
who have one Father in heaven,
and one teacher, the Messiah.

Let your Spirit make our hearts
docile to the challenge of your word,
and let the same mind be in us
that was in Christ Jesus.

We ask this through our Lord
        Jesus Christ, your Son,
who lives and reigns with you
in the unity of the Holy Spirit,
one God for ever and ever. Amen.

Prayer after Reading the Word

To the last as to the first, O God,
you are generous and more than just,
for as high as the heavens are above the earth,
so high are your ways above our ways
and your thoughts above our thoughts.

Open our hearts to the wisdom of your Son,
Fix in our minds his sound teaching,
that, without concern for the cost of discipleship
we may work without ceasing
for the coming of your kingdom.

We ask this through our Lord
        Jesus Christ, your Son,
who lives and reigns with you
in the unity of the Holy Spirit,
one God for ever and ever. Amen.

Weekday Readings

August 25: *2 Thessalonians 1:1–5, 11–12; Matthew 23:13–22*
August 26: *2 Thessalonians 2:1–3a, 14–17; Matthew 23:23–26*
August 27: *2 Thessalonians 3:6–10, 16–18; Matthew 23:27–32*
August 28: *1 Corinthians 1:1–9; Matthew 24:42–51*
August 29: *1 Corinthians 1:17–25; Mark 6:17–29*
August 30: *1 Corinthians 1:26–31; Matthew 25:14–30*

September 1: *1 Corinthians 2:1–5; Luke 4:16–30*
September 2: *1 Corinthians 2:10b–16; Luke 4:31–37*
September 3: *1 Corinthians 3:1–9; Luke 4:38–44*
September 4: *1 Corinthians 3:18–23; Luke 5:1–11*
September 5: *1 Corinthians 4:1–5; Luke 5:33–39*
September 6: *1 Corinthians 4:6b–15; Luke 6:1–5*

**September 8: Feast of the Nativity of
the Blessed Virgin Mary**
  Micah 5:1–4a; Matthew 1:1–16, 18–23
September 9: *1 Corinthians 6:1–11; Luke 6:12–19*
September 10: *1 Corinthians 7:25–31; Luke 6:20–26*
September 11: *1 Corinthians 8:1b–7, 11–13; Luke 6:27–38*
September 12: *1 Corinthians 9:16–19, 22b–27; Luke 6:39–42*
September 13: *1 Corinthians 10:14–22; Luke 6:43–49*

September 15: *1 Corinthians 11:17–26, 33; John 19:25–27*
September 16: *1 Corinthians 12:12–14, 27–31a; Luke 7:11–17*
September 17: *1 Corinthians 12:31 — 13:13; Luke 7:31–35*
September 18: *1 Corinthians 15:1–11; Luke 7:36–50*
September 19: *1 Corinthians 15:12–20; Luke 8:1–3*
September 20: *1 Corinthians 15:35–37, 42–49; Luke 8:4–15*

September 22: *Proverbs 3:27–34; Luke 8:16–18*
September 23: *Proverbs 21:1–6, 10–13; Luke 8:19–21*
September 24: *Proverbs 30:5–9; Luke 9:1–6*
September 25: *Ecclesiastes 1:2–11; Luke 9:7–9*
September 26: *Ecclesiastes 3:1–11; Luke 9:18–22*
September 27: *Ecclesiastes 11:9 — 12:8; Luke 9:43b–45*

September 29: Feast of Michael, Gabriel, and Raphael
  Daniel 7:9–10, 13–14 John 1:47–51
September 30: *Job 3:1–3, 11–17, 20–23; Luke 9:51–56*
October 1: *Job 9:1–12, 14–16; Luke 9:57–62*
October 2: *Job 19:21–27; Matthew 18:1–5, 10*
October 3: *Job 38:1, 12–21; 40:3–5; Luke 10:13–16*
October 4: *Job 42:1–3, 5–6, 12–17; Luke 10:17–24*

October 6: *Galatians 1:6–12; Luke 10:25–37*
October 7: *Galatians 1:13–24; Luke 10:38–42*
October 8: *Galatians 2:1–2, 7–14; Luke 11:1–4*
October 9: *Galatians 3:1–5; Luke 11:5–13*
October 10: *Galatians 3:7–14; Luke 11:15–26*
October 11: *Galatians 3:22–29; Luke 11:27–28*

October 13: *Galatians 4:22–24, 26–27, 31 — 5:1;*
  Luke 11:29–32
October 14: *Galatians 5:1–6; Luke 11:37–41*
October 15: *Galatians 5:18–25; Luke 11:42–46*
October 16: *Ephesians 1:1–10; Luke 11:47–54*
October 17: *Ephesians 1:11–14; Luke 12:1–7*
October 18: Feast of Saint Luke
  2 Timothy 4:10–17b; Luke 10:1–9

October 20: *Ephesians 2:1–10; Luke 12:13–21*
October 21: *Ephesians 2:12–22; Luke 12:35–38*
October 22: *Ephesians 3:2–12; Luke 12:39–48*
October 23: *Ephesians 3:14–21; Luke 12:49–53*
October 24: *Ephesians 4:1–6; Luke 12:54–59*
October 25: *Ephesians 4:7–16; Luke 13:1–9*

October 27: *Ephesians 4:32 — 5:8; Luke 13:10–17*
October 28: Feast of Saint Simon and Saint Jude
  Ephesians 2:19–22; Luke 6:12–16
October 29: *Ephesians 6:1–9; Luke 13:22–30*
October 30: *Ephesians 6:10–20; Luke 13:31–35*
October 31: *Philippians 1:1–11; Luke 14:1–6*
November 1: Solemnity of All Saints
  Revelation 7:2–4, 9–14; 1 John 3:1–3; Matthew 5:1–12a

November 3: *Philippians 2:1–4; Luke 14:12–14*
November 4: *Philippians 2:5–11; Luke 14:15–24*
November 5: *Philippians 2:12–18; Luke 14:25–33*
November 6: *Philippians 3:3–8a; Luke 15:1–10*
November 7: *Philippians 3:17 — 4:1; Luke 16:1–8*
November 8: *Philippians 4:10–19; Luke 16:9–15*

November 10: *Timothy 1:1–9; Luke 17:1–6*
November 11: *Timothy 2:1–8, 11–14; Luke 17:7–10*
November 12: *Timothy 3:1–7; Luke 17:11–19*
November 13: *Philemon 7–20; Luke 17:20–25*
November 14: *2 John 4–9; Luke 17:26–37*
November 15: *3 John 5–8; Luke 18:1–8*

August 31, 2008

READING I   *Jeremiah 20:7—9*

You duped me, O LORD,
> and I let myself be duped;
> you were too strong for me,
> > and you triumphed.
All the day I am an object of laughter;
> everyone mocks me.

Whenever I speak, I must cry out,
> violence and outrage
> > is my message;
the word of the LORD has brought me
> derision and reproach all the day.

I say to myself, I will not
> mention him,
> I will speak in his name no more.
But then it becomes like fire
> burning in my heart,
> imprisoned in my bones;
I grow weary holding it in,
> I cannot endure it.

READING II   *Romans 12:1—2*

I urge you, brothers and sisters, by the mercies of God, to offer your bodies as a living sacrifice, holy and pleasing to God, your spiritual worship. Do not conform yourselves to this age but be transformed by the renewal of your mind, that you may discern what is the will of God, what is good and pleasing and perfect.

GOSPEL   *Matthew 16:21—27*

Jesus began to show his disciples that he must go to Jerusalem and suffer greatly from the elders, the chief priests, and the scribes, and be killed and on the third day be raised. Then Peter took Jesus aside and began to rebuke him, "God forbid, Lord! No such thing shall ever happen to you." He turned and said to Peter, "Get behind me, Satan! You are an obstacle to me. You are thinking not as God does, but as human beings do."

Then Jesus said to his disciples, "Whoever wishes to come after me must deny himself, take up his cross, and follow me. For whoever wishes to save his life will lose it, but whoever loses his life for my sake will find it. What profit would there be for one to gain the whole world and forfeit his life? Or what can one give in exchange for his life? For the Son of Man will come with his angels in his Father's glory, and then he will repay all according to his conduct."

Practice of Prayer

Psalm 63:2, 3—4, 5—6, 8—9 (2b)

R. My soul is thirsting for you,
> O Lord my God.

O God, you are my God whom I seek;
> for you my flesh pines and my soul thirsts
> like the earth, parched,
> > lifeless and without water.   R.

Thus have I gazed toward you in the sanctuary
    to see your power and your glory,
for your kindness is a greater good than life;
    my lips shall glorify you. R.

Thus will I bless you while I live;
    lifting up my hands,
        I will call upon your name.
As with the riches of a banquet
        shall my soul be satisfied,
    and with exultant lips
        my mouth shall praise you. R.

You are my help,
    and in the shadow of your wings
        I shout for joy.
My soul clings fast to you;
    your right hand upholds me. R.

Practice of Hope

"For more than 60 years now, he has organized, marched, prayed, and bled for the social and economic justice of working Americans." So was Monsignor George Higgins described in the year 2000, when he was awarded the Presidential Medal of Freedom. We remember him on this Labor Day weekend. A consultant at the Second Vatican Council, Monsignor Higgins was also a trusted advisor to political and church leaders, a teacher of ethics and theology, a walker of picket lines, and a co-founder of the United Farm Workers Union. He described his work as "a ministry of presence," talking with and listening to both sides in a dispute until common ground could be reached. His wit, tact, and personal warmth helped greatly in this process. Monsignor Higgins took pride in the work of the National Interfaith Committee on Worker Justice, which carries on his legacy. To learn more about them, visit www. nicwj.org.

Scripture Insights

Today, Jeremiah, Peter, and Jesus teach us aqbout responding to suffering that faithfulness to God and one's God-given vocation often brings. Almost always, the suffering comes at the hands of the very ones to whom God's servant is sent. Unable and unwilling to hear God's message, they try to destroy God's messenger.

No prophet in the Old Testament suffered as greatly as did Jeremiah. He was rejected and persecuted by others and inwardly conflicted about his call from God (Jeremiah 26:7–15). Today's first reading—from the so-called confessions of Jeremiah (see Scripture Insight for June 22) recounts one such incident.

So great is Jeremiah's anguish that he is ready to abandon his prophetic call. Yet, God's word is like a fire burning in his heart; his is compelled to speak. He cannot help but be faithful.

Jesus, too, knew distress and anguish in the face of his sufferings (Matthew 26:37–38) and he, too, was faithful to the Father's will, as we see today and later in 26:39–46. It's no wonder that the early believers were reminded of Jeremiah when reflecting on the sufferings of Jesus (see Matthew 16:14). Significantly, Jesus' words about taking up our cross in today's Gospel reading remind us that the way of the disciple can be no different from his, and it is a way that must be shown in one's actions and deeds (or "conduct" as the Lectionary renders the Greek *praxis,* at the end of the reading).

In a similar vein, Paul describes this manner of losing one's life as an offering of one's self, one's very body, as a "living sacrifice." Where else are one's actions and deeds expressed than in and by the body?

A living sacrifice given up to God; suffering not only accepted, but embraced—so Jesus lived and so must those who follow after him.

• How is responsorial Psalm 63 related to the other readings?

• How does the second reading define "losing one's life"?

• The "costs" of discipleship are great. When have you felt as Jeremiah did? When have you felt comfortable with what Paul and Jesus describe?

READING I *Ezekiel 33:7—9*

Thus says the LORD:

You, son of man, I have appointed watchman for the house of Israel; when you hear me say anything, you shall warn them for me. If I tell the wicked, "O wicked one, you shall surely die," and you do not speak out to dissuade the wicked from his way, the wicked shall die for his guilt, but I will hold you responsible for his death. But if you warn the wicked, trying to turn him from his way, and he refuses to turn from his way, he shall die for his guilt, but you shall save yourself.

READING II *Romans 13:8—10*

Brothers and sisters:

Owe nothing to anyone, except to love one another; for the one who loves another has fulfilled the law. The commandments, "You shall not commit adultery; you shall not kill; you shall not steal; you shall not covet," and whatever other commandment there may be, are summed up in this saying, namely, "You shall love your neighbor as yourself." Love does no evil to the neighbor; hence, love is the fulfillment of the law.

GOSPEL *Matthew 18:15—20*

Jesus said to his disciples:

"If your brother sins against you, go and tell him his fault between you and him alone. If he listens to you, you have won over your brother. If he does not listen, take one or two others along with you, so that 'every fact may be established on the testimony of two or three witnesses.' If he refuses to listen to them, tell the church. If he refuses to listen even to the church, then treat him as you would a Gentile or a tax collector. Amen, I say to you, whatever you bind on earth shall be bound in heaven, and whatever you loose on earth shall be loosed in heaven. Again, amen, I say to you, if two of you agree on earth about anything for which they are to pray, it shall be granted to them by my heavenly Father. For where two or three are gathered together in my name, there am I in the midst of them."

Practice of Prayer

Psalm 95:1—2, 6—7, 8—9 (8)

R. If today you hear his voice,
    harden not your hearts.

Come, let us sing joyfully to the LORD;
    let us acclaim the Rock of our salvation.
Let us come into his presence with thanksgiving;
    let us joyfully sing psalms to him.   R.

Come, let us bow down in worship;
    let us kneel before the LORD who made us.
For he is our God,
    and we are the people he shepherds,
        the flock he guides.   R.

Oh, that today you would hear his voice:
    "Harden not your hearts as at Meribah,
    as in the day of Massah in the desert,
Where your fathers tempted me;
    they tested me though
        they had seen my works."   R.

Practice of Charity

For centuries, quilting has been a reason for two or three to gather. Quilters' circles, traditionally formed through churches, have provided fellowship, opportunities for common prayer, and means of artistic expression. For many women, especially during hard times, those qualities of life would otherwise be in short supply.

Tutwiler, in the Mississippi Delta, has long been home to gifted quilters. In 1988, Maureen Delaney, a Sister of the Holy Names of Jesus and Mary, opened a community education center in Tutwiler. She recognized the talent of these women, and since then the artworks of the Tutwiler Quilt Collective have sometimes been exhibited in museums. In addition to bedspreads, the quilters make potholders, table runners, placemats and tote bags to order—you specify the colors you want and let their creativity take it from there. Purchasing their handiwork enables the quilters in this poverty-stricken region to be financially self-sufficient. Learn more at www.tutwilerquilters.org.

Scripture Insights

This Sunday, when we stand for the Alleluia, this Gospel acclamation will be sung: "God was reconciling the world to himself in Christ and entrusting to us the message of reconciliation" (2 Corinthians 5:19).

Peacemaker and reconciler—how often do we see ourselves in that role? Act in that capacity? Yet, this is the message and the work we have been given, the "responsibility" we have for one another.

Note that the directive is given in today's Gospel reading regarding a brother (or sister) in the *Church*. (The Greek word for *Church*, *ekklēsia*, occurs twice in Matthew's account of the Gospel—16:18 and 18:17—and is etymologically related to the verb *kaleō* or *call*.) The Church is the new people of God, called by and gathered around Jesus. "Whoever does the will of my heavenly Father is my brother, and sister, and mother" (Matthew 12:50)—and brothers and sisters of one another. Harmonious relationships with these brothers and sisters are like-wise treated in Matthew 5:22–24.

The phrase "against you," in the first line of our reading, is not found in some of the oldest manuscripts of this passage. This alters the meaning significantly, for then the subject is not so much a personal offense, but rather, any sin. Brothers and sisters are responsible for the conversion of one another. (But note the caveat in Matthew 7:3–5 about the possible beam in one's own eye!).

The "how" of exercising this work of conversion and reconciliation is set forth in the first lines of the Gospel reading and tempered by the second reading, which reminds us that love of neighbor must be the basis of any reconciliation work.

Today's scriptures call us to self-examination, for we are both sinners in need of our own conversion and called to be "prophets" and reconcilers for one another. Let us listen to God's voice—however, whenever, through whomever God speaks, and harden not our hearts.

• What is the interrelationship between "listening" and "speaking" in today's readings?

• When have you acted as a reconciler?

• What attitude do we need in order to receive the prompting of another?

READING I *Numbers 21:4b—9*

With their patience worn out by the journey,
   the people complained against
      God and Moses,
"Why have you brought us up
     from Egypt to die in this desert,
   where there is no food or water?
We are disgusted with this wretched food!"

In punishment the LORD sent
     among the people saraph serpents,
   which bit the people so that
     many of them died.
Then the people came to Moses and said,
   "We have sinned in complaining
     against the LORD and you.
Pray the LORD to take the serpents from us."
So Moses prayed for the people,
    and the LORD said to Moses,
   "Make a saraph and mount it on a pole,
   and if any who have been bitten
     look at it, they will live."
Moses accordingly made a bronze serpent and
    mounted it on a pole,
   and whenever anyone who had
     been bitten by a serpent
   looked at the bronze serpent, he lived.

READING II *Philippians 2:6—11*

Brothers and sisters:
Christ Jesus, though he was in the form of God,
   did not regard equality with God
     something to be grasped.
Rather, he emptied himself,
   taking the form of a slave,
   coming in human likeness;
   and found human in appearance,
   he humbled himself,
   becoming obedient to the point of death,
   even death on a cross.
Because of this, God greatly exalted him
   and bestowed on him the name
   which is above every name,
   that at the name of Jesus
   every knee should bend,
   of those in heaven and on earth
     and under the earth,
   and every tongue confess that
   Jesus Christ is Lord,
   to the glory of God the Father.

GOSPEL *John 3:13 —17*

Jesus said to Nicodemus:
"No one has gone up to heaven
   except the one who has come down from
     heaven, the Son of Man.
And just as Moses lifted up the serpent
    in the desert,
   so must the Son of Man be lifted up,
   so that everyone who believes in him
     may have eternal life."

For God so loved the world that he
    gave his only Son,
   so that he who believes in
     him might not perish
   but might have eternal life.
For God did not send his Son into
    the world to condemn the world,
   but that the world might be
     saved through him.

Practice of Prayer

Psalm 78:1—2, 34—35, 36—37, 38 (see 7b)

R. Do not forget the works of the Lord!

Hearken, my people, to my teaching;
    incline your ears to the words of my mouth.
I will open my mouth in a parable,
    I will utter mysteries from of old.   R.

While he slew them they sought him
    and inquired after God again,
remembering that God was their rock
    and the Most High God, their redeemer.   R.

But they flattered him with their mouths
    and lied to him with their tongues,
though their hearts were not steadfast toward him,
    nor were they faithful to his covenant.   R.

Yet he, being merciful, forgave their sin
    and destroyed them not;
often he turned back his anger
    and let none of his wrath be roused.   R.

Practice of Hope

Faculty and students at Dominican University in River Forest, Illinois, prize its lovely wooded campus. However, construction for a new academic building last year necessitated displacing 40 mature trees—oak, American ash, sugar maple, American elm, and pine. In one of many creative ways found to recycle the wood, Professor Daniel Beach offered to fashion handmade oak crosses for each classroom in the new building. Beach, psychology department chair and accomplished woodworker, says he incorporated Mission-style elements into his unique cross design because Dominican is mission-driven. Also, Mission style complements local architecture. The four points of each cross echo a gothic detail of campus buildings. The design also features a basket weave pattern representing the interconnectedness of everyone on campus. "This design is symbolic of my faith," Beach says, "and crafting the wood is a contemplative experience. The crosses provide a connection between present and future generations who will see them."

Scripture Insights

There is a paradox in the title of today's feast, for as Paul so emphatically points out in his first letter to the Corinthians, the cross is a "stumbling block" for the Jews and "foolishness" for the Gentiles (1 Corinthians 1:23). For the Romans, crucifixion was so shameful and heinous a form of capital punishment, that they would not inflict it upon a Roman citizen. For the Jews, God's word in Deuteronomy had pronounced a curse on anyone who hung upon a tree (Deuteronomy 21:22—23). An entirely different perspective, however, is voiced in the Gospel.

Three times within this account, the evangelist speaks of Jesus being "lifted up" (*hypsōo*) on the cross (3:14; 8:28; 12:32). The Greek verb *hypsōo* has two meanings: "to raise" as in raising up a cross and "to exalt" or to glorify. In John's narrative, the lifting up of Jesus on the cross *is* his exaltation. For on the cross, Jesus' work of salvation is accomplished (19:30). This realization even leads Paul to speak of "boasting" in the cross of Christ in his letter to the Galatians (6:14).

Today's Gospel reading draws a parallel between Moses lifting up the serpent in the desert (today's first reading) and the lifting up of Jesus. Moses' action brought healing to those who had sinned through their lack of faith in the ways of God. Jesus' crucifixion brings eternal life to those who believe in Jesus as *the* "way" of God (John 14:6). No wonder the cross is a universal sign for Christians, that looking at it we remember and embrace the saving work of God in Christ. Let us glory in the cross of Christ, for by it we are saved and made free.

• In Numbers, the people are healed by looking at the bronze serpent; in John, we are redeemed by believing in Jesus. How might looking and believing be related?

• In the second reading, what opposites do you find? What do they tell us about this central mystery of our faith?

• When have you experienced new life arising from deep suffering or death?

• What cross are you carrying now? Can you see any potential for new life from it?

September 21, 2008

READING I   *Isaiah 55:6—9*

Seek the LORD while he may be found,
    call him while he is near.
Let the scoundrel forsake his way,
    and the wicked his thoughts;
let him turn to the LORD for mercy;
    to our God, who is generous in forgiving.
For my thoughts are not your thoughts,
    nor are your ways my ways, says the LORD.
As high as the heavens are above the earth,
    so high are my ways above your ways
    and my thoughts above your thoughts.

READING II   *Philippians 1:20c—24, 27a*

Brothers and sisters:

Christ will be magnified in my body, whether by life or by death. For to me life is Christ, and death is gain. If I go on living in the flesh, that means fruitful labor for me. And I do not know which I shall choose. I am caught between the two. I long to depart this life and be with Christ, for that is far better. Yet that I remain in the flesh is more necessary for your benefit.

Only, conduct yourselves in a way worthy of the gospel of Christ.

GOSPEL   *Matthew 20:1—16a*

Jesus told his disciples this parable:

"The kingdom of heaven is like a landowner who went out at dawn to hire laborers for his vineyard. After agreeing with them for the usual daily wage, he sent them into his vineyard. Going out about nine o'clock, the landowner saw others standing idle in the marketplace, and he said to them, 'You too go into my vineyard, and I will give you what is just.' So they went off. And he went out again around noon, and around three o'clock, and did likewise. Going out about five o'clock, the landowner found others standing around, and said to them, 'Why do you stand here idle all day?' They answered, 'Because no one has hired us.' He said to them, 'You too go into my vineyard.' When it was evening the owner of the vineyard said to his foreman, 'Summon the laborers and give them their pay, beginning with the last and ending with the first.' When those who had started about five o'clock came, each received the usual daily wage. So when the first came, they thought that they would receive more, but each of them also got the usual wage. And on receiving it they grumbled against the landowner, saying, 'These last ones worked only one hour, and you have made them equal to us, who bore the day's burden and the heat.' He said to one of them in reply, 'My friend, I am not cheating you. Did you not agree with me for the usual daily wage? Take what is yours and go. What if I wish to give this last one the same as you? Or am I not free to do as I wish with my own money? Are you envious because I am generous?' Thus, the last will be first, and the first will be last."

Practice of Prayer

Psalm 145:2–3, 8–9, 17–18 (18a)

R. The Lord is near to all who call upon him.

Every day will I bless you,
    and I will praise your name forever and ever.
Great is the LORD and highly to be praised;
    his greatness is unsearchable. R.

The LORD is gracious and merciful,
    slow to anger and of great kindness.
The LORD is good to all
    and compassionate toward all his works. R.

The LORD is just in all his ways
    and holy in all his works.
The LORD is near to all who call upon him,
    to all who call upon him in truth. R.

Practice of Charity

Today, three billion people live on less than $2 a day. Whether in remote villages of Mozambique, in Guatemalan shantytowns, or on depleted farmland in Peru, many of these people live in families headed by heavily burdened women. Such women not only carry most of the responsibility for childcare and household chores, but often are the primary wage earners as well. They can earn crucially needed income by selling food door to door or selling homemade craft items. But micro-businesses such as these need startup income, and even $40 can constitute a woman's entire life savings. Banks do not make loans to people in these situations. However, Acción International, a nonprofit organization, has assisted over three million women with micro loans of $50 to $150. Prosperity results for the business owner, her family, and her community. A remarkable 97 percent of borrowers repay their loans on time. Learn more at www.accion.org.

Scripture Insights

"I long to depart this life and be with Christ," says Paul in the second reading. What do these words say to us about the depth, the faith, the prayer of the man who uttered them? Paul is not speaking out of depression, even though he is imprisoned at the time he writes this (Philippians 1:7, 17). His words come from a deep desire within his heart and a strong conviction of faith. "For to me life is Christ, and death is gain."

As a Pharisee (Philippians 3:5), Paul would have believed in the resurrection of the dead even prior to his conversion to Christ (Acts 23:6). But it is not just resurrected life for which Paul longs; it is to be with Christ in the fullness of his glory. Not only had the risen Christ appeared to him at his conversion, Paul had even glimpsed the glory of paradise in some type of mystical prayer experience, described in 2 Corinthians 12:1–4.

Paul's personal experience of Christ rooted him firmly in Christ. "I consider everything as a loss because of the supreme good of knowing Christ Jesus my Lord" (Philippians 3:8). One could even say that Paul lived and breathed Christ: "I live, no longer I, but Christ lives in me" (Galatians 2:20).

What a model for us to ponder! But how does one attain such Christ-centeredness? To be sure, Paul's personal experience of Jesus was gift and grace. But it is also true that we can open ourselves to grace in various ways—by being faithful to prayer, reading scripture, fasting, meditating on the sacred, and other acts of devotion which help to cultivate a personal relationship with the Lord Jesus. Certainly Paul was a man of prayer and devotion. Let us cultivate practices that we, too, may be open to the graces, the nearness of Christ.

◆ How might the first reading help us understand the parable in the Gospel reading?

◆ What are some practices that have helped you cultivate a personal relationship with the Lord Jesus?

◆ What understanding and feelings do you have about death?

September 28, 2008

READING I *Ezekiel 18:25—28*

Thus says the LORD:

You say, "The LORD's way is not fair!" Hear now, house of Israel: Is it my way that is unfair, or rather, are not your ways unfair? When someone virtuous turns away from virtue to commit iniquity, and dies, it is because of the iniquity he committed that he must die. But if he turns from the wickedness he has committed, and does what is right and just, he shall preserve his life; since he has turned away from all the sins that he has committed, he shall surely live, he shall not die.

READING II *Philippians 2:1—11*

Shorter: Philippians 2:1– 5

Brothers and sisters:

If there is any encouragement in Christ, any solace in love, any participation in the Spirit, any compassion and mercy, complete my joy by being of the same mind, with the same love, united in heart, thinking one thing. Do nothing out of selfishness or out of vainglory; rather, humbly regard others as more important than yourselves, each looking out not for his own interests, but also for those of others.

Have in you the same attitude
    that is also in Christ Jesus,
        Who, though he was in the form of God,
        did not regard equality with God
        something to be grasped.
    Rather, he emptied himself,
        taking the form of a slave,
        coming in human likeness;
        and found human in appearance,
    he humbled himself,
        becoming obedient to the point of death,
        even death on a cross.

Because of this, God greatly exalted him
    and bestowed on him the name
    which is above every name,
    that at the name of Jesus
    every knee should bend,
    of those in heaven and on earth
        and under the earth,
    and every tongue confess that
    Jesus Christ is Lord,
    to the glory of God the Father.

GOSPEL *Matthew 21:28—32*

Jesus said to the chief priests and elders of the people:

"What is your opinion? A man had two sons. He came to the first and said, 'Son, go out and work in the vineyard today.' He said in reply, 'I will not,' but afterwards changed his mind and went. The man came to the other son and gave the same order. He said in reply, 'Yes, sir,' but did not go. Which of the two did his father's will?" They answered, "The first." Jesus said to them, "Amen, I say to you, tax collectors and prostitutes are entering the kingdom of God before you. When John came to you in the way of righteousness, you did not believe him; but tax collectors and prostitutes did. Yet even when you saw that, you did not later change your minds and believe him."

Practice of Prayer

Psalm 25:4—5, 6—7, 8—9 (6a)

R. Remember your mercies, O Lord.

Your ways, O Lord, make known to me;
    teach me your paths,
guide me in your truth and teach me,
    for you are God my savior. R.

Remember that your compassion, O Lord,
    and your love are from of old.
The sins of my youth and
        my frailties remember not;
    in your kindness remember me,
    because of your goodness,
        O Lord. R.

Good and upright is the Lord;
    thus he shows sinners the way.
He guides the humble to justice,
    and teaches the humble his way. R.

Practice of Hope

California's Folsom State Prison, confining 5,000 inmates, is a fear-some place. Beyond the forbidding environment, regimentation, gang tensions, and overcrowding is the incessant noise. Violent yelling is frequent. Six years ago a small group of men searching for quiet discovered a room above the chapel. A volunteer introduced them to Father Thomas Keating's book, *Open Mind, Open Heart,* which teaches the meditation technique of Centering Prayer. After going through a maze of procedures, the men obtained permission for a regular Friday night prayer group. As the group grew, its members convened an unprecedented meeting of all the prison's rival gang leaders. The prayer group was declared neutral turf, exempt from the territorial boundaries between racial groups. The Contemplative Fellowship now numbers 400, and it has made a life-changing difference to many inmates. Learn about Centering Prayer at www.centeringprayer.com.

Scripture Insights

"Doing the will of the Father" is a recurring theme in the Gospel according to Matthew. It is the gauge of our relationship with Jesus: "For whoever does the will of my heavenly Father is my brother, and sister, and mother" (Matthew 12:50). It is the criterion by which people will be judged worthy of entering the kingdom of heaven. "Not everyone who says to me, 'Lord, Lord' will enter the kingdom of heaven, but only the one who does the will of my Father in heaven" (Matthew 7:21).

By means of the parable in today's Gospel reading, Jesus had the chief priests and elders—the leaders of the people—pass judgment on themselves. Interestingly, the point of reference is not Jesus' preaching, but that of John the Baptist.

The context of today's Gospel story is significant. It takes place in Jerusalem, in the final week of Jesus' life. Earlier in chapter 21, Matthew recounts Jesus' entry into Jerusalem and his cleansing of the temple. The chief priests and scribes are "indignant" when the people acclaim Jesus as the "Son of David"—a title with clear messianic overtones (21:15). This reading is part of a tense discussion with the chief priests and elders about Jesus' authority that begins in verse 23. It is here that Jesus first brings up their refusal to believe John the Baptist.

At the time John was baptizing, "Jerusalem, all Judea and the whole region around the Jordan were going out to him and were being baptized . . . as they acknowledged their sins," but the Pharisees and Sadducees were notable exceptions (3:5–10). They would not recognize "the way of righteousness" John preached. Tax collectors, scorned as agents of the Roman government, and prostitutes, notorious sinners, did recognize it. They are the ones who did the will of the Father and produced good fruit as evidence of their repentance. Our response can be no less.

♦ Why is Psalm 25 an appropriate response to today's readings?

♦ How can we know God's will?

♦ In what ways do you have difficulty doing what God asks?

READING I   *Isaiah 5:1—7*

Let me now sing of my friend,
    my friend's song concerning his vineyard.
My friend had a vineyard
    on a fertile hillside;
he spaded it, cleared it of stones,
    and planted the choicest vines;
within it he built a watchtower,
    and hewed out a wine press.
Then he looked for the crop of grapes,
    but what it yielded was wild grapes.

Now, inhabitants of Jerusalem and
      people of Judah,
    judge between me and my vineyard:
What more was there to do for my vineyard
    that I had not done?
Why, when I looked for the crop of grapes,
    did it bring forth wild grapes?
Now, I will let you know
    what I mean to do with my vineyard:
take away its hedge, give it to grazing,
    break through its wall, let it be trampled!
Yes, I will make it a ruin:
    it shall not be pruned or hoed,
    but overgrown with thorns and briers;
I will command the clouds
    not to send rain upon it.
The vineyard of the LORD of hosts
      is the house of Israel,
    and the people of Judah
      are his cherished plant;
he looked for judgment, but see, bloodshed!
    for justice, but hark, the outcry!

READING II   *Philippians 4:6—9*

Brothers and sisters:

Have no anxiety at all, but in everything, by prayer and petition, with thanksgiving, make your requests known to God. Then the peace of God that surpasses all understanding will guard your hearts and minds in Christ Jesus.

Finally, brothers and sisters, whatever is true, whatever is honorable, whatever is just, whatever is pure, whatever is lovely, whatever is gracious, if there is any excellence and if there is anything worthy of praise, think about these things. Keep on doing what you have learned and received and heard and seen in me. Then the God of peace will be with you.

GOSPEL   *Matthew 21:33—43*

Jesus said to the chief priests and the elders of the people:

"Hear another parable. There was a landowner who planted a vineyard, put a hedge around it, dug a wine press in it, and built a tower. Then he leased it to tenants and went on a journey. When vintage time drew near, he sent his servants to the tenants to obtain his produce. But the tenants seized the servants and one they beat, another they killed, and a third they stoned. Again he sent other servants, more numerous than the first ones, but they treated them in the same way. Finally, he sent his son to them, thinking, 'They will respect my son.' But when the tenants saw the son, they said to one another, 'This is the heir. Come, let us kill him and acquire his inheritance.' They seized him, threw him out of the vineyard, and killed him. What will the owner of the vineyard do to those tenants when he comes?" They answered him, "He will put those wretched men to a wretched death and lease his vineyard to other tenants who will give him the produce at the proper times." Jesus said to them, "Did you never read in the Scriptures:

The stone that the builders rejected
    has become the cornerstone;
by the Lord has this been done,
    and it is wonderful in our eyes?

Therefore, I say to you, the kingdom of God will be taken away from you and given to a people that will produce its fruit."

Practice of Prayer

Psalm 80:9, 12, 13—14, 15—16, 19—20
(Isaiah 5:7a)

R. The vineyard of the Lord is the house of Israel.

A vine from Egypt you transplanted;
    you drove away the nations and planted it.
It put forth its foliage to the Sea,
    its shoots as far as the River.   R.

Why have you broken down its walls,
    so that every passer-by plucks its fruit,
the boar from the forest lays it waste,
    and the beasts of the field feed upon it?   R.

Once again, O Lord of hosts,
    look down from heaven, and see;
take care of this vine,
    and protect what your right hand has planted,
    the son of man whom
        you yourself made strong.   R.

Then we will no more withdraw from you;
    give us new life, and we will call
        upon your name.
O Lord, God of hosts, restore us;
    if your face shine upon us,
        then we shall be saved.   R.

Practice of Charity

In 1977, Wangari Maathai founded the Green Belt Movement. Deforestation in Kenya had brought dwindling water supplies, soil degradation, and hardships for millions of rural women. Dr. Maathai's organization hired these women to plant trees.

Her plan made a difference in many lives; it also brought attacks from the authoritarian government. Despite imprisonment, in 2002 she was elected to Parliament with 98 percent of the vote. In 2004, with 30 million new trees planted, Dr. Maathai was awarded the Nobel Peace Prize. For $20, Green Belt Movement International can support two women to plant 20 trees. Visit www.greenbeltmovement.org.

Scripture Insights

"The vineyard of the Lord of hosts is the house of Israel," says Isaiah toward the end of today's reading. There can be no doubt that Matthew also speaks of the vineyard of the house of Israel. Matthew's focus, however, is not so much the vineyard, which becomes the kingdom of God at the end of the reading, but rather, its tenants. The Lectionary omits a later verse, which clearly identifies the chief priests and scribes with the tenants. In the course of Matthew's account of the Gospel, the Jewish leaders' opposition to Jesus steadily increased and culminated in Jesus' death. It is to them that the parable is addressed.

In today's reading, the chief priests and scribes pronounce judgment on themselves. But later in chapter 23, Jesus will pronounce judgment on the Jewish leaders, the wretched tenants of God's vineyard. Like the tenants in the parable, the Jewish leaders rejected and killed the Son. Matthew, ever ready to present Jesus as the fulfillment of the Old Testament, portrays him drawing on a verse from Psalm 118 to demonstrate the triumph of God's plan: "The stone that the builders rejected has become the cornerstone. . . ." The Greek phrase *kephalen gonias*, translated as "cornerstone" is best understood as "keystone," that stone at the center of an arch which holds the structure together. The early Christians especially loved this text as a description of Jesus (Acts 4:11; 1 Peter 2:7), and it expresses their understanding of themselves as a building built and supported by him.

Today's readings call us to examine ourselves. What kind of tenants are we? May we never be found negligent.

◆ Jesus has used the imagery of vines and grapes in other places. What additional meaning might that lend to today's readings?

◆ How might the "servants" sent by the Lord be rejected today?

◆ How do you see yourself and your faith community as tenants of the kingdom?

READING I   *Isaiah 25:6—10a*

On this mountain the LORD of hosts
> will provide for all peoples
a feast of rich food and choice wines,
> juicy, rich food and pure, choice wines.
On this mountain he will destroy
> the veil that veils all peoples,
the web that is woven over all nations;
> he will destroy death forever.
The Lord GOD will wipe away
> the tears from every face;
the reproach of his people he will remove
> from the whole earth;
> > for the LORD has spoken.
> On that day it will be said:
"Behold our God, to whom we looked to
> > save us!
> This is the LORD for whom we looked;
> let us rejoice and be glad that he has
> > saved us!"
For the hand of the LORD will rest
> on this mountain.

READING II   *Philippians 4:12—14, 19—20*

Brothers and sisters: I know how to live in humble circumstances; I know also how to live with abundance. In every circumstance and in all things I have learned the secret of being well fed and of going hungry, of living in abundance and of being in need. I can do all things in him who strengthens me. Still, it was kind of you to share in my distress.

My God will fully supply whatever you need, in accord with his glorious riches in Christ Jesus. To our God and Father, glory forever and ever. Amen.

GOSPEL   *Matthew 22:1—14*

Shorter: Matthew 22:1–10

Jesus again in reply spoke to the chief priests and elders of the people in parables, saying, "The kingdom of heaven may be likened to a king who gave a wedding feast for his son. He dispatched his servants to summon the invited guests to the feast, but they refused to come. A second time he sent other servants, saying, 'Tell those invited: "Behold, I have prepared my banquet, my calves and fattened cattle are killed, and everything is ready; come to the feast." ' Some ignored the invitation and went away, one to his farm, another to his business. The rest laid hold of his servants, mistreated them, and killed them. The king was enraged and sent his troops, destroyed those murderers, and burned their city. Then he said to his servants, 'The feast is ready, but those who were invited were not worthy to come. Go out, therefore, into the main roads and invite to the feast whomever you find.' The servants went out into the streets and gathered all they found, bad and good alike, and the hall was filled with guests. But when the king came in to meet the guests, he saw a man there not dressed in a wedding garment. The king said to him, 'My friend, how is it that you came in here without a wedding garment?' But he was reduced to silence. Then the king said to his attendants, 'Bind his hands and feet, and cast him into the darkness outside, where there will be wailing and grinding of teeth.' Many are invited, but few are chosen."

Practice of Prayer

Psalm 23:1–3a, 3b–4, 5, 6 (6cd)

R. I shall live in the house of the
          Lord all the days of my life.

The Lord is my shepherd; I shall not want.
     In verdant pastures he gives me repose;
beside restful waters he leads me;
     he refreshes my soul.   R.

He guides me in right paths
     for his name's sake.
Even though I walk in the dark valley
     I fear no evil; for you are at my side
with your rod and your staff
     that give me courage.   R.

You spread the table before me
     in the sight of my foes;
you anoint my head with oil;
     my cup overflows.   R.

Only goodness and kindness follow me
     all the days of my life;
and I shall dwell in the house of the Lord
     for years to come.   R.

Practice of Charity

In filling out their online wedding gift registry, Justin Alexander and Jenny Elliott made some unusual requests. The couple, who had met doing volunteer work on the West Bank, told a reporter for the *Chicago Tribune* that they plan to return to humanitarian service in the Middle East eventually. "The life we lead is rather transient," Justin said, "and it has allowed us to realize that we are not really the ones in need." So instead of china or silver, the couple requested donations to various charities. Their thoughtfulness reflects a concern among some young people about the lavishness of some weddings. The I Do Foundation, a non-profit agency, offers couples a variety of ways to share part of their wedding spending with charities. For instance, brides can donate their dresses, and favors for guests at the reception can instead be charitable donations made in the couple's name. Learn more at www.idfoundation.org.

Scripture Insights

As told by Jesus, the parables were stories that left his listeners "hanging," having to ponder the meaning for themselves. As retold in the Gospels, the parables often include the interpretations given them by the early Church. The parable in today's Gospel both interprets and leaves us hanging.

The predominant image in today's parable is the wedding feast. The Greek noun *gamos* (marriage) occurs eight times, although unfortunately, this is not evident in the English translation. In the Old Testament, God's covenant with Israel is often described as a marriage relationship (Isaiah 54:6, 62:5; Hosea 2:16–22). The New Testament continues this image, often speaking of Jesus as the bridegroom.

Today's parable points to the new reality that has come about through the presence, teaching, and ministry of Jesus. The promises of old are fulfilled: "The kingdom of heaven is at hand" (Matthew 4:17), the bridegroom is among us. Emmanuel, God, is with us. "The feast is ready."

This Good News was first announced to the Jewish people, but not all believed. The reference to the armed attack and burning of the city in today's Gospel reading has been understood with reference to the destruction of Jerusalem by the Romans in 70 AD—an event Matthew's community saw as divine punishment for the Jewish leaders' rejection of Jesus. At the end of Matthew's account of the Gospel, the disciples are sent to "invite" all nations (Matthew 28:19), that is, the Gentiles, to the wedding feast. Many of them believed, and some were members of Matthew's community.

What about our response to the invitation? Do we have our "wedding garment"? May we live now in such a way that we will never be "cast out."

• How does "God's banquet" appear in today's other readings?

• What attire is required of us for the royal wedding banquet?

• How have you accepted or refused the invitations God has given you?

October 19, 2008

READING I *Isaiah 45:1, 4—6*

Thus says the LORD to his anointed, Cyrus,
   whose right hand I grasp,
subduing nations before him,
   and making kings run in his service,
opening doors before him
   and leaving the gates unbarred:
For the sake of Jacob, my servant,
   of Israel, my chosen one,
I have called you by your name,
   giving you a title, though you knew
      me not.
I am the LORD and there is no other,
   there is no God besides me.
It is I who arm you, though you know me not,
   so that toward the rising and
      the setting of the sun
   people may know that there
      is none besides me.
I am the LORD, there is no other.

READING II *1 Thessalonians 1:1—5b*

Paul, Silvanus, and Timothy to the church of the Thessalonians in God the Father and the Lord Jesus Christ: grace to you and peace. We give thanks to God always for all of you, remembering you in our prayers, unceasingly calling to mind your work of faith and labor of love and endurance in hope of our Lord Jesus Christ, before our God and Father, knowing, brothers and sisters loved by God, how you were chosen. For our gospel did not come to you in word alone, but also in power and in the Holy Spirit and with much conviction.

GOSPEL *Matthew 22:15—21*

The Pharisees went off and plotted how they might entrap Jesus in speech. They sent their disciples to him, with the Herodians, saying, "Teacher, we know that you are a truthful man and that you teach the way of God in accordance with the truth. And you are not concerned with anyone's opinion, for you do not regard a person's status. Tell us, then, what is your opinion: Is it lawful to pay the census tax to Caesar or not?" Knowing their malice, Jesus said, "Why are you testing me, you hypocrites? Show me the coin that pays the census tax." Then they handed him the Roman coin. He said to them, "Whose image is this and whose inscription?" They replied, "Caesar's." At that he said to them, "Then repay to Caesar what belongs to Caesar and to God what belongs to God."

Practice of Prayer

Psalm 96: 1, 3, 4—5, 7—8, 9—10 (7b)

R. Give the Lord glory and honor.

Sing to the LORD a new song;
    sing to the LORD, all you lands.
Tell his glory among the nations;
    among all peoples, his wondrous deeds. R.

For great is the LORD and highly to be praised;
    awesome is he, beyond all gods.
For all the gods of the nations are things of nought,
    but the LORD made the heavens. R.

Give to the LORD, you families of nations,
    give to the LORD glory and praise;
    give to the LORD the glory due his name!
Bring gifts, and enter his courts. R.

Worship the LORD, in holy attire;
    tremble before him, all the earth;
say among the nations: The LORD is king,
    he governs the peoples with equity. R.

Practice of Faith

Christ instructs, "Repay to Caesar what belongs to Caesar and to God what belongs to God." In response, every four years since 1976 the Catholic Bishops of the United States have produced a statement in advance of the election: "Faithful Citizenship: A Catholic Call to Political Responsibility." The 2004 edition of this document states, "Politics in this election year and beyond should be about an old idea with new power—the common good. The central question should not be, 'Are you better off than you were four years ago?' It should be, 'How can we—all of us, especially the weak and vulnerable—be better off in the years ahead? How can we protect and promote human life and dignity? How can we pursue greater justice and peace?'" The document details principles of Catholic social teaching to serve as yardsticks for voters. Before you vote, read this year's statement at www.usccb.org.

Scripture Insights

Initially, today's first reading may take us by surprise. Cyrus? The Lord's anointed? Cyrus was the Persian king who conquered Babylon during the exile, thus winning freedom for the Jewish people. Isaiah speaks of him as the Lord's "anointed" (literally, *messiah*), the agent God used on behalf of his chosen people even though Cyrus did not "know" God (Isaiah 45:4,5); that is, was not in covenant relationship with him as a member of the chosen people).

The books of Ezra and Nehemiah recount the Jews' return to Jerusalem and re-building of the temple and city, showing how the people appropriately "repaid" both God and the government their respective dues. There was no doubt, however, that God was God and no other ruler was more supreme.

In today's Gospel reading, the conflict between Jesus and the Jewish leaders continues. Today, the Pharisees are in the spotlight. Enlisting the aid of the Herodians, who were supporters of the ruling dynasty of Herod the Great and thus loyal to Rome, the Pharisees are trying to put allegiance to the government in conflict with covenant ("lawful") fidelity to God. In effect, the Pharisees are playing from both sides in order to entrap Jesus. In response, Jesus affirms the just claims of both, "Repay to Caesar what belongs to Caesar and to God what belongs to God."

What belongs to God is, of course, everything and everyone. How fittingly today's responsorial psalm acclaims, "Give the Lord glory and honor. . . . The gods of the nations are things of naught. . . . The Lord is king." Let us pray, this day, for a heightened awareness that *all* belongs to God. Let us render the tribute that is rightly due.

◆ How does the psalm echo the first reading and Gospel reading?

◆ Could any current world leaders be viewed as God's "anointed"? Why or why not?

◆ What do today's scriptures suggest about our own involvement in the civic or political arena?

October 26, 2008

READING I *Exodus 22:20—26*

Thus says the LORD:

"You shall not molest or oppress an alien, for you were once aliens yourselves in the land of Egypt. You shall not wrong any widow or orphan. If ever you wrong them and they cry out to me, I will surely hear their cry. My wrath will flare up, and I will kill you with the sword; then your own wives will be widows, and your children orphans.

"If you lend money to one of your poor neighbors among my people, you shall not act like an extortioner toward him by demanding interest from him. If you take your neighbor's cloak as a pledge, you shall return it to him before sunset; for this cloak of his is the only covering he has for his body. What else has he to sleep in? If he cries out to me, I will hear him; for I am compassionate."

READING II *1 Thessalonians 1:5c—10*

Brothers and sisters:

You know what sort of people we were among you for your sake. And you became imitators of us and of the Lord, receiving the word in great affliction, with joy from the Holy Spirit, so that you became a model for all the believers in Macedonia and in Achaia. For from you the word of the Lord has sounded forth not only in Macedonia and in Achaia, but in every place your faith in God has gone forth, so that we have no need to say anything. For they themselves openly declare about us what sort of reception we had among you, and how you turned to God from idols to serve the living and true God and to await his Son from heaven, whom he raised from the dead, Jesus, who delivers us from the coming wrath.

GOSPEL *Matthew 22:34—40*

When the Pharisees heard that Jesus had silenced the Sadducees, they gathered together, and one of them, a scholar of the law, tested him by asking, "Teacher, which commandment in the law is the greatest?" He said to him, "You shall love the Lord, your God, with all your heart, with all your soul, and with all your mind. This is the greatest and the first commandment. The second is like it: You shall love your neighbor as yourself. The whole law and the prophets depend on these two commandments."

Practice of Prayer

Psalm 18:2–3, 3–4, 47, 51 (2)

R. I love you, Lord, my strength.

I love you, O LORD, my strength
   O LORD, my rock, my fortress,
      my deliverer. R.

My God, my rock of refuge,
   my shield, the horn of
      my salvation, my stronghold!
Praised be the LORD, I exclaim,
   and I am safe from my enemies. R.

The LORD lives and blessed be my rock!
   Extolled be God my savior.
You who gave great victories to your king
   and showed kindness to your anointed. R.

Practice of Charity

Today's reading from Exodus conveys God's concern for widows and orphans. In contemporary times, the Joint United Nations Programme on HIV/AIDS conveys the same concern, estimating that by 2010 the number of AIDS orphans will total at least 25 million. This is a population larger than many nations! In the meantime, economies of nations suffering high rates of the disease are slowed drastically as skilled workers die. Shortages of farm workers to tend the crops mean a dwindling food supply.

Catholic Relief Services (CRS) works to combat conditions that give AIDS a foothold: poverty, lack of knowledge, and inequality. Various CRS projects in more than forty countries serve nearly two million people who have the disease. In Nigeria, CRS has built an HIV/AIDS prevention center. In South Africa, the organization works to improve home health care for infected persons. And in Ethiopia, CRS supports AIDS orphans. To contribute or to learn more, visit www.crs.org.

Scripture Insights

Sometimes it helps to spell things out—that is exactly what today's first reading does with respect to the Gospel reading. It's easy to assume that we're obeying the two great commandments. Of course we love God and our neighbors! But what if the theoretical is brought down to the practical level? That practical level was important to Israel—and to Jesus.

The laws Jesus recites in today's Gospel reading appear in the Old Testament: the first, in Deuteronomy 6:5, part of the Shema (Hebrew for *hear*), a prayer that Jews recited three times a day; the second, in Leviticus 19:18, one of many laws of conduct meant to keep Israel set apart or consecrated to the Lord.

The first reading from Exodus is also an excerpt from the Laws. In fact, from Exodus 19:1 to Numbers 10:10 the Laws continue, following the description of Israel's encampment at Mt. Sinai on the way to the Promised Land. While many of those Laws come from a later period, their placement alongside the original ones suggests that they were understood to show how the people remained faithful to the covenant in new situations, such as when they settled in the new land.

Today's readings might be summarized as follows: Do unto others as I have done unto you; for I am compassionate. The Israelites had only to remember that they had once been slaves to recall what God had done for them. This they must do for others.

The Gospel reading is, again, tense with conflict. Jesus is questioned, literally "tested," by a "scholar of the law," an expert. How ironic—the "scholar of the law" testing the Son of the Giver of the Law, the one who came "not to abolish but to fulfill" the law and the prophets! Let us pray that we might always live in a manner that is indeed the fulfillment of the "law and the prophets."

◆ How does today's first reading "translate" for our own time?

◆ What sort of experience would inspire the author of today's responsorial psalm?

◆ What exactly does it mean to show compassion? When have you experienced compassion?

November 2, 2008

READING I   *Wisdom 3:1—9*

See Lectionary for alternate readings.

The souls of the just are in the hand of God,
  and no torment shall touch them.
They seemed, in the view of the foolish, to be dead;
  and their passing away was
    thought an affliction
  and their going forth from us,
    utter destruction.
But they are in peace.
For if before men, indeed they be punished,
  yet is their hope full of immortality;
chastised a little, they shall be greatly blessed,
  because God tried them
  and found them worthy of himself.
As gold in the furnace, he proved them,
  and as sacrificial offerings he
    took them to himself.
In the time of their visitation they shall shine,
  and shall dart about as sparks through stubble;
they shall judge nations and rule over peoples,
  and the LORD shall be their King forever.
Those who trust in him shall understand truth,
  and the faithful shall abide with him in love:
Because grace and mercy are with his holy ones,
  and his care is with the elect.

READING II   *Romans 5:5—11*

See Lectionary for alternate readings.

Brothers and sisters:
Hope does not disappoint,
  because the love of God has been
    poured out into our hearts
  through the Holy Spirit that has
    been given to us.
For Christ, while we were still helpless,
  died at the appointed time for the ungodly.
Indeed, only with difficulty does
    one die for a just person,
  though perhaps for a good person
  one might even find courage to die.
But God proves his love for us
  in that while we were still
    sinners Christ died for us.

How much more then, since we are
    now justified by his Blood,
  will we be saved through him from the wrath.
Indeed, if, while we were enemies,
  we were reconciled to God
    through the death of his Son,
  how much more, once reconciled,
  will we be saved by his life.
Not only that,
  but we also boast of God through
    our Lord Jesus Christ,
  through whom we have now
    received reconciliation.

GOSPEL   *Matthew 11:25—30*

See Lectionary for alternate readings.

At that time Jesus exclaimed:
"I give praise to you, Father, Lord of
    heaven and earth,
  for although you have hidden these things
    from the wise and the learned
  you have revealed them to little ones.
Yes, Father, such has been your gracious will.
All things have been handed over
    to me by my Father.
No one knows the Son except the Father,
  and no one knows the Father except the Son
  and anyone to whom the Son
    wishes to reveal him.

"Come to me, all you who labor and are burdened,
  and I will give you rest.
Take my yoke upon you and learn from me,
  for I am meek and humble of heart;
  and you will find rest for yourselves.
For my yoke is easy, and my burden light."

Practice of Prayer

Psalm 23:1 — 3a, 3b — 4, 5, 6 (1) (4ab)
See Lectionary for alternate readings.

R. The Lord is my shepherd;
    there is nothing I shall want. or

R. Though I walk in the valley of darkness,
    I fear no evil, for you are with me.

The LORD is my shepherd; I shall not want.
    In verdant pastures he gives me repose;
beside restful waters he leads me;
    he refreshes my soul.   R.

He guides me in right paths
    for his name's sake.
Even though I walk in the dark valley
    I fear no evil; for you are at my side
with your rod and your staff
    that give me courage.   R.

You spread the table before me
    in the sight of my foes;
you anoint my head with oil;
    my cup overflows.   R.

Only goodness and kindness follow me
    all the days of my life;
and I shall dwell in the house of the LORD
    for years to come.   R.

Practice of Faith

Yesterday we celebrated God's own ingathering: the saints. Today we remember the faithful departed. Having in common the tender care of God, together we all form one magnificent community, the communion of saints. Mexican families celebrate this communion with zest, picnicking in cemeteries during *Días de los Muertos,* the Days of the Dead. In your home, you could display photos of your family's beloved dead this November. Near the photos, place a white candle on a white cloth, recalling Easter Resurrection. Burn your Easter candle while telling favorite stories about each remembered loved one.

Scripture Insights

Today's scriptures offer us beautiful imagery with which to pray and to hope on behalf of our departed loved ones. "The souls of the just are in the *hand* of God." — and how loving that hand is, the hand that created and formed us (Isaiah 43:1), the hand that takes us to himself (last line, second stanza of the Wisdom reading). God's hand leads us through the dark valley (in today's psalm) to streams of life-giving water, and sets before us a heavenly banquet. *This* is the destiny for which God's hand has created us—and to which he ever faithfully leads us.

Today's scriptures also speak of our eternal destiny as *rest.* The Greek noun *anapausis* (Psalm 23:3; Matthew 11:29) and its related verb *anapauo* (Matthew 11:28) mean rest and repose, but also refreshment, revival. Yet another image of revival and transformation occurs in today's first reading. In verse 7, the souls of the just are said to shine and be like sparks. Similar imagery is found in Daniel 12:3, where "those who sleep in the dust of the earth shall awake" and the righteous will shine like stars. In Daniel 8:10, the stars are angelic beings. Daniel and the author of the book of Wisdom believe that after death, the just will be transformed into angelic beings. This same view is expressed by Jesus in the Gospels, as in Mark 12:25.

What glory awaits us! What joy and peace! Today, let us pray for those who have died. Let us ask for the intercession of those who are in the kingdom for our faithful departed and for ourselves. May we never lose sight of our destiny.

• What is the basis of our hope according to Romans 5?

• How do you understand "eternal rest"?

• Which images from today's scriptures would be especially helpful to use when praying with someone who has recently lost a loved one?

• Which of these scriptures is particularly helpful to you in contemplating your own death?

READING I   Ezekiel 47:1—2, 8—9, 12

The angel brought me
     back to the entrance of the temple,
     and I saw water flowing out
     from beneath the threshold of
         the temple toward the east,
     for the facade of the temple was
         toward the east;
     the water flowed down from the
         southern side of the temple,
     south of the altar.
He led me outside by the north gate,
     and around to the outer gate facing the east,
     where I saw water trickling from
         the southern side.
He said to me,
     "This water flows into the eastern district
         down upon the Arabah,
     and empties into the sea, the salt waters,
         which it makes fresh.
Wherever the river flows,
     every sort of living creature that
         can multiply shall live,
     and there shall be abundant fish,
     for wherever this water comes,
         the sea shall be made fresh.
Along both banks of the river, fruit trees of
         every kind shall grow;
     their leaves shall not fade, nor their fruit fail.
Every month they shall bear fresh fruit,
     for they shall be watered by the
         flow from the sanctuary.
Their fruit shall serve for food, and
     their leaves for medicine."

READING II   1 Corinthians 3:9c—11, 16—17

Brothers and sisters:
You are God's building.
According to the grace of God given to me,
     like a wise master builder I laid a foundation,
     and another is building upon it.

But each one must be careful how
         he builds upon it,
     for no one can lay a foundation other than
         the one that is there,
     namely, Jesus Christ.

Do you not know that you are the temple of God,
     and that the Spirit of God dwells in you?
If anyone destroys God's temple,
     God will destroy that person;
     for the temple of God, which you are, is holy.

GOSPEL   John 2:13—22

Since the Passover of the Jews was near,
     Jesus went up to Jerusalem.
He found in the temple area those who sold
         oxen, sheep, and doves,
     as well as the money changers seated there.
He made a whip out of cords
     and drove them all out of the temple area,
with the sheep and oxen,
     and spilled the coins of the money changers
     and overturned their tables,
     and to those who sold doves he said,
     "Take these out of here,
     and stop making my Father's
         house a marketplace."
His disciples recalled the words of Scripture,
     Zeal for your house will consume me.
At this the Jews answered and said to him,
     "What sign can you show us for doing this?"
Jesus answered and said to them,
     "Destroy this temple and in
         three days I will raise it up."
The Jews said,
     "This temple has been under construction
         for forty-six years,
     and you will raise it up in three days?"
But he was speaking about the temple of his Body.
Therefore, when he was raised from the dead,
     his disciples remembered that he had said this,
     and they came to believe the Scripture
     and the word Jesus had spoken.

Practice of Prayer

Psalm 46:3, 4, 5—6, 8, 11 (5)

R. The waters of the river gladden the city of God,
the holy dwelling of the Most High.

God is our refuge and our strength,
    an ever-present help in distress.
Therefore we fear not, though the earth be shaken
    and mountains plunge into the
        depths of the sea. R.

There is a stream whose runlets
    gladden the city of God,
  the holy dwelling of the Most High.
God is in its midst; it shall not be disturbed;
  God will help it at the break of dawn. R.

The LORD of hosts is with us;
    our stronghold is the God of Jacob.
Come! behold the deeds of the LORD,
    the astounding things he has
        wrought on earth. R.

Practice of Hope

Today as we ponder a very special house of God, let us also give thanks for Mercy Housing. In 1981, the Sisters of Mercy of Omaha, Nebraska, founded Mercy Housing, a nonprofit corporation which has since grown to provide quality housing for families, seniors, the formerly homeless, and those suffering from HIV/AIDS and mental illness. Other Sisters of Mercy groups and other women religious have joined them as co-sponsors. Mercy Housing aims to build stable, healthy communities by networking with other agencies to provide social services at the properties. It manages its own properties, provides loans to builders of affordable housing, and advocates for affordable housing. Mercy properties can be found in the Midwest, the Southeast, the Southwest, California, Washington, and Idaho. Learn more at http://www.mercyhousing.org.

Scripture Insights

On this feast of the dedication of the basilica that is the seat of the Bishop of Rome, our Pope, we have a triptych of scripture texts on the dwelling places of God.

The Jerusalem temple figures prominently in both the first reading and the Gospel. Built at the time of King Solomon, it was a monumental shrine to the God of Israel (see 1 Kings 6:12–13; 7:13—8:66). Tragically, the temple was destroyed at the time of the Babylonian conquest of Jerusalem in the sixth century before Christ (see 2 Kings 25).

It was during this time that Ezekiel prophesied, and in chapters 40 to 47 he recounts his visions of a restored temple. What a message of hope this must have been to a despairing people! The focus of today's verses is clearly the life-giving water that flows from the temple. Not only will there be a restoration of the temple, but abundant life and healing for all.

Today's Gospel reading depicts Jesus in the rebuilt temple, driving out the moneychangers and sellers. In the last several lines of the reading there is a play on words: "he was speaking about the temple of his body." Jesus, the Incarnate Son, the Word made flesh, is the living, dwelling place of God (John 1:32–33; 14:10). We recall that water pours forth from his side as he hangs on the cross (John 19:34)—life and healing flow from him as they do from the temple in Ezekiel's vision!

Earlier in John's account of the Gospel, Jesus says: "Whoever loves me will keep my word, and my Father will love him, and we will come to him and make our *dwelling* with him" (John 14:23, emphasis added).

It is in this light that Paul, in today's second reading, can speak of the community of believers as the dwelling place of God. What an awe-inspiring reality and what a tremendous responsibility!

◆ How does Paul develop the image of the community as the temple of God in today's reading?

◆ In what places or people have you encountered God in a strong way?

◆ What care is to be shown to God's temple?

READING I   Proverbs 31:10—13, 1—20, 30—31

When one finds a worthy wife,
    her value is far beyond pearls.
Her husband, entrusting his heart to her,
    has an unfailing prize.
She brings him good, and not evil,
    all the days of her life.
She obtains wool and flax
    and works with loving hands.
She puts her hands to the distaff,
    and her fingers ply the spindle.
She reaches out her hands to the poor,
    and extends her arms to the needy.
Charm is deceptive and beauty fleeting;
    the woman who fears the LORD
        is to be praised.
Give her a reward for her labors,
    and let her works praise her at
        the city gates.

READING II   1 Thessalonians 5:1—6

Concerning times and seasons, brothers and sisters, you have no need for anything to be written to you. For you yourselves know very well that the day of the Lord will come like a thief at night. When people are saying, "Peace and security," then sudden disaster comes upon them, like labor pains upon a pregnant woman, and they will not escape.

But you, brothers and sisters, are not in darkness, for that day to overtake you like a thief. For all of you are children of the light and children of the day. We are not of the night or of darkness. Therefore, let us not sleep as the rest do, but let us stay alert and sober.

GOSPEL   Matthew 25:14—30

Shorter: Matthew 25:14—15, 19—21

Jesus told his disciples this parable:

"A man going on a journey called in his servants and entrusted his possessions to them. To one he gave five talents; to another, two; to a third, one—to each according to his ability. Then he went away. Immediately the one who received five talents went and traded with them, and made another five. Likewise, the one who received two made another two. But the man who received one went off and dug a hole in the ground and buried his master's money.

"After a long time the master of those servants came back and settled accounts with them. The one who had received five talents came forward bringing the additional five. He said, 'Master, you gave me five talents. See, I have made five more.' His master said to him, 'Well done, my good and faithful servant. Since you were faithful in small matters, I will give you great responsibilities. Come, share your master's joy.' Then the one who had received two talents also came forward and said, 'Master, you gave me two talents. See, I have made two more.' His master said to him, 'Well done, my good and faithful servant. Since you were faithful in small matters, I will give you great responsibilities. Come, share your master's joy.' Then the one who had received the one talent came forward and said, 'Master, I knew you were a demanding person, harvesting where you did not plant and gathering where you did not scatter; so out of fear I went off and buried your talent in the ground. Here it is back.' His master said to him in reply, 'You wicked, lazy servant! So you knew that I harvest where I did not plant and gather where I did not scatter? Should you not then have put my money in the bank so that I could have got it back with interest on my return? Now then! Take the talent from him and give it to the one with ten. For to everyone who has, more will be given and he will grow rich; but from the one who has not, even what he has will be taken away. And throw this useless servant into the darkness outside, where there will be wailing and grinding of teeth.'"

Practice of Prayer

Psalm 128:1–2, 3, 4–5 (see 1a)

R. Blessed are those who fear the Lord.

Blessed are you who fear the LORD,
    who walk in his ways!
For you shall eat the fruit of your handiwork;
    blessed shall you be, and favored.   R.

Your wife shall be like a fruitful vine
    in the recesses of your home;
your children like olive plants
    around your table.   R.

Behold, thus is the man blessed
    who fears the LORD.
The LORD bless you from Zion:
    may you see the prosperity of Jerusalem
    all the days of your life.   R.

Practice of Charity

Today's Gospel reading, which calls for the prudent use of resources, applies well to the work of the Catholic Campaign for Human Development (CCHD). CCHD was founded by the Catholic Bishops of the United States to ensure that the most precious resources of all, human industry and talent, have opportunities for expression. Since it began in 1970, CCHD has funded over seventy-eight hundred grants to self-help projects developed by grassroots groups of needy persons. The results have significantly changed lives. CCHD projects invite clients to participate in decisions and actions that affect their lives.

In most dioceses of the United States, the CCHD collection will take place at next weekend's liturgies at www.usccbcc.org/cchd.

Scripture Insight

Today's scriptures praise industriousness, whether it is the tireless "worthy" wife of Proverbs or the ingenious servants in the Gospel who doubled their master's investment. In contrast, there is no tolerance for the paralyzing fear that leads to inactivity, as we learn from the master's response to the third servant in the Gospel reading.

Today's Gospel reading is ultimately about the return of the Lord and the final judgment. The "man" in the first line has become the "master" (in the Greek, *kýrios* or *Lord*) later in verse 19. At the end of the reading, mention of the "darkness outside" and the "wailing and grinding of teeth" refer to the realm of punishment *outside* of the kingdom of God. (See also Matthew 8:12; 13:42, 50 and 24:51.)

The Lectionary's juxtaposition of the Proverbs text with today's Gospel invites us to look beyond the literal level of meaning (the kind of wife every Jewish man should have). If not for last Sunday's feast, we would have heard the first parable in Matthew 25:1–13 about the wedding feast. In that reading and elsewhere in the scriptures, Jesus is the bridegroom and the Church is his bride (Matthew 9:15; Revelation 21:2). In that light, the Proverbs text is a description of what the Church must be like if she would be "worthy" of the groom.

The wife of Proverbs, like the husband of today's responsorial psalm, is someone whose reverence for and obedience to the Lord leads to fidelity and love for God and others. Truly are these blessed; truly will they be rewarded.

• What do today's scriptures call the Church to be and do until the Lord returns?

• What industriousness is the Lord calling forth from you?

• In what ways could your church be more industrious?

• How are you investing your talents for the Lord?

READING I   *Ezekiel 34:11—12, 15—17*

Thus says the Lord GOD:

I myself will look after and tend my sheep. As a shepherd tends his flock when he finds himself among his scattered sheep, so will I tend my sheep. I will rescue them from every place where they were scattered when it was cloudy and dark. I myself will pasture my sheep; I myself will give them rest, says the Lord GOD. The lost I will seek out, the strayed I will bring back, the injured I will bind up, the sick I will heal, but the sleek and the strong I will destroy, shepherding them rightly.

As for you, my sheep, says the Lord GOD, I will judge between one sheep and another, between rams and goats.

READING II   *1 Corinthians 15:20—26, 28*

Brothers and sisters:

Christ has been raised from the dead, the first-fruits of those who have fallen asleep. For since death came through man, the resurrection of the dead came also through man. For just as in Adam all die, so too in Christ shall all be brought to life, but each one in proper order: Christ the first-fruits; then, at his coming, those who belong to Christ; then comes the end, when he hands over the kingdom to his God and Father, when he has destroyed every sovereignty and every authority and power. For he must reign until he has put all his enemies under his feet. The last enemy to be destroyed is death. When everything is subjected to him, then the Son himself will also be subjected to the one who subjected everything to him, so that God may be all in all.

GOSPEL   *Matthew 25:31—46*

Jesus said to his disciples:

"When the Son of Man comes in his glory, and all the angels with him, he will sit upon his glorious throne, and all the nations will be assembled before him. And he will separate them one from another, as a shepherd separates the sheep from the goats. He will place the sheep on his right and the goats on his left. Then the king will say to those on his right, 'Come, you who are blessed by my Father. Inherit the kingdom prepared for you from the foundation of the world. For I was hungry and you gave me food, I was thirsty and you gave me drink, a stranger and you welcomed me, naked and you clothed me, ill and you cared for me, in prison and you visited me.' Then the righteous will answer him and say, 'Lord, when did we see you hungry and feed you, or thirsty and give you drink? When did we see you a stranger and welcome you, or naked and clothe you? When did we see you ill or in prison, and visit you?' And the king will say to them in reply, 'Amen, I say to you, whatever you did for one of the least brothers of mine, you did for me.' Then he will say to those on his left, 'Depart from me, you accursed, into the eternal fire prepared for the devil and his angels. For I was hungry and you gave me no food, I was thirsty and you gave me no drink, a stranger and you gave me no welcome, naked and you gave me no clothing, ill and in prison, and you did not care for me.' Then they will answer and say, 'Lord, when did we see you hungry or thirsty or a stranger or naked or ill or in prison, and not minister to your needs?' He will answer them, 'Amen, I say to you, what you did not do for one of these least ones, you did not do for me.' And these will go off to eternal punishment, but the righteous to eternal life."

Practice of Prayer

Psalm 23:1—2, 2—3, 5—6 (1)

R. The Lord is my shepherd;
   there is nothing I shall want.

The LORD is my shepherd; I shall not want.
   In verdant pastures he gives me repose. R.

Beside restful waters he leads me;
   he refreshes my soul.
He guides me in right paths
   for his name's sake. R.

You spread the table before me
   in the sight of my foes;
you anoint my head with oil;
   my cup overflows. R.

Only goodness and kindness follow me
   all the days of my life;
and I shall dwell in the house of the LORD
   for years to come. R.

Practice of Hope

Twentieth-century writer Caryll Houselander once saw a series of powerful spiritual images reminiscent of our Gospel reading today. As she describes in her autobiography, *A Rocking-Horse Catholic,* she was walking in London one evening and saw what she later called a living icon: "Christ was lifted above the world in our drab street . . . filling the sky, His arms reaching, as it seemed, from one end of the world to the other, the wounds on his hands and feet rubies, Christ Himself, with His head bowed down by the crown, brooding over the world." Soon after, riding in a crowded subway, she experienced Christ in all persons, "living in them, dying in them, rejoicing in them, sorrowing in them."

These images shaped her subsequent writings and all aspects of her life. Because of her great compassion, psychiatrists she knew sometimes sent her their most difficult patients for counseling.

Scripture Insights

The scriptures for Christ the King seem to focus more on shepherds than kings! However, in biblical tradition, the king is often described as a shepherd. This probably begins with King David, the shepherd boy who was called by God to "shepherd my people Israel" (2 Samuel 5:2; Psalm 78:71). Shepherd imagery is also found in the prophets, usually directed against the kings who have failed in their pastoral responsibilities (Jeremiah 23:1–4; Ezekiel 34:1–10). Their failure leads God to say: "I myself will pasture my sheep" (Ezekiel 34:15; see also Isaiah 40:11; Jeremiah 31:10, and today's Psalm 23), an action fulfilled by Jesus, the Good Shepherd (Matthew 9:36; John 10:1–10; Revelation 7:17).

This same shepherd image underlies today's Gospel where royal imagery is also found: the king, the throne, and the kingdom. Note that this king-shepherd is also called "the Son of Man." The phrase occurs frequently in the four Gospel accounts with reference to Jesus, and when associated with angels, glory, and throne language, it recalls Daniel 7:13–14 with its vision of the end-time and the exaltation of one "like a Son of Man." Matthew's message is clear: Jesus, Son of David (1:1; 9:27; 21:9), the Son of Man (9:6; 11:19; 17:22), will come in glory at the end of time (16:27–28), and he shall be king. As king, he will sit in judgment (13:41; 19:28).

The judgment motif predominates in today's Gospel reading, in words that call us to account—both as individuals and as church. The criterion of judgment is not a matter of dogma, but of action (see Matthew 7:21). In effect, we are called to be shepherds of one another after God's own example. May we never be found wanting in our charge.

• How does the theme of kingship figure in today's second reading?

• What is your experience with the corporal works of mercy described in today's Gospel passage? Are there reasons beyond saving our souls that we should practice them?

• Does the image of Christ as King speak to you? Why or why not?

Information on the License to Reprint from At Home with the Word 2008

The low bulk-rate prices of *At Home with the Word 2008* are intended to make quantities of the book affordable. Single copies are $10.00 each; 5–99 copies, $9.00 each; 100 or more copies, $8.00. We encourage parishes to buy quantities of this book.

However, Liturgy Training Publications makes a simple reprint license available to parishes that would find it more practical to reproduce some parts of this book. Scripture Insights, Practice of Faith, Hope, or Charity, prayers titled Prayer before Reading the Word and Prayer after Reading the Word and lists of Weekday Readings may be duplicated for the parish bulletin or reproduced in other formats. These may be used every week or as often as the license-holder chooses.

The license granted is for the period beginning with the First Sunday of Advent—December 2, 2007—through the solemnity of Christ the King—November 23, 2008.

Please note that the license does *not* cover scripture readings or psalms (Practice of Prayer) from the Lectionary. See the acknowledgments page at the beginning of this book for the name of that copyright owner.

The materials reprinted under license from LTP may not be sold, may not be used in connection with any program or event for which a fee is charged, and may be used only among the members of the community obtaining the license. The license may not be purchased by a diocese for use in its parishes. No reprinting may be done by the parish until the license is signed by both parties and the fee is paid. Copies of the license agreement will be sent on request. The fee varies with the number of copies to be reproduced on a regular basis:

Up to 100 copies: $100
101 to 500 copies: $300
501 to 1,000 copies: $500
More than 1,000 copies: $800

For further information, call the reprint permissions department at 773-486-8970, ext. 261, or fax your request to 773-486-7094, att: reprint permissions.

Daily Prayer 2008
Rev. Michael J.K. Fuller

Paperback, 6 x 9, 432 pages
978-1-56854-616-2
Order Code: DP08

Single copy: **$12**
2–9 copies: **$10**
10 or more: **$9**

At Home with the Word 2008
Large Print Edition

**Anne Elizabeth Sweet, ocso,
Mary Ellen Hynes, Margaret Ralph,
Jennifer Willems**

Paperback, 8⅜ x 10⅞
978-1-56854-614-8
Order code: AHW08L

1–4 copies: **$10** each
5–99: **$9** each
100 or more: **$8** each

❝ I will want a copy of this book for the little shrine where I say my morning prayers. It will help me to direct the rest of my day. It is a luminous book; one might even call it a new form of the breviary. ❞

— Andrew Greeley

Daily Prayer 2008 provides an order of prayer for each day of the liturgical year from the First Sunday of Advent, December 2, 2007, to December 31, 2008.

This portable and easy-to-use book is the ultimate resource for praying every day of the liturgical year. Using a familiar order of prayer (psalmody, scripture, brief reflection, Prayer of the Faithful, Lord's Prayer, and closing prayer) this annual publication is ideal for personal and communal reflection upon the word of God. Daily Prayer is a great introduction to Catholic prayer for catechumens and candidates as well as an easy way for high school students, teachers, and parishioners to get into the habit of daily prayer. It also includes intercessions that are in accordance with GIRM, making it a great resource for the Prayer of the Faithful.

This large print edition of *At Home with the Word* invites you to read and ruminate on the Sunday scriptures, by yourself or with others. Whether you use the book for meditation or study, it will nourish you as you prepare to hear the scripture proclaimed at Sunday liturgy. This edition of *At Home with the Word 2008* has been approved for use by the National Association for the Visually Handicapped. A portion of the proceeds will go to the association.

Children's Daily Prayer 2007–2008
Suzanne M. Lewis

Paperback, 8⅜ x 10⅞, 384 pages
978-1-56854-615-5
Order Code: CDP08

Single copy: **$15**
2–9 copies: **$13** each
10 or more: **$12** each (net)

Daily Prayer 2008 is ideal for
- older students
- teachers and catechists
- youth groups
- Confirmation candidates
- religious education programs with older students
- RCIA
- adult formation and prayer groups
- prayer with the aged, sick, and homebound

Children's Daily Prayer includes
- a clear, easy-to-follow format
- prayer for every day of the school year with a reading taken from the Mass of the day
- an opening that explains the reading, describes its background, defines difficult vocabulary, and highlights feasts of the day
- a psalm with responses that may be photocopied
- silent reflection questions
- prayer services for feasts and special occasions
- extra psalms and canticles

At bookstores or 800-933-1800
www.LTP.org

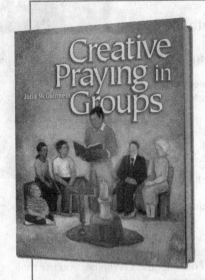

Creative Praying in Groups
Julia McGuinness

Paperback, 8½ x 10⅞, 112 pages
978-1-56854-253-9
Order code: CPRAYG **$10.95**

Creative Praying in Groups is an accessible resource for those looking for fresh ways of praying in a group setting: Bible study group, Confirmation or adult education group, retreat, class assembly at school. This valuable tool for prayer preparation offers various ways to begin parish gatherings with prayer. It is organized in two parts: prayers to be used at meetings and prayers used throughout the year. Each part contains multiple services, thematically organized.

Each service includes

- directions for how to prepare the service,

- scripture verses that you can use,

- parts for the prayer leader and those participating in the prayer,

- a list of items that you will need for the prayer (specific visual aids, suggestions for music, water, bowls, candles, etc.)

Living the Lectionary: Links to Life and Literature
Geoff Wood

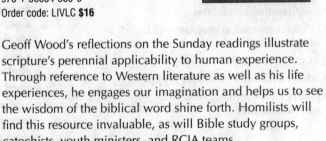

Year A
Paperback, 6 x 9, 160 pages
978-1-56854-523-3
Order code: LIVLA **$16**

Year B
Paperback, 6 x 9, 168 pages
978-1-56854-527-1
Order code: LIVLB **$16**

Year C
Paperback, 6 x 9, 160 pages
978-1-56854-365-9
Order code: LIVLC **$16**

Geoff Wood's reflections on the Sunday readings illustrate scripture's perennial applicability to human experience. Through reference to Western literature as well as his life experiences, he engages our imagination and helps us to see the wisdom of the biblical word shine forth. Homilists will find this resource invaluable, as will Bible study groups, catechists, youth ministers, and RCIA teams.

At bookstores or 800-933-1800
www.LTP.org